THE FUNDAMENTAL SCHOOL CURRICULUM IN THE AGE OF AI

Sienna Reed

Contents

Foreword

We are standing at the edge of the most profound transformation in the history of education. For centuries, the classroom has been a relatively stable environment, evolving slowly through reform movements, philosophical shifts, and changes in pedagogy. But now, in the span of just a few years, we are witnessing a change so fundamental that it does not merely adjust the content of our curriculum—it demands we redefine what education is, who it serves, and how it prepares the next generation for a world shaped by intelligence that is no longer exclusively human.

This book is not a forecast. It is not an opinion piece on the benefits or risks of technology. It is a deeply researched, stage-by-stage examination of what must change—and what must be built—in order for our children not only to survive but to flourish in the age of artificial intelligence. It is a call to educators, policymakers, and most importantly, parents, to recognize that the future is no longer a distant concept. It is present. It is shaping our children's development in real time. And it requires an immediate, coordinated, and deeply human response.

As the author of this book, I bring not only research and analysis, but urgency, experience, and a profound respect for both the technological innovation reshaping our world and the human values that must guide it. I do not write this as a technologist alone, nor as a reformer disconnected from practice, but as someone who believes the convergence of AI and education presents both a historic risk and a historic opportunity. If we design this shift intentionally, we can unlock new levels of equity, creativity, and global progress. If we ignore it, we risk producing a generation trained for a world that no longer exists.

This book is written for those who care not only about academic outcomes, but about the development of conscious, capable, ethical human beings. It is for parents trying to raise children in a world they barely understand. It is for teachers struggling to reconcile outdated standards with intelligent platforms. It is for school boards, superintendents, and legislators who must make decisions that will echo for decades. It is for the student who asks, "Why do I have to learn this?" and deserves an answer rooted not in compliance, but in vision.

I have written this book to serve as both a framework and a tool. Each chapter builds from the last, tracing the cognitive, emotional, and ethical development of a child from birth through high school graduation. Along the way, I explore the psychological foundations of learning, the technological disruptions underway, the policies in play, and the responsibilities we all share in shaping what comes next. It is not just a curriculum reimagined—it is an education redefined.

We will begin by acknowledging where we are—beyond speculation, beyond theory, already immersed in an intelligent system. From there, we will examine the collapse of the traditional curriculum, analyze the AI impact equation, and proceed through a comprehensive redesign of education at every stage of childhood development. We will explore what it means to raise a child in this age, what new metrics of success must replace the old, and what roles educators and parents must assume in the decades ahead. Finally, we will conclude not with optimism or fear, but with a structured call to action—because a future designed with intention is far more powerful than one inherited by default.

This is not a book about artificial intelligence. This is a book about human intelligence in an artificial age. And it begins with the one question that matters most: **Are we preparing our children for the world they are entering, or the one we remember?**

If your answer is the former, then this book is for you.

The Future Is Already Here

"We are not preparing for the future of education. We are already inside it."

The modern education system has long operated with a delayed sense of reality. It often functions as if it has time (time to adapt, time to respond, time to catch up). But this illusion is no longer sustainable. We have crossed the threshold where education reform is optional. The world that our children are growing up in is no longer an extension of the one we knew; it is a new ecosystem entirely. It is shaped by artificial intelligence, driven by decentralized information flows, and governed by tools and technologies that learn faster than institutions can update their policies. We are not preparing students for the future. We are attempting to raise and educate children inside it—and most of our systems are still pretending that this revolution is somewhere over the horizon, rather than already in our homes, devices, and minds.

This introduction serves as a necessary confrontation. The changes that we discuss throughout this book are not theoretical projections or distant trends. They are the living conditions of a new digital-human era. The goal of this chapter is to establish, with clarity and without fear-mongering, that artificial intelligence is not coming for education—it has already claimed its place inside it. It is influencing what children learn, how they learn it, who delivers it, and what outcomes are valued. This is no longer a speculative conversation. It is a logistical, philosophical, and societal emergency that requires us to respond with both urgency and design.

We begin here not to stoke fear, but to remove any false comfort that we have the luxury of waiting. For too long, education has operated in reaction mode—lagging years or decades behind technological, industrial, and societal evolution. But with artificial intelligence, the stakes are categorically different. This is not simply a tool. It is an ecosystem. It is not one trend among many. It is the infrastructure beneath nearly every sector of modern life—from healthcare to transportation, finance to national security, and certainly, from early childhood development through postsecondary learning and workforce training. To pretend otherwise is not naivety—it is negligence.

What this book proposes is not a simple update to existing curriculum models. It is a recognition that we must now approach education as an entirely new design challenge. We must consider how intelligence is defined, how skills are developed, how ethics are taught, and how technology is integrated into human development. The schools, classrooms, policies, and learning strategies that were functional in the 20th century are no longer viable. They are not flawed—they are obsolete. And there is no reform capable of saving a system whose foundation was never built to coexist with intelligent machines.

Parents, teachers, school administrators, and legislators are already seeing the signs. They are noticing that students are using AI tools to complete homework assignments. They are watching as essays, coding projects, and even visual art are being generated by software rather than human effort. They are noticing that students are no longer asking adults for answers, but querying models that can offer not just one response, but multiple perspectives. This is not the future. This is now. And yet, few are prepared to articulate what it means for learning outcomes, for childhood development, for assessments, and for equity. Most conversations remain reactive. Some are paralyzed by fear. Others adopt the tools blindly without understanding the implications. Neither of these extremes is sustainable.

What is required now is a third option: **an intentional redefinition of education**. That is what this book offers—a developmental framework, informed by research, guided by ethics, and rooted in a belief that human intelligence, when elevated with AI, can become something profoundly more impactful. But before we can move forward, we must understand the present moment clearly. We must dispel the myth that AI is a phase, a feature, or a tech trend. It is none of those things. It is a structural reordering of what it means to know, to teach, to learn, and to grow. And it is already reshaping our children's minds.

To grasp this, we must step back from headlines and daily usage patterns and consider the broader arc of civilization. Just as the printing press democratized knowledge, and electricity reshaped industrial production, artificial intelligence is now redefining the limits of cognition. But unlike previous revolutions, which took decades or centuries to fully integrate, AI is unfolding at an exponential pace. It took humanity over 1,000 years to move from the abacus to the modern calculator. It took only 18 months for GPT-3 to evolve into multimodal GPT-4o with speech, vision, and reasoning capabilities that rival professional human performance in dozens of domains. This is not a curve. It is a cliff. And education is standing at its edge.

The future, as it relates to learning, is therefore not a destination we are preparing for. It is a condition we are already immersed in. Our children are not growing up in the world of our childhoods. They are growing up inside a network of constant feedback, infinite content, and machine-guided learning curves. They are interacting with intelligent systems before they fully develop the ability to regulate their emotions or evaluate truth. Their understanding of self, society, knowledge, and reality is being mediated by algorithms we do not fully understand—and yet, most school systems have not meaningfully adjusted to this fact.

Consider the average elementary classroom. Despite the prevalence of AI outside the school walls, most students are still evaluated on handwritten essays, memorized math facts, and rigid timelines of progression. The curriculum remains siloed: math at 9:00, reading at 10:00, science in the afternoon. There is little room for creativity, cross-disciplinary exploration, or ethical reasoning. And above all, there is minimal integration of AI as a learning partner—not because it isn't possible, but because the system hasn't adapted. Teachers are exhausted, not because they are resistant to technology, but because they are trying to prepare students for a world that the curriculum no longer understands.

And so we arrive at a paradox. Our children are developing inside an intelligent environment while being educated by an unintelligent system. This misalignment is not merely inefficient—it is damaging. It creates confusion, anxiety, disengagement, and mistrust. Students know that the world they live in is far more dynamic than the worksheets they are asked to complete. They sense the disconnect. Many check out. Others comply, but silently disengage. And increasingly, the most capable students are using AI to navigate school rather than learn from it.

To solve this, we must redesign the learning experience from the ground up—beginning not with tools, but with **principles**. We must ask: What is education for in the age of AI? What does it mean to be intelligent, creative, ethical, or successful when machines can mimic so much of what we once called knowledge? What should we be cultivating in our children if we can no longer define excellence as content mastery alone? And how do we create learning environments that prepare them not just for future careers, but for civic leadership, emotional well-being, and ethical decision-making in a world shaped by artificial cognition?

These are the questions this book seeks to answer—not in the abstract, but across every stage of development. Each chapter builds upon the last, outlining how learning should evolve from early childhood through high school in an AI-powered world. We examine how parenting must change, how assessments must adapt, and how policies must be reimagined. We explore the role of teachers, the responsibilities of school boards, and the infrastructure of a new national curriculum. We do so not as a theoretical exercise, but as a practical necessity. Because education cannot remain a system of habits. It must become a system of design.

This book is for those ready to build that system. It is for parents who feel overwhelmed, for teachers who feel unsupported, for policymakers who feel the pressure of change, and for students who sense that what they're learning does not yet match who they're becoming. It is not a book about machines. It is a book about children—and the systems we must build to ensure they do not inherit a world they are unprepared to lead.

We are already inside the future. The question is not whether we are ready for it (but whether we are willing to design education accordingly).

The tension between the present and the past is no longer theoretical—it is institutional.

To appreciate just how significant the current educational shift is, we must first understand how rigid the existing model has been. The modern school system—particularly in the United States and across much of the Western world—was not designed with adaptability in mind. It was designed with uniformity. It was structured during the industrial era to reflect industrial values: standardization, efficiency, hierarchy, and predictability. Schools were not merely institutions of learning; they were tools of social sorting and economic preparation. The goal was to produce a compliant, moderately skilled, and hierarchically organized workforce capable of performing repetitive tasks within emerging corporate and manufacturing systems. That model, for its time, served its function. It educated the masses, lifted literacy rates, and contributed to industrial progress.

But it also cemented a deep rigidity into the heart of education. That rigidity manifested in age-based grouping, subject-specific instruction, time-bound progression, and externally measured assessments. These structures became the scaffolding for nearly every aspect of the school experience. They dictated not only what children learned but how they learned, when they learned, and in what sequence. Teachers were expected to deliver content. Students were expected to absorb and replicate it. Success was measured in uniformity—how closely a child's outputs matched the expectations of the system.

For over a century, this model persisted with minor reforms. The introduction of technology—computers in the classroom, digital whiteboards, online homework portals—gave the appearance of evolution. But underneath the cosmetic upgrades, the foundation remained unchanged. The logic of education continued to rest on a basic assumption: that knowledge was a static commodity, passed from expert to novice, and that schools were the primary gatekeepers of that commodity.

That assumption has now collapsed.

With the rise of artificial intelligence, knowledge is no longer static. It is dynamic, conversational, and multimodal. It is accessible to anyone, anywhere, on demand. A student in a rural town with a smartphone now has access to the same information—and in many cases, the same personalized tutoring—as a student in a top-tier private school. AI has eliminated the monopoly schools once held over access to knowledge. It has democratized explanation, creativity, and critical reasoning in ways that traditional education was never designed to accommodate.

This does not render schools obsolete. But it does render their traditional role insufficient.

In a world where any child can generate an essay, solve a complex math problem, or code an app using natural language inputs, the value of education can no longer be defined by the transmission of information. It must be defined by something deeper—by the cultivation of discernment, originality, ethical reasoning, and collaborative problem-solving. In other words, education must shift from teaching what to think to teaching how to think, how to choose, and how to lead.

This is not a trivial pivot. It is a complete reorientation of priorities, structures, and values. It challenges every layer of the current system—from curriculum design to teacher training, from funding models to college admissions. It requires us to stop measuring intelligence through regurgitation and start nurturing it through complexity. It asks us to trust students with creative autonomy, to support teachers with evolving roles, and to build schools not as factories of uniformity but as ecosystems of individualized learning and ethical development.

Many educators and school leaders understand this intuitively. They see how AI is changing the landscape. But they are trapped in a paradox: while the world is demanding rapid transformation, the system they operate within is constrained by slow-moving bureaucracy, outdated accountability structures, and resistance to ambiguity. Teachers are expected to innovate without institutional permission. Parents are asked to support schools that no longer reflect the world their children are preparing to enter. Policymakers are tasked with regulating tools they barely understand.

This dissonance creates friction at every level. It breeds frustration, burnout, skepticism, and inertia. It also reinforces inequity. Schools with more resources are adapting faster. They are integrating AI tools, retraining faculty, and reimagining learning environments. Schools with fewer resources are left behind, widening the digital divide not just in terms of access but in terms of future readiness. This is the new fault line of educational injustice—not access to books or even broadband, but access to **systems that are designed for an intelligent future.**

We must not underestimate the stakes. Children are not waiting for policy. They are already forming cognitive and emotional patterns based on the world around them. When schools fail to reflect the complexity, dynamism, and ethical questions of this world, students disengage. They learn to perform rather than to think. They learn to hide their use of AI rather than understand its implications. They learn to navigate two parallel realities: one inside the classroom that is rigid, linear, and slow, and one outside of it that is adaptive, intuitive, and fast. This dissonance is not a minor problem. It is an identity crisis. And it will shape not just educational outcomes, but civic engagement, mental health, and societal cohesion for decades to come.

The great lie of this moment is that we have time. We do not. Every year that we delay systemic redesign, we produce another generation of students misaligned with their future. We cannot afford to tinker around the edges. We must build a new architecture—one that respects human complexity, integrates intelligent systems, and prepares students not for yesterday's benchmarks but for tomorrow's reality. This will require courage, clarity, and collective will. It will require new kinds of partnerships—between parents and teachers, between schools and startups, between public agencies and ethical technologists. It will require a reimagining of what we call success and a redefinition of what we mean by school.

But above all, it will require honesty. We must be willing to admit that our current system is not simply behind—it is incompatible with the world it claims to prepare students for. That admission is not a failure. It is the beginning of transformation.

This book is your companion in that transformation. It does not offer quick fixes. It offers frameworks, language, and actionable insight. It traces the arc of childhood development in the AI era. It explores what must change in parenting, in teaching, in assessment, and in governance. It lays out the scaffolding of a new curriculum and the ethical responsibilities of a society raising children in a world no longer defined by scarcity of information, but by abundance of intelligent interaction.

The introduction ends here not with resolution but with invitation: to join the work of rebuilding education for a world that is not waiting for us to catch up. Because the future, in every meaningful way, is already here.

Understanding the foundational truth: curriculum, cognition, and context must all be redefined together.

One of the most dangerous myths perpetuated within the educational reform movement is the idea that you can update the tools of learning without fundamentally redefining the context and cognition surrounding that learning. Far too many school systems have fallen into the trap of adding AI as a supplement—an enrichment program, a coding module, a lab experiment—while leaving the core curriculum untouched. This is equivalent to installing a high-performance engine in a car with flat tires and a rusted frame. The vehicle may look updated, but it is not built to move forward.

Artificial intelligence is not a peripheral technology—it is an intelligence amplifier. It rewrites the relationships between questions and answers, between effort and output, between human intention and machine execution. As a result, the content of education cannot simply be adjusted—it must be **rebuilt around new assumptions**. The old assumption, that students need to memorize, recall, and replicate large bodies of information, collapses under the presence of AI. Today's intelligent tools can retrieve, summarize, explain, and even personalize knowledge faster than any human teacher. This forces us to confront a new imperative: education must now prioritize **what cannot be automated.**

This leads us to the emerging cognitive frontier. If AI can handle information delivery, what then becomes the role of human learning? The answer is not singular—it is multidimensional. Human cognition must now specialize in the qualities machines lack or cannot replicate in full: ethical reasoning, emotional intelligence, contextual judgment, value alignment, long-term goal-setting, creative synthesis, and self-awareness. These are not soft skills. They are survival skills in a world of artificial cognition. They are the new currency of capability. And yet, most school systems do not formally teach them, let alone assess or celebrate them.

Parents, too, have been caught in a narrative trap. Many still define success through traditional lenses: high test scores, admission to elite universities, mastery of academic content. But what if those benchmarks no longer correlate with future-readiness? What if the child who is best prepared for the AI age is not the one with the best grades, but the one who knows how to collaborate with intelligent systems while maintaining ethical boundaries, emotional balance, and long-term adaptability? This paradigm shift is not only uncomfortable—it is disorienting. It requires us to let go of decades of inherited assumptions about what school is for and what it means to be intelligent.

Consider this real-world tension: a parent enrolls their child in a highly ranked STEM magnet school. The curriculum emphasizes rote memorization of math theorems, regimented coding syntax, and test-based validation. The student excels. But meanwhile, that same student spends evenings exploring GPT-based tools to generate business ideas, solve logic puzzles, write stories, or even build basic web applications using drag-and-drop AI frameworks. The school rewards linear logic; the AI ecosystem rewards synthesis and iteration. The student is living a dual life—one structured, sanctioned, and outdated; the other experimental, intuitive, and future-aligned. Eventually, the child begins to question why the school still operates with such rigid boundaries. If left unaddressed, this leads to boredom, disillusionment, or quiet rebellion. What's worse, it can cause the student to devalue their own educational journey, believing that formal school is a system to outsmart, not to grow within.

This dissonance must be resolved—and not by stifling students 'curiosity or banning AI tools. It must be resolved by realigning the curriculum to reflect the world outside the classroom. That requires more than a policy shift. It requires an entire architectural rebuild. Curriculum, cognition, and context must now evolve together.

Curriculum must center around challenge-based learning, interdisciplinary integration, and ethical inquiry. It must shift from information-heavy modules to systems thinking, creativity, adaptability, and human-AI co-creation. A science unit should no longer be about memorizing phases of matter—it should be about modeling ecological systems, predicting change, and assessing solutions. A history unit should no longer be about timelines—it should be about analyzing narratives, deconstructing bias, and simulating diplomacy.

Cognition must be redefined to emphasize the meta-skills of thinking: self-regulation, question framing, ethical judgment, collaboration, and the ability to engage with uncertainty. We must teach students not just to answer well, but to ask better. We must prioritize learning how to learn, unlearn, and reframe in environments that will continuously evolve.

Context must shift from top-down instruction to co-designed learning ecosystems. Classrooms should become innovation studios, ethical sandboxes, and feedback-rich labs. Teachers become curators, facilitators, and developmental coaches—not just information deliverers. Students become co-creators of knowledge rather than passive recipients. The boundaries between subjects must become porous, and the boundaries between school and life must begin to dissolve. Authentic learning should happen everywhere—not just in classrooms, but in homes, libraries, community hubs, virtual reality labs, and simulated policy chambers.

And through it all, we must build a culture that values human uniqueness over replication. Because in a world where AI can imitate human behavior with increasing precision, the goal of education must not be to produce uniformity—it must be to cultivate **irreducible individuality**.

This individuality is not simply about expression or creativity. It is about identity. It is about producing humans who are capable of making meaning, sustaining relationships, resisting manipulation, and navigating complexity without losing their sense of purpose. This is no longer a philosophical ideal—it is a psychological necessity. Children growing up in the AI era must be equipped not just with knowledge but with **narrative strength**. They must be able to tell the story of who they are, what they value, and how they will contribute—despite living in a world that can algorithmically predict, profile, and provoke their decisions.

That narrative begins not in college, not in high school, but in the earliest moments of life. And that is where our book will go next—beginning with the cradle, moving through childhood, adolescence, and into civic maturity. At each stage, we will explore what education must become, how AI should be integrated, what parents must know, and what policy must support. It will be granular, real, and designed for implementation. Because inspiration without structure is not transformation. It is sentiment. And our children deserve more than sentiment.

They deserve an educational system that sees them not as data points or passive learners but as sovereign, intelligent, ethical beings preparing to lead in a world where intelligence is no longer uniquely human—but leadership still is.

Why urgency must replace hesitation—and why hesitation is a luxury our children can no longer afford.

Across history, education has always lagged behind innovation. During the Industrial Revolution, long after factories were mechanized and the workforce stratified, schools finally mirrored the production line—bells, rows, rote memorization, hierarchical structure. During the Information Age, long after computers entered homes and businesses, schools slowly introduced computer labs, word processors, and eventually internet-enabled learning platforms. The inertia was always present, but the consequences were survivable. Catching up was difficult, but possible. In the age of AI, however, the delay is no longer survivable. It is existential.

Artificial intelligence is not an external event. It is an embedded infrastructure now shaping language, media, business, law, healthcare, transportation, and governance. It is learning faster than children, and if our educational systems do not adapt in real time, we will raise generations whose mental models are shaped by obsolete paradigms. That is not simply inefficient—it is unjust. To educate a child in a system that does not account for the actual world they will enter is to commit a form of institutional malpractice.

Why then, despite mounting evidence, do so many systems hesitate?

The answer lies in the nature of institutional psychology. Large systems, especially those built on public governance, are not designed to be agile. They are designed to be stable, equitable, and predictable. But the very principles that once preserved fairness are now reinforcing stagnation. Education systems hesitate because they are afraid of inequity. If only wealthy districts can afford AI integration, won't that widen the gap? If only the most progressive teachers feel empowered to innovate, won't that create inconsistency? These are real concerns. But the answer is not to delay adaptation—it is to democratize it. It is to build frameworks, funding structures, and training systems that make intelligent education **accessible, not exclusive**.

Other systems hesitate because of fear—fear of disruption, job loss, ethical misuse. What happens if students use AI to cheat? What if teachers are replaced? What if hallucinations or bias in models misinform learning? Again, these concerns are valid. But avoiding integration will not eliminate these risks—it will multiply them. If students are left to explore AI tools without ethical guidance, contextual framing, or human scaffolding, they will make meaning from algorithmic randomness. If teachers are not trained to collaborate with AI, the profession will suffer—not because machines are superior, but because humans were not empowered to evolve.

The only rational response is proactive transformation. It is not enough to tolerate AI in the classroom—it must be integrated **ethically, structurally, and pedagogically.** We must design systems where AI enhances—not replaces—human agency. Where it supports differentiated learning, expands access, sparks creativity, and promotes empathy. We must build ethical guidelines, user agreements, and model evaluation tools that are transparent and youth-appropriate. We must hold technology providers accountable while also equipping educators and parents with the language, mindset, and training to lead.

None of this will happen if we wait for consensus. Transformation begins with those bold enough to lead before it is popular. The education system does not need more pilot programs or five-year committees. It needs a movement—a decisive shift in mindset where urgency replaces hesitation and experimentation replaces perfectionism. The risks of doing nothing far outweigh the risks of intelligent, incremental redesign.

At the heart of this redesign is a fundamental truth: **the most powerful technology in education will always be the teacher.** But the role of the teacher is changing. No longer a content gatekeeper, the teacher must become a coach of cognition, a mentor of meaning, and a model of ethical intelligence. This requires new training pathways, new compensation models, and new metrics of excellence. It requires that we elevate the teaching profession to reflect its true complexity—not just as a transmitter of standards, but as a cultivator of future humans in an intelligent world.

Parents, too, must be redefined in the system. No longer just supporters of homework or fundraisers for field trips, parents must become strategic co-educators. They must be briefed, equipped, and respected as part of the learning ecosystem. They must understand the tools their children are using, the philosophies that underlie new curricula, and the psychological shifts occurring in AI-mediated learning environments. Parenting in the AI age is not about digital policing—it is about ethical coaching. It is about forming a coherent framework of values, emotional resilience, and cognitive agility that guides children through a world of algorithmic influence.

This book provides that framework. It begins with early childhood—those precious years where identity, attachment, and language are formed—and carries through the stages of learning where complexity, independence, and worldview are built. At each level—Head Start, early elementary, upper elementary, middle school, and high school—we present the necessary shifts in curriculum, parenting, teacher practice, and policy design. We align development with design, reality with readiness, and theory with tools.

We do not ignore the hard questions. We face them directly: Should students be allowed to use ChatGPT in class? Should exams be open-AI? How do you measure originality when machines can simulate it? What happens when AI tutors outperform human instructors? What happens to equity when some students have more advanced AI literacy than others? These questions do not have simple answers—but they are answerable. And they are only unmanageable if we continue pretending this future is optional.

It is not.

The longer we delay, the greater the dissonance between what students experience outside school and what they are asked to do inside of it. That dissonance will breed disengagement. It will fuel inequality. It will erode trust in education and in the adults who manage it.

But if we act—intelligently, collaboratively, and urgently—we can create an educational future where AI is not a threat, but a co-architect of a more human world.

That is the purpose of this book.

From disruption to design: anchoring the mission of raising future-ready children in an era of artificial intelligence.

The true challenge of this moment is not technical—it is philosophical. We know how to build AI. We know how to integrate systems. What we have not yet done, collectively, is decide what it means to be educated in the presence of intelligence that can outperform us in memory, language generation, and even creative composition. This book asserts that education must now shift from producing correct answers to producing courageous, ethical, and adaptive humans.

And that shift cannot be achieved by simply layering AI on top of old standards. It demands a full reimagination of purpose.

If the old system sought to sort students—into winners and losers, advanced and behind, gifted and delayed—the new system must aim to **elevate all learners** by identifying and cultivating uniquely human capacities. The measure of intelligence will no longer be determined by speed of recall, but by **depth of thought, clarity of values, and the capacity to build meaning in an information-saturated world.**

This transformation begins before school ever does.

Long before a child steps foot into a kindergarten classroom, they are already learning how to process the world—emotionally, socially, linguistically. They are absorbing values from their caregivers, scripts from their devices, attention patterns from their environment. In an age where digital content is embedded into every aspect of early development, parenting has become the first line of curriculum. Understanding how to raise a child with AI is now as important as choosing a school. This book begins there.

But we do not stop there. Because education does not occur in silos.

From the moment formal schooling begins, the child becomes part of a much larger system. That system is increasingly disconnected from the future it claims to prepare students for. Math taught through memorized formulas rather than applied modeling. English taught through five-paragraph essays rather than multimodal storytelling. Science taught through recall rather than simulation. The disconnect is not in content—but in context. It is not in subject—but in structure.

This book examines the architecture of schooling across every stage of development. For each phase—early childhood, elementary, middle school, and high school—we analyze the developmental psychology at play, the AI disruptions emerging, and the curriculum redesigns required. We integrate neuroscience, education theory, case studies, and tech ethics to create a blueprint for what school must now become. We provide not just critique but design. Not just alarm—but alignment.

In addition to curriculum and stage-specific insights, this book offers something more: a **strategic guide for parents**.

We believe that raising an AI-ready child is no longer the exclusive domain of schools. In fact, the most important training ground is the home. The language parents use, the questions they ask, the way they frame success—all of these shape the child's inner operating system long before any formal system takes hold. Parents must be equipped, not just with tools, but with **a worldview**. This book gives them that worldview. It shows them how to prepare children to work with AI, not fear it. To collaborate with machines without outsourcing their identity. To use tools with discernment and purpose.

And finally, this book speaks to those in power: policymakers, school board leaders, curriculum designers, education secretaries. It makes clear that the future of education is not a partisan issue. It is a **civilizational issue.** If we fail to design a coherent national or global framework for education in the age of intelligence, we will not just lose innovation—we will lose stability. We will fracture society into those who can think with AI, and those who are controlled by it. That gap will not be economic alone—it will be cognitive, cultural, and existential. This book demands action now—before that gap becomes irreversible.

We must be clear-eyed: the transformation of education in the AI era will not be clean or linear. It will be disruptive, messy, and at times uncomfortable. It will require new vocabulary, new metrics, and new courage. It will require those who believe in the child—not the system—to take the lead.

If you are reading this book, it is because you are one of those leaders.

Whether you are a parent, teacher, policymaker, or student yourself—this is your call. You are living at the inflection point. You are the bridge between two worlds. One that is collapsing, and one that has not yet been built.

Chapter 1

The Death of the Traditional Curriculum

The traditional curriculum, as structured and implemented in most educational institutions throughout the twentieth and early twenty-first centuries, is no longer suitable for the cognitive, economic, or technological demands of the contemporary era. Its foundations were laid during the Industrial Age and refined during the Information Age, but it has failed to evolve in proportion to the acceleration of artificial intelligence and digital systems that now shape all aspects of human development. What once served as a framework for standardizing knowledge acquisition has become a constraint, limiting both the potential of learners and the relevance of education itself.

The original purpose of the standardized curriculum was to produce functional citizens equipped with a consistent base of literacy, numeracy, and civic understanding. Subjects were compartmentalized—language arts, mathematics, science, and social studies—each defined by linear progression and discrete skill mastery. Success was measured through uniform assessments that prioritized recall over reasoning, replication over reflection. Such a structure mirrored the needs of an industrial economy, where predictability, obedience, and specialized roles were considered essential. At that time, this model fulfilled a civic function: it provided access to structured knowledge in an era when such access was scarce.

However, the modern world no longer suffers from a scarcity of information. It suffers from a surplus of it. The proliferation of intelligent systems has transformed the relationship between learner and knowledge. Artificial intelligence has rendered memorization and procedural calculation largely obsolete. Machines now perform these functions with greater speed, precision, and scalability. What remains uniquely human—and increasingly vital—is the capacity to synthesize information, evaluate context, form ethical judgments, and create original insights in collaboration with intelligent tools.

In this new paradigm, the traditional curriculum appears increasingly antiquated. It prioritizes stability over adaptability, conformity over creativity, and measurable outcomes over meaningful engagement. Its subjects are often detached from lived experience and global complexity. Students are taught historical events without understanding geopolitical causality. Mathematical instruction often excludes real-world applications, such as data analysis or financial literacy. Science is frequently reduced to static content, rather than a method for inquiry and experimentation. The curriculum remains largely indifferent to interdisciplinary thinking, which is essential in a world shaped by systems-level challenges such as climate change, algorithmic bias, and technological displacement.

The persistence of this model is not merely a matter of tradition. It is sustained by institutional inertia, bureaucratic accountability frameworks, and a risk-averse culture within public education systems. Policymakers continue to rely on standardized assessments to determine funding allocations and educator effectiveness. University admissions processes reinforce curricular rigidity by prioritizing grade-point averages and test scores. Teacher preparation programs often fail to equip educators with the tools necessary for integrating emerging technologies or for designing learning experiences that mirror the dynamism of real-world problem-solving.

Furthermore, the curriculum's emphasis on static knowledge fails to prepare students for the fluidity of future employment. The labor market increasingly demands adaptive learners, creative thinkers, and digital collaborators. Roles once considered stable have been rendered obsolete, while entirely new fields—such as algorithmic ethics, human-centered design, and quantum computing—emerge without corresponding curricular representation. Students are being prepared for a world that no longer exists, using a system that no longer applies.

This misalignment creates cognitive dissonance for learners. Many students, particularly those with access to intelligent tools outside the classroom, recognize the irrelevance of traditional instruction. They encounter AI systems capable of answering complex questions, generating essays, composing music, and performing tasks once reserved for top-tier academic achievers. When such capabilities exist at the fingertips of young people, a curriculum that requires passive absorption of content appears not only outdated but insulting to their potential.

The death of the traditional curriculum is not a metaphor. It is a necessary transition. A curriculum that fails to evolve in the presence of technological transformation becomes an artifact of a prior era—educationally inert and ethically indefensible. The task ahead is not to mourn its decline, but to design a replacement capable of addressing the realities of intelligence amplification, cognitive diversity, and global interdependence.

The reimagined curriculum must center around core competencies that machines cannot replicate: ethical decision-making, emotional intelligence, metacognitive awareness, interdisciplinary synthesis, and collaborative problem-solving. These competencies are not soft skills; they are survival skills. They define human agency in an age of artificial cognition. Moreover, they must be integrated not as supplemental programs, but as foundational elements of educational design.

To accomplish this, subject boundaries must be restructured. Traditional disciplines should no longer operate in isolation. For example, a unit on climate science should incorporate statistical modeling, ethical debate, historical context, and policy analysis. A project on media literacy should involve coding, psychology, language analysis, and digital ethics. This approach, often referred to as transdisciplinary or thematic learning, better reflects the integrated nature of real-world challenges and the cognitive processes required to address them.

Assessment practices must also be overhauled. Traditional metrics such as multiple-choice exams, time-limited essays, and standardized tests no longer serve as accurate proxies for intelligence, creativity, or readiness. Instead, authentic assessments—portfolios, project-based demonstrations, collaborative simulations, and long-term inquiry reports—offer a more accurate representation of student capacity. These formats emphasize process over product and depth over breadth. They encourage students to engage in sustained inquiry, iterate on feedback, and present work that reflects both academic rigor and personal relevance.

Additionally, curriculum design must account for personalization. The advent of AI makes this both possible and necessary. Students differ not only in learning styles but also in cognitive pacing, cultural frameworks, and emotional development. A static, one-size-fits-all curriculum undermines these differences and perpetuates inequality. AI-enabled systems, when ethically deployed, can support differentiated learning paths, provide real-time formative feedback, and adapt instruction to meet diverse learner profiles. These tools must not replace human educators but rather augment their ability to meet individual needs at scale.

Finally, the curriculum must be rooted in values. In an era defined by rapid technological evolution, students must grapple with questions of meaning, responsibility, and power. What does it mean to be human in an intelligent world? How should society govern the use of algorithmic decision-making? What ethical frameworks should inform the design and deployment of emerging technologies? These are not questions for the future; they are questions for the present. The curriculum must make space for them—not in extracurricular clubs or elective seminars, but within the core educational experience.

The death of the traditional curriculum creates a profound opportunity. It allows educators, parents, and policymakers to co-create a new educational blueprint—one that honors the complexity of the world, the capacity of young minds, and the ethical imperatives of human development. The challenge is significant, but the alternative is unacceptable. A society that fails to update its curriculum in the face of such profound change does not merely risk irrelevance—it risks collapse.

Education is not merely the transmission of knowledge; it is the formation of character and capacity. As artificial intelligence accelerates, this formation must become more intentional, more inclusive, and more aligned with the demands of the present and future. The traditional curriculum, with all its structure and history, must now give way to a new architecture—one capable of preparing not just students, but citizens, creators, and leaders in the age of intelligence.

In the global context, the limitations of the traditional curriculum become even more pronounced when evaluated against rapid international advancements in educational innovation. Nations that have invested in adaptive curriculum models and AI integration—such as Singapore, Finland, South Korea, and Estonia—have demonstrated not only superior academic outcomes but also greater learner engagement, digital fluency, and system resilience. These systems have moved beyond the passive transmission of content toward dynamic, inquiry-based frameworks grounded in real-world problem-solving and technological adaptation. Meanwhile, systems adhering rigidly to the conventional model increasingly fall behind—not due to lack of intelligence among their student populations, but due to institutional stagnation.

This stagnation has broader implications beyond test scores or academic performance. The global economy now operates on principles of innovation, rapid iteration, and constant re-skilling. Traditional curricula, with their slow revision cycles and bureaucratic gatekeeping, cannot keep pace with the demands of emerging industries. Fields such as AI ethics, blockchain infrastructure, biotechnology, green engineering, and immersive computing evolve on timelines measured in months, not years. Curricula that are updated only every decade—or even every five years—place students at a structural disadvantage upon graduation. The time lag between innovation and curricular adoption ensures that learners are trained for outdated roles while being unprepared for the complex decision-making required in future leadership.

Furthermore, the cultural narratives embedded within the traditional curriculum often fail to reflect the diversity of the societies they serve. Textbooks and teaching materials continue to center dominant historical perspectives, omitting or marginalizing contributions from underrepresented communities. In doing so, curricula perpetuate exclusion, reinforce structural bias, and hinder the development of global consciousness. In an age where social justice, environmental stewardship, and intercultural competence are prerequisites for sustainable development, such omissions are not merely oversights—they are liabilities.

Curriculum redesign must begin with a redefinition of purpose. If the aim of education is merely to transmit a fixed body of knowledge, then the traditional model may have merit. However, if the purpose of education is to cultivate autonomous thinkers capable of navigating ambiguity, coexisting with difference, and contributing meaningfully to society, then a complete reorientation is necessary. This reorientation must begin at the level of national policy, but it must also permeate classroom practice, parental expectations, teacher education programs, and digital infrastructure.

One of the most significant barriers to reform is the false assumption that curricular rigor is synonymous with difficulty. Many educational institutions cling to archaic standards under the belief that challenge equals excellence. However, difficulty derived from irrelevance, abstraction, or outdated delivery methods does not yield deeper understanding. It yields disengagement. True rigor lies in the complexity of thought required, not in the obscurity of content. A curriculum can be rigorous while remaining adaptive, personalized, and technologically integrated. In fact, such a curriculum is likely to produce greater intellectual resilience than one rooted in rote memorization and high-stakes testing.

Moreover, the traditional curriculum is structurally misaligned with the cognitive realities of the digital generation. Learners today are not merely consumers of information; they are participants in complex media ecosystems. They interact with dynamic content, multidirectional communication channels, and algorithmically curated knowledge. As a result, attention patterns, memory retention, and conceptual framing differ significantly from previous generations. A curriculum that fails to acknowledge these neurological and sociotechnical shifts is not only ineffective—it is neurologically mismatched to the students it serves.

Educational neuroscience has made considerable progress in identifying optimal learning conditions, yet these insights have rarely been translated into curricular design. For example, research consistently demonstrates that emotion, social relevance, and experiential context dramatically increase knowledge retention and cognitive flexibility. However, most traditional curricula remain emotion-neutral, socially detached, and abstractly structured. Students are expected to memorize vocabulary without narrative, solve equations without application, and analyze literature without contemporary relevance. This pedagogical approach undermines the brain's natural learning architecture, wasting both time and developmental potential.

A curriculum designed for the AI age must integrate these neuroscientific insights. It must also redefine the teacher's role not as an information provider, but as a facilitator of critical engagement, emotional development, and intellectual agency. In this redefined role, educators must be empowered—not only through professional development but through systemic trust and curricular autonomy. Teachers must be given the tools to co-design learning experiences with students, to utilize AI platforms without fear of replacement, and to foster classrooms where curiosity supersedes compliance.

The structural design of school schedules also reveals the obsolescence of traditional curricula. Time remains fragmented into fifty-minute intervals, subject divisions remain rigid, and student transitions are governed by bells rather than by cognitive flow. This structure fragments attention, discourages deep work, and prevents the kind of cross-disciplinary inquiry necessary for real-world problem-solving. Curriculum redesign must also include redesigning time. Block scheduling, thematic learning periods, intersessional projects, and extended inquiry modules offer alternatives that promote sustained engagement and intellectual depth.

In addressing the death of the traditional curriculum, it is also necessary to explore the ethical imperative of change. The continued implementation of obsolete curricula in full awareness of their limitations constitutes a breach of ethical responsibility. Institutions that knowingly perpetuate models of education that disempower learners are complicit in a form of intellectual disenfranchisement. Ethical education requires constant reflection, responsive adaptation, and humility in the face of transformative discovery. As such, every educational leader, policymaker, and parent must confront the question: does the current curriculum serve the best interest of children, or merely the convenience of legacy systems?

The death of the traditional curriculum must not be interpreted as a descent into chaos or academic nihilism. Rather, it should be viewed as a necessary evolution—a shedding of rigid forms in favor of flexible structures. The new curriculum must prioritize competencies over content, adaptability over uniformity, and meaning over memorization. It must center the learner not only as a recipient of knowledge but as a designer of knowledge ecosystems.

A new curriculum architecture must therefore be grounded in five core pillars:

1. **Interdisciplinary Relevance** – Every unit must integrate at least two disciplines and connect to real-world problems.
2. **AI-Enabled Personalization** – Learning trajectories must be adaptive, using ethical AI to provide differentiated pacing and feedback.
3. **Ethical Inquiry** – Every major theme must incorporate questions of justice, responsibility, and human impact.
4. **Authentic Assessment** – Evaluation must be performance-based, demonstrating application and reflection rather than regurgitation.
5. **Human-AI Collaboration** – Tools must be treated as extensions of human cognition, not replacements for human agency.

These pillars are not theoretical. They have been implemented successfully in model schools, international innovation hubs, and experimental classroom frameworks across diverse cultural contexts. What remains is the political and institutional will to scale such innovation beyond the margins and into the mainstream.

The transition will require significant investment—in infrastructure, teacher training, curricular redesign, and policy overhaul. However, the cost of inaction far exceeds the cost of transformation. If systems persist in clinging to outdated models, society will continue producing graduates who are misaligned with both the workforce and the democratic fabric of their communities. Disengagement will deepen. Innovation will stall. Inequality will widen.

By contrast, a bold curricular reinvention offers the promise of relevance, agency, and alignment with the future. It signals to students that their education is not a relic of a bygone era but a living, responsive, and dignified journey toward purposeful participation in the world.

The death of the traditional curriculum is not a tragedy. It is a release. It is an invitation to imagine, design, and implement an education worthy of the world unfolding before us.

In assessing the failures of the traditional curriculum, one must also analyze the role of educational policy and its reliance on outdated accountability mechanisms. Standardized testing remains the dominant metric by which student proficiency, teacher effectiveness, and institutional success are judged. This dependency, initially intended to promote equity and transparency, has inadvertently restricted curricular innovation and distorted the educational experience. Teachers, pressed to improve test scores, often forgo exploratory learning, critical discussion, and creative inquiry in favor of teaching to the test. Students, in turn, become passive recipients of rehearsed responses, deprived of the freedom to question or co-create knowledge.

The psychological toll of this emphasis on high-stakes assessment cannot be overstated. Research has consistently demonstrated a correlation between excessive standardized testing and elevated anxiety, diminished motivation, and student disengagement. In an environment dominated by extrinsic evaluation, intrinsic curiosity withers. Instead of fostering a lifelong love for learning, the traditional curriculum often promotes short-term compliance, where success is defined by the ability to replicate answers rather than to generate ideas.

This problem is particularly acute in marginalized communities, where schools often receive fewer resources and are subjected to more punitive forms of accountability. Rather than receiving enriched, innovative instruction that cultivates critical thinking and creativity, students in underfunded districts are often confined to rigid remediation programs focused solely on test preparation. In this way, the traditional curriculum not only fails to prepare students for the future—it actively reinforces cycles of inequality and cognitive suppression.

A reimagined curriculum must address these structural inequities head-on. It must reject the notion that uniform testing yields fair evaluation. Instead, equity must be defined as the capacity of all students to access rigorous, relevant, and personalized learning experiences that align with their individual strengths, cultural identities, and life aspirations. This requires a fundamental redesign of curriculum development processes to include the voices of communities historically excluded from educational decision-making. Parents, students, and educators from diverse backgrounds must serve as co-architects of the new curriculum, ensuring that it reflects the complexity of the world and the dignity of every learner.

The integration of technology, particularly artificial intelligence, must be approached with the same rigor. AI presents unprecedented opportunities for curriculum enhancement—ranging from real-time feedback systems and language modeling to immersive simulations and intelligent tutoring platforms. However, without intentional design and ethical guardrails, these tools risk replicating and amplifying the biases embedded in the current system. Curriculum developers must therefore become literate in both pedagogy and machine learning, understanding how algorithmic decisions are made, what data is used, and how outputs can be interpreted or misinterpreted by learners.

This dual fluency—educational and technological—represents the new frontier of curriculum leadership. School districts must invest in the training and certification of curriculum designers who can navigate this intersection. These professionals must not only possess content knowledge but also understand cognitive development, systems thinking, and human-computer interaction. In their hands lies the responsibility of crafting learning environments that are not only intellectually rigorous but also emotionally and ethically sound.

Moreover, the curriculum must respond to the existential questions that define this era. As society grapples with the implications of automation, climate collapse, digital surveillance, and geopolitical instability, students must be equipped to think critically about the systems in which they live. Education must no longer avoid controversy in the name of neutrality. Rather, it must embrace complexity, teaching students to analyze competing narratives, evaluate sources of information, and engage in respectful civic discourse. These capacities are not supplementary—they are foundational to functioning in a democratic society increasingly shaped by algorithmic power and systemic uncertainty.

To this end, educators must be prepared not only to teach but to moderate, facilitate, and mentor. The role of the teacher becomes that of a cognitive coach and ethical guide, supporting learners as they navigate complex ideas and form their own intellectual identities. This shift in responsibility requires corresponding shifts in teacher preparation programs, which must now include training in AI ethics, trauma-informed pedagogy, cross-cultural communication, and design-based learning. Only then can teachers function as catalysts within a restructured curricular ecosystem.

Another essential component of curriculum renewal lies in the reconceptualization of student agency. Traditional education often positions students as objects of instruction—passive recipients of predefined knowledge paths. A modern curriculum must reverse this logic, positioning students as co-creators of their learning journeys. This does not mean abandoning structure, but rather designing frameworks that allow for autonomy, exploration, and iteration. Students should have input into the questions they pursue, the media through which they express understanding, and the metrics by which they are assessed. Such empowerment fosters ownership, responsibility, and deeper cognitive engagement.

Curriculum designers can leverage AI tools to facilitate this agency. For instance, adaptive learning platforms can analyze student choices, performance trends, and reflective input to generate customized content maps. Generative AI can assist students in developing research prompts, visualizations, or coding sequences, provided that such tools are used as amplifiers of human intellect, not as replacements for thinking. When properly integrated, these technologies can democratize access to advanced forms of inquiry that were once limited to elite institutions.

Despite these advantages, curriculum transformation cannot be technocentric. The core of any effective educational framework remains human connection. Students learn most deeply when they feel seen, respected, and challenged. Therefore, any curriculum reform must place relational pedagogy at its center. Emotional intelligence, social-emotional learning, and ethical literacy must be embedded not only in specific programs but throughout every content area. The AI-augmented classroom must still be a space where human values are taught, modeled, and refined.

This holistic approach requires systemic coherence. The curriculum cannot be transformed in isolation. Changes to assessment, scheduling, infrastructure, teacher evaluation, and parent communication must align with curricular reform. Otherwise, even the most visionary curricula will be undermined by misaligned systems. Policymakers must therefore adopt an ecosystemic approach, recognizing the interdependencies between curriculum and broader educational structures.

To facilitate this transition, education systems should pilot model schools or innovation zones where the new curriculum can be developed, tested, and refined before scaling. These pilots should be supported by robust research partnerships, community feedback loops, and iterative design cycles. Documentation of successes and failures must be shared transparently across districts and regions to accelerate collective learning.

The transition away from the traditional curriculum will not occur overnight. It will require phases of experimentation, resistance, recalibration, and growth. But the urgency is clear. The traditional curriculum has exhausted its utility. Its continued implementation is an act of inertia, not intention. In contrast, a new curriculum—one built on relevance, responsiveness, and responsibility—offers the promise of an education that prepares learners not just for the jobs of tomorrow, but for the moral and intellectual complexities of the human future.

If educational systems continue to operate on obsolete assumptions, society risks producing generations of citizens who are disconnected from the intellectual, emotional, and ethical demands of the era in which they live. The traditional curriculum was constructed in an age of print, hierarchy, and limited access to information. In contrast, the contemporary world operates in a decentralized, interconnected digital ecosystem. As such, the knowledge economy now demands not static mastery, but constant reinvention.

This distinction has significant implications for how curriculum must be designed in both form and function. Static curriculum models, often bound in annual textbooks or sequenced through yearly syllabi, are incapable of responding to the velocity of change now experienced globally. In contrast, dynamic curriculum models must function more like living documents—continuously iterated, data-informed, and learner-responsive. These models must be platform-based, modular, and designed with the assumption that new tools, perspectives, and realities will emerge midstream.

The infrastructure to support this dynamism already exists. Learning management systems, AI-assisted planning software, and open educational resources can be harnessed to create real-time curricular updates, personalized learner pathways, and feedback-informed content adaptation. However, without the proper policy frameworks, many schools remain locked into bureaucratic approval cycles that prevent curricular evolution. A central policy priority must be the decentralization of curricular decision-making to allow schools, and even classrooms, the flexibility to evolve in accordance with learner needs and contextual developments.

In this emergent model, curation becomes just as important as creation. Teachers will need to operate as expert curators of content, evaluating, modifying, and assembling materials from a range of digital and physical sources. They must be trained to assess quality, bias, and relevance—not simply to follow scripted lesson plans. Curricular autonomy becomes essential, not as a threat to standardization, but as a necessary component of relevance. When teachers are given ownership over curriculum implementation, they are more likely to engage in continuous professional growth, experimentation, and collaboration.

Moreover, as students take on increased responsibility for their learning, the boundaries between curriculum and experience will begin to blur. Experiential learning—through internships, digital projects, community engagement, and interdisciplinary challenges—must be seen not as extracurricular, but as central to the curriculum itself. Learners must be empowered to apply what they learn to authentic situations, reflect on the outcomes, and iterate based on real consequences. This type of situated learning fosters deeper transfer of knowledge and helps to close the gap between school and society.

In parallel, curriculum must also recognize and support different modalities of intelligence. The traditional model privileges linguistic and logical-mathematical reasoning, often at the expense of spatial, kinesthetic, interpersonal, and intrapersonal intelligences. In doing so, it marginalizes a vast portion of student potential. The emerging curriculum must be multimodal—providing students with diverse ways of demonstrating understanding and contributing value. AI systems, particularly those capable of processing voice, gesture, movement, and expression, can be leveraged to support these alternative modalities in ways that were previously unimaginable.

This expanded definition of intelligence also requires a rethinking of how success is measured. Instead of relying on summative grades or standardized test results, curriculum must support formative, process-oriented assessment that prioritizes growth, creativity, collaboration, and self-reflection. Digital portfolios, peer review systems, and performance exhibitions must become the norm. These forms of assessment not only provide a more accurate picture of student capacity, but also foster metacognitive skills that are essential in an age of self-directed learning and constant adaptation.

Attention must also be given to the ethical implications of curricular decisions. Every inclusion and omission in the curriculum sends a message about what society values. In an age of global crisis and technological disruption, the curriculum must address themes such as ecological stewardship, human rights, global interdependence, digital citizenship, and mental well-being. These are not peripheral concerns—they are existential imperatives. Failing to include them in the core curriculum is not only a pedagogical oversight; it is a moral failure.

Curriculum must also address the phenomenon of misinformation, digital manipulation, and ideological polarization. Students must be trained to interrogate sources, identify logical fallacies, and understand the economic and political forces that shape the information landscape. Critical media literacy must become a foundational skill—taught with the same intensity and rigor as mathematics or language. In doing so, the curriculum supports not just academic development, but the cultivation of informed, resilient democratic citizens.

Another emerging priority is the inclusion of systems thinking. As global problems become increasingly interconnected, students must learn to analyze issues not in isolation but as components of larger ecosystems. Whether addressing climate change, economic instability, or algorithmic bias, curriculum must support learners in identifying feedback loops, cascading effects, and unintended consequences. This cognitive approach fosters humility, curiosity, and strategic awareness—traits essential for future leadership.

As the traditional curriculum fades into obsolescence, it is vital to ensure that its replacement is not simply a digitized version of the same underlying structure. A true transformation requires new epistemologies, new relationships between teacher and learner, and a new narrative about what education is for. Education must be reconceived not as preparation for a specific job or standardized role, but as a lifelong process of becoming—intellectually, ethically, socially, and spiritually.

The curriculum must serve as a guide for that becoming. It must help learners develop the capacity to ask meaningful questions, to form interdisciplinary connections, to confront uncertainty with courage, and to act with integrity in complex environments. In short, it must prepare learners not only to thrive in an AI-dominated world, but to shape that world with wisdom and compassion.

This is the challenge—and opportunity—presented by the death of the traditional curriculum. It is a moment of reckoning, of possibility, and of profound responsibility. The decisions made in the coming years will determine whether education remains a mechanism of compliance or evolves into a platform for liberation. It is not enough to reform around the edges. The entire curricular structure must be reimagined.

To do so will require courage—from policymakers, from educators, from communities, and from learners themselves. It will require the abandonment of familiar comfort zones and the embrace of experimentation. It will require significant investment, robust debate, and a willingness to admit that past models, no matter how revered, no longer suffice.

But most importantly, it will require a collective reassertion of a simple yet powerful idea: that education matters. That how societies educate their young determines not only what they know, but who they become. And in an age of intelligent machines, this truth matters more than ever.

Education must now transcend the transmission of knowledge and become the practice of wisdom. It must transcend preparation for work and become the foundation for ethical citizenship. It must transcend the delivery of answers and become the cultivation of questions.

The death of the traditional curriculum is therefore not the end of education. It is the beginning of its rebirth.

Chapter 2

The Rise of Intelligent Learning Systems

The emergence of artificial intelligence in education marks a pivotal transformation not only in the tools that learners and educators use, but in the very architecture of knowledge delivery, assessment, and development. This transformation is not theoretical; it is already unfolding in classrooms, platforms, and policy initiatives across the globe. The rise of intelligent learning systems represents a fundamental shift away from static, uniform instructional models and toward dynamic, responsive, and individualized experiences. Understanding this shift requires an examination of the technological innovations driving it, the pedagogical opportunities it presents, and the ethical and structural implications that follow.

Intelligent learning systems are broadly defined as technology-enabled platforms that use algorithms, machine learning, and real-time data analytics to adapt content, pacing, and instruction to meet the specific needs of individual learners. Unlike traditional educational software, which operates through fixed sequences and static rules, intelligent systems can analyze learner behavior, identify patterns, make predictions, and adjust in real time. This capability transforms the one-size-fits-all paradigm into a dynamic continuum of learning pathways tailored to the evolving profile of each student.

The genesis of these systems can be traced to developments in three foundational technologies: natural language processing, neural networks, and predictive analytics. Natural language processing allows machines to interpret, analyze, and respond to human language in meaningful ways, enabling AI tutors and chat-based learning assistants to communicate effectively with students. Neural networks, inspired by the human brain's architecture, enable machines to "learn" from vast datasets, improving their performance over time without explicit reprogramming. Predictive analytics, meanwhile, allows these systems to anticipate learner needs and outcomes based on historical performance, engagement levels, and other behavioral indicators.

When integrated into learning environments, these technologies facilitate the construction of adaptive learning platforms. Such platforms continuously assess a student's performance across a variety of tasks—whether multiple-choice questions, essay responses, spoken dialogue, or interactive simulations—and adjust the content, feedback style, difficulty level, and instructional approach accordingly. This form of adaptation mimics the personalized attention that only the most skilled human tutors have traditionally been able to provide, but at scale and with unprecedented precision.

One of the most transformative aspects of intelligent learning systems is their ability to transcend traditional conceptions of time in education. In conventional classrooms, all students are expected to progress at the same pace regardless of prior knowledge, cognitive development, or emotional readiness. This uniform pacing disproportionately disadvantages students who require either more time to master foundational concepts or accelerated pathways to remain engaged. Intelligent learning systems dissolve these artificial constraints by allowing students to progress based on mastery rather than schedule. Mastery-based progression ensures that learning is not superficial or time-dependent but grounded in demonstrable competence.

Additionally, intelligent systems offer the potential to democratize access to high-quality instruction. In many regions, educational inequality stems from disparities in teacher quality, classroom size, and instructional resources. AI-powered platforms can serve as equalizers, delivering consistent, research-backed instructional strategies to students irrespective of geographic location or socioeconomic status. For example, an AI-based reading assistant can provide instant pronunciation correction, vocabulary reinforcement, and comprehension questioning to a student in a rural village as readily as to one in an elite urban academy. In doing so, these systems can bridge the gap between educational aspiration and systemic limitation.

However, the benefits of intelligent learning systems are not confined to students alone. Educators also stand to gain from the integration of

AI into instructional practice. Intelligent systems can serve as diagnostic assistants, identifying which students are struggling, in what areas, and why. They can automate routine tasks such as grading, content delivery, and administrative recordkeeping, thereby freeing educators to focus on higher-order pedagogical responsibilities such as facilitating discussion, mentoring, and designing interdisciplinary projects. Furthermore, intelligent systems can provide teachers with real-time dashboards that visualize student progress, recommend interventions, and suggest differentiated strategies—all based on live data.

It is essential, however, to recognize that intelligent learning systems are not a substitute for educators. Rather, they are tools that enhance the capacity of educators to serve the diverse and complex needs of their students. The most effective implementations of AI in education treat the technology as a collaborator rather than a replacement. This human-in-the-loop model ensures that ethical judgment, emotional intelligence, and cultural responsiveness remain central to the learning process, while allowing AI to handle tasks better suited to automation and data analysis.

Despite the advantages offered by intelligent learning systems, their adoption raises significant ethical, technical, and philosophical questions. Chief among these is the issue of data privacy. These systems collect extensive data on student behavior, performance, emotion, and even biometric indicators. The use, storage, and sharing of such data must be governed by stringent ethical frameworks that prioritize student rights, transparency, and informed consent. Without such safeguards, the same systems that promise personalized learning could become instruments of surveillance, manipulation, or discriminatory profiling.

Moreover, intelligent learning systems must be critically examined for algorithmic bias. Machine learning models are only as unbiased as the data on which they are trained. If training datasets reflect existing societal inequalities or cultural blind spots, then the systems will replicate and reinforce these biases. For instance, an AI reading tutor trained predominantly on Western English-language texts may struggle to interpret or support students from linguistically diverse backgrounds. Ensuring that intelligent systems are inclusive, culturally responsive, and globally representative is not a technical afterthought—it is a moral imperative.

The rise of intelligent learning systems also forces a reevaluation of the human dimensions of education. If machines can deliver content more efficiently and assess performance more precisely than humans, what then is the unique value of human educators? The answer lies in the realms of relationship, meaning, and identity formation. Education is not merely the transfer of information; it is the cultivation of personhood. It is through dialogue, mentorship, and moral example that students develop character, resilience, and purpose. No algorithm, regardless of sophistication, can replace the formative power of a trusted human guide. Therefore, the deployment of intelligent systems must be balanced by a deep investment in the emotional and ethical development of teachers and students alike.

Furthermore, there is a philosophical tension between the efficiency offered by AI and the messiness inherent in authentic learning. Human learning is nonlinear, emotionally driven, and context-dependent. It often includes moments of confusion, contradiction, and failure that are difficult to quantify or model. Over-reliance on intelligent systems risks reducing learning to a series of optimizations, thereby neglecting the transformative potential of struggle, ambiguity, and reflection. Education must resist the temptation to equate intelligence with correctness or speed. True intelligence includes the capacity to question, to doubt, and to imagine differently.

As intelligent learning systems continue to evolve, they must also be embedded within a broader educational ecosystem that includes family, community, and culture. Learning does not occur in a vacuum. Students bring with them a lifetime of experiences, beliefs, and values that shape how they engage with knowledge. AI systems must be designed to honor these complexities rather than flatten them. This means allowing for local customization, multilingual interfaces, and culturally embedded content. It also means designing systems that support—not replace—human connection.

At the policy level, governments must play a proactive role in regulating the development and implementation of intelligent learning systems. This includes establishing standards for transparency, equity, and accessibility. It also includes funding research on long-term outcomes, supporting the development of open-source platforms, and ensuring that underserved communities are not left behind in the AI transformation. Education cannot be allowed to become a privilege of the technologically fluent. It must remain a universal right, enriched by technology but not determined by it.

Finally, the rise of intelligent learning systems requires a redefinition of what it means to be educated. Traditional models have emphasized the accumulation of knowledge and the reproduction of established norms. In contrast, intelligent systems invite a vision of education as adaptive, interactive, and co-created. This vision aligns more closely with the realities of the 21st century, where knowledge is abundant, information is dynamic, and the ability to learn continuously is more valuable than any static credential.

To further comprehend the transformative power of intelligent learning systems, one must explore their influence on curriculum design and content delivery. Traditional curricula, structured around rigid scopes and sequences, often fail to account for variations in student background knowledge, interest levels, and learning preferences. Intelligent systems, by contrast, can disaggregate curriculum into modular units, each of which can be dynamically assembled in response to learner profiles. These profiles are not static constructs but are continuously updated through data generated by the learner's interactions with the system. As a result, each learner receives a tailored curriculum pathway, optimized not only for content mastery but for cognitive engagement and emotional readiness.

This modularization allows for the integration of interdisciplinary content that reflects the complexity of real-world problems. In place of isolated lessons in science, mathematics, language, or history, intelligent systems can facilitate learning experiences that weave these disciplines together around central questions or challenges. For instance, a unit on climate change might incorporate scientific modeling, statistical analysis, persuasive writing, and historical context. Such integration cultivates holistic thinking, one of the most essential skills in an era defined by complexity and uncertainty.

Moreover, intelligent learning systems can embed formative assessment into every aspect of the learning process. Rather than relying on end-of-unit tests or periodic standardized exams, these systems provide continuous, low-stakes feedback that enables students to understand their own learning progress in real time. Immediate feedback, tailored to the specific error or misconception, has been shown to significantly improve retention and understanding. It also reduces the fear of failure, encouraging students to take intellectual risks and explore difficult concepts without the anxiety associated with high-stakes assessments.

From a teacher's perspective, the availability of real-time performance data across multiple dimensions—comprehension, engagement, emotional state, and pacing—can inform instructional decisions with a degree of precision that traditional classroom observation cannot match. Teachers can intervene earlier, differentiate more effectively, and engage in proactive support rather than reactive remediation. These insights also facilitate professional development by highlighting areas in which the teacher's instructional strategies may require refinement or adaptation.

Importantly, intelligent learning systems can also play a pivotal role in addressing learning loss and educational recovery following disruptions such as the COVID-19 pandemic. During periods of remote learning, many students experienced significant academic setbacks due to inconsistent access to instruction, lack of digital infrastructure, and socio-emotional challenges. Intelligent systems can identify these learning gaps at an individual level and generate recovery plans that prioritize foundational concepts, integrate scaffolded instruction, and track progress toward closure. This personalized approach stands in stark contrast to blanket remediation models that often bore advanced students and overwhelm those in need.

The use of intelligent systems in early childhood education presents another frontier of opportunity. During the formative years of cognitive development, children benefit from responsive environments that adapt to their emergent needs and interests. AI-powered learning tools designed for young learners can interpret vocalizations, facial expressions, and interaction patterns to provide age-appropriate stimulation and support. These systems can reinforce phonemic awareness, number sense, and emotional regulation while collecting data that informs parental engagement and educator interventions. However, their use must be carefully moderated to ensure that screen time does not displace critical elements of early learning, such as physical activity, imaginative play, and social interaction.

In middle and high school contexts, intelligent learning systems offer powerful tools for career exploration and pathway alignment. By analyzing a student's academic performance, preferences, and behavioral indicators, AI systems can suggest potential career trajectories and the academic or technical competencies required for each. These insights can then be used to personalize elective choices, internship placements, and extracurricular involvement. Moreover, intelligent systems can connect students with industry mentors, virtual job shadowing opportunities, and real-world problem-solving scenarios, thereby making education more relevant and motivational.

In higher education and lifelong learning, the integration of intelligent systems is revolutionizing the concept of credentialing. Traditional degree programs, often costly and time-bound, are giving way to micro-credentials, digital badges, and competency-based certifications. These alternatives are more flexible, modular, and aligned with the demands of the labor market. AI systems can track a learner's mastery across diverse learning experiences—formal and informal—and generate a verified portfolio that demonstrates real-world skills. This shift places value on what a learner can do, rather than where or how long they studied.

A parallel development is the emergence of AI-enabled peer learning communities. Intelligent platforms can analyze learner profiles and match students for collaborative projects, discussion forums, and peer tutoring. These peer networks enhance motivation, deepen understanding, and cultivate social-emotional competencies that are critical for success in both academic and professional environments. Unlike traditional group work, which often suffers from misaligned abilities or interests, AI-driven peer matching increases the likelihood of productive and mutually beneficial interactions.

Despite these advancements, it is essential to maintain a critical perspective on the implementation of intelligent systems in education. Technological innovation alone cannot resolve the systemic inequalities that shape educational access and outcomes. In fact, without deliberate efforts to ensure equitable access to AI infrastructure, there is a risk that intelligent systems will exacerbate existing divides. Schools serving affluent communities may have the bandwidth, devices, and support systems to fully implement intelligent learning, while under-resourced schools struggle with basic connectivity. Policymakers must therefore prioritize funding models that enable equitable access, digital inclusion, and ongoing support for technology integration in marginalized communities.

Ethical literacy must also be built into the design and use of intelligent systems. Students, teachers, and parents must be educated about how these systems work, what data they collect, how algorithms make decisions, and what rights users have. Transparency in algorithmic processes is not only a matter of fairness but of democratic accountability. Intelligent learning systems must be auditable, interpretable, and responsive to user feedback. Moreover, there must be clear channels for redress in cases where students are unfairly classified, recommended, or assessed.

Institutional culture represents another barrier to the effective adoption of intelligent systems. Many educators are understandably wary of new technologies, particularly when they feel imposed rather than integrated. Professional development must therefore be robust, ongoing, and co-constructed with teachers. Rather than positioning AI as a replacement for teacher expertise, training programs must frame it as a tool that enhances teacher autonomy, efficacy, and impact. Teachers must also be given the time and space to experiment with these systems, reflect on their use, and contribute to their evolution.

The implementation of intelligent learning systems also raises important questions about the role of government and private industry in shaping the educational landscape. Many of the most advanced platforms are developed by private technology companies, whose motivations may not always align with public educational goals. Governments must establish frameworks for procurement, evaluation, and partnership that prioritize student well-being, pedagogical integrity, and long-term sustainability. Public-private partnerships can yield powerful innovations, but only when guided by clear ethical standards and rigorous public oversight.

Finally, the global dimension of intelligent learning systems cannot be ignored. While much of the research and development has emerged from technologically advanced countries, the benefits of intelligent learning must extend to the global South, to indigenous communities, and to multilingual populations. This requires the development of culturally responsive AI models, multilingual datasets, and localized content. It also requires collaboration across borders, disciplines, and sectors to ensure that the AI-powered education revolution is inclusive, diverse, and globally just.

Chapter 3

The New Role of the Teacher

The technological transformation underway in global education systems has not only reshaped curriculum and learning environments, but has also profoundly redefined the role of the teacher. In an age characterized by artificial intelligence, adaptive platforms, and data-driven personalization, the responsibilities, expectations, and identity of educators are undergoing a fundamental recalibration. No longer confined to the roles of information deliverers and classroom managers, teachers must now evolve into strategic facilitators, learning architects, ethical mentors, and collaborative designers of future-ready learners. This chapter explores the multifaceted evolution of the teacher's role, examines the professional competencies required in the AI era, and proposes a framework for cultivating empowered educators within intelligent learning ecosystems.

Historically, the image of the teacher has been closely aligned with the concept of authority. Teachers were regarded as the primary source of knowledge, the enforcers of discipline, and the gatekeepers of academic achievement. Their authority was derived from content mastery and institutional status. In traditional classroom settings, the teacher stood at the front, delivered instruction to passive recipients, administered assessments, and determined outcomes. The classroom functioned as a knowledge hierarchy, with the teacher positioned at the apex.

This instructional paradigm has been destabilized by the exponential growth of accessible knowledge, the rise of digital content platforms, and the democratization of learning resources. Students today can access world-class lectures, simulation tools, and AI tutors at any time, from virtually any location. In such an environment, the monopoly on knowledge held by teachers has been eroded. However, rather than diminishing the importance of educators, this shift has elevated their function to a new level of sophistication and strategic relevance.

In the AI-enhanced classroom, the teacher's role is no longer to transmit facts but to cultivate wisdom. Educators must guide students through the process of inquiry, help them make sense of abundant information, and support the development of critical thinking, ethical reasoning, and emotional intelligence. The modern teacher serves as a curator of experiences, a coach of cognition, and a builder of learning communities. This evolution requires not only a change in skill set but a transformation in professional identity.

One of the central roles of the teacher in the intelligent learning system is that of a learning engineer. Teachers must now collaborate with AI platforms to design learning pathways that are personalized, adaptive, and aligned with both curricular goals and student interests. This requires fluency not only in pedagogical theory but in data interpretation, instructional design, and digital tool integration. Teachers must analyze real-time data from intelligent systems to identify student strengths, gaps, and engagement patterns, then adjust strategies accordingly. This design process is iterative, evidence-based, and deeply learner-centered.

In this context, educators become co-pilots of the learning journey, continuously making decisions based on data, student input, and contextual variables. They must balance the algorithmic recommendations of AI platforms with their professional judgment and understanding of students as whole human beings. Where the system sees trends and probabilities, the teacher sees nuance, motivation, trauma, and potential. This human-in-the-loop model is essential for ensuring that intelligent learning remains ethical, empathetic, and developmentally appropriate.

The teacher's role also expands to include that of a mentor and relationship builder. Social-emotional learning has emerged as a core priority in contemporary education, driven by an increasing recognition of the interdependence between academic success and psychological well-being. Teachers must create emotionally safe learning environments where students feel seen, respected, and supported. They must build trust through consistent communication, model empathy in classroom interactions, and coach students in conflict resolution, resilience, and self-awareness.

These relational competencies cannot be replicated by machines. While AI systems can detect emotional states through voice tone or facial expression, they cannot form bonds of genuine care or model ethical behavior. Only human educators can respond with compassion to a student's fear of failure, offer encouragement in moments of doubt, or inspire purpose through personal example. These human connections are not ancillary to learning—they are foundational. In the absence of emotional safety and belonging, even the most sophisticated instructional design will fail to achieve its goals.

Another emergent function of the teacher is that of a facilitator of metacognition. As students engage with intelligent systems that adjust content, pace, and difficulty level in real time, they must also learn to monitor their own understanding, regulate their learning strategies, and reflect on their cognitive processes. Teachers must explicitly teach these skills, providing students with the language, tools, and habits to become self-directed learners. This includes helping students set goals, track progress, identify learning preferences, and develop personalized strategies for overcoming challenges.

Metacognitive development is particularly critical in the context of lifelong learning, where individuals must continually acquire new competencies in response to evolving technological and economic demands. Teachers must prepare students not just for content mastery but for learning how to learn. This recursive, reflective capacity is what will enable students to remain agile and adaptive in a world of constant change.

In parallel, teachers must also become cultural navigators. As classrooms become more diverse and globalized, educators must possess the intercultural competence to honor multiple identities, perspectives, and epistemologies. They must integrate culturally sustaining pedagogies that affirm students 'backgrounds and connect academic content to lived experience. In the AI era, where algorithms may unintentionally reproduce dominant cultural narratives or marginalize minority voices, the teacher's role in ensuring cultural inclusivity becomes even more vital.

This requires a deep understanding of social justice, systemic inequities, and the historical contexts that shape educational experience.

Teachers must be trained not only in inclusive curriculum design but in the critical interrogation of educational technology itself. Who designs the AI? Whose knowledge is represented in the training data? What assumptions are encoded into the platform? Educators must become advocates for equity, pushing back against technological determinism and ensuring that the digital tools used in classrooms serve the interests of all learners.

Furthermore, the teacher of the future must function as a community connector. Intelligent systems, while powerful, operate within the digital realm. Teachers must help students bridge the gap between virtual learning and real-world application. This includes facilitating service-learning projects, organizing community-based challenges, and building partnerships with local organizations. It also includes involving families in the learning process, using technology to maintain open lines of communication, and supporting parents in understanding the tools and strategies being used to educate their children.

The future teacher must also engage in continuous professional learning. The pace of technological change necessitates that educators remain intellectually agile, continuously updating their knowledge and refining their practice. This requires professional development that is ongoing, personalized, and embedded in daily work. AI can support this by providing teachers with real-time feedback, suggesting targeted resources, and connecting them with peer learning communities. However, systems and policies must be put in place to support teacher well-being, prevent burnout, and sustain morale in the face of rapid change.

To support the evolution of teacher identity, educational systems must rethink the ways in which teachers are recruited, trained, and retained. Pre-service teacher education must integrate technology fluency, design thinking, and systems-level analysis alongside traditional pedagogy. It must also emphasize emotional intelligence, ethical reasoning, and social justice. Mentorship programs, induction pathways, and career advancement models must recognize and reward the expanded skill sets that educators are now expected to demonstrate.

Compensation structures, professional recognition, and workplace culture must evolve to reflect the increasing complexity and importance of the teacher's role. Educators must be seen not as implementers of external mandates but as co-creators of the future of learning. They must be granted professional autonomy, respected as intellectuals, and empowered to lead innovation within their schools and districts. Without this revaluation of the teaching profession, the promise of intelligent learning systems will remain unfulfilled.

Finally, the teacher must be envisioned as a moral compass. In a world where artificial intelligence can outpace human reasoning in computation and prediction, educators must ensure that learning remains grounded in values, purpose, and collective well-being. Teachers must help students confront ethical dilemmas, understand the societal impact of technology, and grapple with questions that have no clear answers. They must model integrity, courage, and humility. In short, teachers must cultivate not only knowledge, but wisdom.

To fully appreciate the magnitude of the teacher's evolving role in an AI-augmented education system, one must examine the intersection of pedagogy and ethics. The capacity for educators to serve as ethical stewards within data-rich learning environments is increasingly essential. Intelligent learning systems operate on the basis of algorithms, many of which lack transparency to both users and implementers. These systems, while capable of tailoring instruction and automating tasks, cannot independently make ethical decisions about learning equity, cultural representation, or fairness in student assessment. The human teacher must assume responsibility for mediating the ethical implications of AI use in education.

This mediation involves the critical evaluation of digital platforms and their alignment with pedagogical values. Teachers must interrogate whether these technologies reinforce narrow definitions of success, perpetuate cultural biases, or devalue non-quantifiable aspects of learning such as creativity, empathy, and collaboration. A system that rewards speed and correctness above deep understanding and social learning may inadvertently reshape student priorities in detrimental ways. Teachers must act as counterbalances to such tendencies, ensuring that learning remains aligned with the holistic development of the learner.

In addition to ethical mediation, the teacher must now operate as a translator between technological outputs and human understanding. Intelligent systems often generate complex visualizations of learning data, including engagement maps, performance dashboards, and behavioral heatmaps. While these tools offer valuable insights, they can overwhelm or mislead if not properly interpreted. Teachers must possess the data literacy to extract actionable insights, identify anomalies, and contextualize information within the broader narrative of each learner's journey. This requires ongoing professional development in data analytics, educational measurement, and system-level evaluation.

Moreover, teachers serve a critical function in the personalization of instruction. While AI can identify what content a student struggles with, it lacks the nuanced understanding of *why*. Only human educators can interpret how a student's cultural background, emotional state, previous trauma, or social dynamics are influencing their learning behavior. Teachers must use this contextual intelligence to customize interventions, modify expectations, and scaffold experiences in ways that technology alone cannot achieve. This personalization requires a deep commitment to knowing each student—not only through data points but through sustained relational engagement.

The role of teacher as researcher has also gained prominence. In dynamic learning ecosystems, educators must adopt a mindset of inquiry and experimentation. They must collect and analyze evidence of what works in their context, adapt strategies accordingly, and contribute findings to the broader professional community. This action research orientation transforms teachers into agents of innovation and continuous improvement. It also reinforces the importance of practitioner voice in shaping the future of education policy and practice.

In support of this, schools and districts must create conditions in which teacher-led inquiry is valued and resourced. Professional learning communities, research partnerships with universities, and collaborative design labs can provide platforms for teachers to share insights, test hypotheses, and co-create new models of practice. These structures affirm the professional agency of educators and elevate their contributions beyond the confines of the classroom.

The teacher's new responsibilities also extend to digital citizenship education. In a world where students navigate a vast digital landscape filled with misinformation, cyberbullying, surveillance capitalism, and algorithmic manipulation, teachers must equip learners with the critical tools to engage responsibly. This includes fostering media literacy, teaching ethical online behavior, and helping students understand how their data is collected, used, and monetized. Teachers must create spaces for dialogue about digital identity, privacy rights, and the societal impact of emerging technologies.

These conversations must not be limited to surface-level discussions of safety or etiquette. Rather, they must delve into the power structures that shape digital life, the commercial interests that drive platform design, and the civic responsibilities of users in democratic societies. Teachers must support students in becoming not only consumers of information but ethical participants in digital ecosystems. This dimension of the teacher's role is especially critical in preparing students to live with, and not merely in, artificial intelligence.

As technology further integrates into the physical classroom environment through augmented reality, virtual reality, and sensor-based systems, the teacher's responsibility for environmental orchestration increases. Physical space must be optimized not only for collaboration and movement but for the strategic placement of devices, wearables, and immersive tools. Teachers must understand the affordances and limitations of each modality and design learning environments that balance stimulation with focus, novelty with clarity, and interactivity with reflection.

In remote and hybrid learning models, teachers must also develop competencies in digital presence. The absence of physical proximity in online spaces challenges traditional methods of engagement, motivation, and classroom management. Teachers must learn to build community through screens, maintain relational connection in asynchronous contexts, and design digital learning experiences that are not merely transmissive but participatory. This requires proficiency in platform navigation, content curation, video facilitation, and digital empathy.

Professional identity for teachers must be reimagined to reflect this new constellation of roles. Teaching must be recognized not as a static occupation but as a dynamic profession that intersects with data science, psychology, design, ethics, and community leadership. This expanded identity must be supported by updated licensure frameworks, certification pathways, and leadership pipelines that recognize the evolving competencies required in the AI era.

Mentorship and leadership development within the teaching profession are essential to cultivating this next generation of educators. Veteran teachers must be equipped to mentor newer colleagues not only in pedagogy but in technology integration and cultural responsiveness. Distributed leadership models can empower teachers to lead innovation efforts, coach peers, and contribute to systemic transformation. This flattening of organizational hierarchy fosters a culture of shared responsibility and mutual learning, both of which are essential in fast-changing environments.

Teacher well-being must also be prioritized. The expansion of roles, coupled with the emotional labor of supporting students in an uncertain world, places significant demands on educators. Institutions must provide mental health support, manageable workloads, and professional autonomy. Without such supports, the demands of the modern teaching role may lead to burnout, attrition, and a loss of institutional memory.

In addition, compensation models must reflect the increased complexity and value of the teaching profession. Teachers who design AI-enhanced curricula, manage learning platforms, lead professional development, and serve as ethical stewards should be recognized and rewarded accordingly. Failure to elevate the profession economically will result in talent shortages and diminished educational quality, undermining the very innovations AI promises to enable.

Finally, the teacher must be seen as a visionary. While AI can project trends and generate forecasts, only human educators can articulate visions of education rooted in dignity, justice, and human flourishing. Teachers must help shape the moral direction of educational innovation, ensuring that it serves not only efficiency but equity, not only automation but aspiration. In doing so, they must remain steadfast in their commitment to the transformative power of education as a deeply human endeavor.

Chapter 4

Preparing the AI-Ready Parent

In the rapidly evolving educational landscape shaped by artificial intelligence, the involvement of parents has become more critical than ever. No longer limited to traditional roles of support and supervision, parents must now embrace a transformative function: that of informed collaborators, ethical guides, and lifelong learning facilitators. The modern child's relationship with learning begins not in the classroom but in the home, long before formal education commences. Consequently, the preparedness of parents to engage with AI-enhanced education systems has a direct impact on the trajectory of a child's academic, cognitive, and emotional development.

To prepare the AI-ready parent, one must first define what this designation entails. An AI-ready parent is one who understands the technologies shaping their child's learning experiences, possesses the literacy to evaluate educational tools critically, and contributes meaningfully to decisions regarding the integration of artificial intelligence in educational contexts. More than a passive participant, the AI-ready parent is a proactive stakeholder who champions equity, safeguards data rights, and fosters adaptive learning behaviors at home. The capacity to fulfill this role requires both mindset shifts and structural support.

The emergence of intelligent learning systems has reconfigured the traditional boundaries between school and home. Learning no longer adheres to strict temporal or physical constraints. Students can access personalized educational content at any hour, from any device, in any setting. As a result, the home has become a de facto extension of the classroom. This shift necessitates a reconceptualization of parental engagement. The AI-ready parent must not only monitor screen time or assist with homework but must cultivate an environment that supports curiosity, inquiry, and resilience in a technology-mediated learning process.

Digital literacy forms the foundation of parental readiness. Parents must develop the ability to understand how artificial intelligence operates in educational tools—the nature of algorithms, the function of machine learning, and the implications of data-driven personalization. This literacy is not intended to transform parents into programmers, but to equip them with the critical faculties necessary to interpret how and why their children are being recommended certain content, assessed in specific ways, or nudged toward particular learning paths. Awareness of how algorithmic decisions are made empowers parents to ask informed questions and advocate for transparent, fair, and inclusive educational practices.

This digital literacy must extend to data privacy and protection. Intelligent systems often rely on extensive data collection, including behavioral, biometric, and performance metrics. Parents must understand what data is being gathered, how it is stored, who has access to it, and how it may be used beyond the immediate educational purpose. Schools and technology providers have a responsibility to communicate this information clearly, but parents must also assume a watchdog role, insisting on consent protocols, deletion rights, and accountability mechanisms. The AI-ready parent must be vigilant against the commodification of their child's data and the potential for surveillance masquerading as personalization.

Beyond technical understanding, the AI-ready parent must cultivate a deep pedagogical partnership with educators. In AI-enhanced classrooms, learning plans may shift dynamically in response to student performance. This fluidity demands more frequent and nuanced communication between school and home. Traditional parent-teacher conferences are insufficient in frequency or scope to maintain alignment. Instead, ongoing digital channels must be established, and parents must actively participate in interpreting learning analytics, setting goals, and reinforcing school-based learning at home. This partnership transforms parents from spectators to collaborators in their child's educational journey.

In practical terms, this collaboration may involve reviewing dashboard summaries, engaging with progress alerts, or co-constructing learning plans alongside teachers and intelligent systems. It also includes contributing context that AI systems cannot access—insights into a child's emotional state, home responsibilities, language background, or special needs. These human variables often influence learning outcomes more than any algorithmic recommendation, and the parent is uniquely positioned to interpret and communicate them.

The emotional landscape of the child must also be a core focus of parental involvement. While intelligent systems can detect engagement levels, they cannot replace the affective labor provided by parents. The AI-ready parent must serve as an emotional anchor, offering reassurance, encouragement, and validation in moments of frustration or uncertainty. They must also help children process the emotional implications of AI use, including comparisons with algorithmic judgments, perceptions of fairness, and fears of surveillance. These conversations build psychological resilience and ethical discernment—skills that are as important as cognitive mastery in an AI-saturated world.

To this end, parents must also model digital ethics. Children learn not only from direct instruction but from observation. The AI-ready parent demonstrates responsible technology use, respects digital boundaries, and engages in critical discussions about online behavior, misinformation, and identity. They introduce children to the concept of digital footprints, encourage skepticism toward algorithmically curated content, and reinforce the importance of consent in digital interactions. These lessons extend far beyond school performance; they prepare children for the civic responsibilities of participation in a technologically mediated society.

Creating a home environment conducive to intelligent learning also requires intentional design. Parents must ensure access to reliable internet, devices suited for educational use, and quiet spaces for focused engagement. They must manage technology use in ways that balance learning with play, screen time with movement, and independence with oversight. While intelligent systems offer flexibility, they also demand structure. Children must be guided in setting routines, establishing boundaries, and reflecting on their progress. The parent serves not as a passive host but as an orchestrator of habits that support sustainable, self-regulated learning.

Parents must also foster metacognitive awareness in their children.

Intelligent systems may present personalized content, but it is the parent who can guide reflection on what was learned, how it was learned, and why it matters. These conversations transform learning from a transactional activity into a meaning-making process. Parents who ask open-ended questions, encourage journaling, and support goal setting reinforce the reflective habits that enable students to thrive not only in school but across the lifespan.

Moreover, AI readiness includes future orientation. Parents must understand the broader trends shaping education and work in the twenty-first century. They must anticipate how automation, globalization, and climate change will influence job markets, social dynamics, and skill requirements. This foresight allows them to support educational choices that are not merely compliant with school mandates but strategically aligned with future opportunities. Whether selecting electives, evaluating extracurriculars, or navigating career pathways, the AI-ready parent must adopt a long-term perspective that connects current learning to future relevance.

This future-oriented mindset also involves redefining success. In a world where machines increasingly handle routine cognitive tasks, human strengths such as creativity, empathy, collaboration, and adaptability become paramount. The AI-ready parent must therefore resist narrow definitions of academic achievement and instead celebrate holistic growth. They must affirm progress in communication, curiosity, and ethical reasoning as indicators of a successful learner. This values shift is essential to counteract the risk that data-driven systems will reduce children to scores, ranks, or predictions.

The cultivation of adaptive parenting strategies becomes imperative in light of the dynamic educational environment shaped by artificial intelligence. The capacity to respond constructively to change, to remain open to emerging tools, and to embrace iterative learning as a family unit represents the mindset required of twenty-first century parents. Adaptability is not synonymous with compliance; it is the deliberate choice to meet complexity with resilience, experimentation, and collaboration. The AI-ready parent models this disposition, not only in their interactions with school systems but in their personal learning journey as well.

To that end, lifelong learning must not be regarded as an abstract concept but as an embodied parental practice. Parents must actively pursue opportunities to expand their understanding of artificial intelligence, education policy, digital ethics, and the social implications of emerging technologies. Whether through reading, community workshops, online courses, or professional development, the AI-ready parent embraces learning as a civic duty. In doing so, they send a powerful message to their children: that growth is not bound by age, that intellectual humility is a strength, and that participation in the future requires intentional preparation.

Community infrastructure plays a crucial role in supporting this parental transformation. Public institutions—including libraries, community centers, and local education agencies—must provide accessible programs to help parents gain technological fluency and pedagogical confidence. These initiatives must be inclusive in design, recognizing the socioeconomic, linguistic, and cultural diversity of families. Equity in AI education begins at home, and without targeted support, existing disparities will only deepen. The AI-ready parent cannot emerge solely from personal initiative; structural support must be provided to democratize access to tools, knowledge, and networks.

Furthermore, policy frameworks must evolve to recognize and institutionalize the role of parents as educational partners. Parent councils, advisory committees, and school governance bodies must include deliberation on AI integration and digital equity. Clear guidelines regarding data consent, algorithmic transparency, and ethical oversight should be co-developed with families, not imposed unilaterally by educational institutions or technology vendors. The AI-ready parent is not a passive recipient of policy but a co-author of the ethical, pedagogical, and governance standards that shape intelligent education.

The influence of parents on early learning is particularly critical. Long before children encounter formal AI tools in school, their cognitive and emotional development is shaped by the home environment. From infancy through early childhood, language exposure, emotional security, exploration opportunities, and parent-child interaction form the foundation upon which all later learning rests. The

AI-ready parent must be intentional in these formative years, fostering habits of attention, curiosity, and emotional regulation that will enable children to benefit from personalized learning technologies later in life.

This early-stage preparation must avoid screen dependency and instead emphasize interactive play, verbal engagement, and emotional attunement. As children grow older, technology can be introduced gradually and strategically, guided by developmental readiness rather than market pressure. The AI-ready parent exercises discernment in technology adoption, prioritizing tools that reinforce learning goals and align with family values. They maintain an active role in co-viewing, co-creating, and co-reflecting on digital content, ensuring that technology enhances rather than replaces human interaction.

In addition, the parenting role must expand to include career guidance in a context of accelerating change. Traditional models of linear career planning are becoming obsolete in the face of rapid technological disruption. The AI-ready parent must help children explore emerging fields, understand the interplay between automation and employment, and cultivate transferable skills such as problem-solving, interdisciplinary thinking, and emotional intelligence. This includes exposing children to a variety of career narratives, facilitating mentorship opportunities, and encouraging entrepreneurial exploration.

Financial literacy also intersects with AI-readiness. Parents must understand how AI is reshaping economic systems, influencing job markets, and transforming personal finance. They must equip children with foundational knowledge of digital currencies, algorithmic trading, gig economies, and automation-related job displacement. In doing so, they prepare children to make informed decisions about education, employment, and investment in a volatile and opportunity-rich economic landscape.

Parental advocacy extends beyond the household into broader civic engagement. The AI-ready parent participates in public discourse about education reform, joins community coalitions advocating for ethical technology use, and holds institutions accountable for inclusive, transparent practices. They understand that systemic change requires collective action and that their voice, when amplified in coordination with others, can shape policy, resource allocation, and curriculum design. This dimension of the parenting role transforms it into a form of civic leadership, where care for one's own child becomes inseparable from care for the community.

The spiritual and philosophical dimensions of parenting also require consideration in the AI era. As machines gain capabilities that once belonged exclusively to humans—such as creativity, language generation, and strategic planning—questions arise about the nature of consciousness, the meaning of work, and the essence of human identity. The AI-ready parent engages children in these existential inquiries, fostering reflection on what it means to be human in a world of artificial agency. They introduce values-based frameworks for decision-making, discuss the moral implications of technology, and encourage discernment in choosing when and how to use intelligent tools.

To facilitate this, parents may draw from religious traditions, philosophical systems, or cultural narratives that provide grounding in purpose, dignity, and responsibility. These frameworks serve as counterweights to the efficiency-driven logic of AI systems, reminding children that human flourishing involves more than optimized outcomes. The AI-ready parent positions technology as a tool for service, growth, and justice, rather than as an end in itself.

Moreover, intergenerational dynamics must be acknowledged. Many parents raising children today were not themselves educated in digitally immersive environments. The speed of technological change has created a generational knowledge gap that can lead to feelings of inadequacy or disconnection. The AI-ready parent confronts this gap not with resignation but with openness. They embrace opportunities to learn from their children, to co-navigate new tools, and to model humility in the face of complexity. In doing so, they normalize learning as a relational process and strengthen family bonds through mutual exploration.

Schools can support this dynamic by providing intergenerational learning experiences, such as family coding nights, joint project exhibitions, and digital storytelling workshops. These events validate parental involvement, honor the contributions of both generations, and reinforce the idea that education is a shared endeavor. When parents and children learn together, a culture of continuous growth and mutual respect is established.

Finally, the AI-ready parent must embrace the long view. Educational outcomes shaped by artificial intelligence may not always be immediately visible or easily quantified. Personalized learning may take unconventional forms, including project-based work, asynchronous exploration, or self-directed inquiry. The parent must resist the urge to over-structure, over-monitor, or over-correct. Instead, they must trust the developmental process, affirm the intrinsic motivation of the learner, and create space for autonomy to emerge.

This requires a fundamental redefinition of control. Rather than dictating content or pace, the AI-ready parent scaffolds habits, values, and decision-making capacities. They create boundaries that protect well-being, offer guidance when sought, and remain present as a stable force in an unpredictable world. Their legacy is not in the micromanagement of outcomes but in the cultivation of character, curiosity, and courage.

Chapter 5

Personalized Learning Pathways in the Age of Algorithms

The emergence of artificial intelligence has ushered in a paradigmatic shift in how education is conceptualized, delivered, and experienced. One of the most transformative developments within this shift is the rise of personalized learning pathways—adaptive, data-informed, student-centered trajectories designed to meet individual learners where they are and guide them toward mastery. At the core of this transformation lies algorithmic intelligence, capable of analyzing vast datasets in real time and recommending precise, individualized instructional strategies. However, while the potential of these systems is immense, the implications are equally profound. To responsibly implement personalized learning in the AI era, it is essential to explore its philosophical foundations, technical infrastructure, pedagogical shifts, ethical considerations, and long-term societal implications.

Personalized learning, in its most accurate definition, refers to the customization of learning experiences based on each learner's needs, strengths, interests, and pace. Traditionally, educators have attempted to differentiate instruction through small group work, leveled texts, and scaffolding techniques. However, the scalability of such efforts has remained constrained by time, resources, and class sizes. AI-driven platforms now offer the potential to democratize personalization by automating diagnostic assessments, adapting content in real-time, and recommending just-in-time supports. These platforms are capable of identifying gaps in understanding, tracking behavioral engagement, and forecasting future performance trajectories.

The foundation of these systems is data. Learning management systems, digital assessments, gamified platforms, and wearable technologies collect thousands of microdata points—from keystroke speed to answer confidence, from eye movement to time-on-task. These data are processed through machine learning algorithms to build comprehensive learner profiles, which in turn guide content delivery, pacing, and remediation. At their most advanced, these systems do not merely adjust the difficulty level of questions but dynamically reconfigure entire sequences of instruction based on predictive models of student comprehension.

Such capabilities, while promising, raise critical questions about the definition of learning. If content delivery becomes increasingly mediated by algorithms, then human educators must clarify their roles in constructing meaning, nurturing motivation, and shaping moral judgment. Learning is not a mere transaction of information; it is a transformation of the self. Personalized pathways must not become individualized echo chambers wherein students are fed only what they are comfortable with or already inclined toward. The true goal of personalized learning is not to make learning easier but to make it *deeper*, more relevant, and more enduring.

To achieve this, personalization must move beyond content adaptation and incorporate multimodal engagement. This includes offering students a range of media through which to explore concepts—text, video, simulation, collaborative projects—and allowing them to demonstrate mastery in varied formats such as essays, presentations, prototypes, or digital portfolios. Such flexibility not only honors diverse learning preferences but cultivates the metacognitive skills necessary for lifelong learning. An algorithm can propose a path, but it is the learner who must choose how to walk it. Personalized systems must therefore include opportunities for reflection, goal setting, and iterative feedback.

Furthermore, effective personalization requires the integration of formative and summative assessment in meaningful ways. Traditional models rely heavily on standardized testing, which offers limited insight into individual growth. Intelligent systems, however, can embed continuous assessment into the learning process, capturing insights from student interactions, peer discussions, and project-based tasks. This continuous data stream enables a more holistic understanding of learner progress and permits real-time intervention. Nevertheless, assessment must remain a tool for growth rather than a mechanism of surveillance. Transparent feedback, student ownership of data, and growth-oriented language are essential to preserving trust and engagement.

Another critical dimension of personalized learning in the AI era is the alignment of learning paths with long-term goals and values. Too often, personalization is equated with hyper-efficiency—accelerating students through content as quickly as possible. This approach risks reducing education to a series of benchmarks devoid of purpose. Instead, learning paths must be designed with intentional connections to students 'aspirations, civic responsibilities, and ethical development. AI systems must be guided by human-designed frameworks that embed social-emotional learning, global competence, and character education into algorithmic recommendations.

Moreover, equity must be a central concern in the design and deployment of personalized learning systems. Without careful attention, these systems may reproduce or exacerbate existing inequities. Algorithms trained on biased data may misinterpret student behaviors, under-identify potential, or recommend limiting pathways. For example, students from underrepresented backgrounds may be disproportionately channeled into remedial tracks based on predictive models that fail to account for contextual factors. To prevent such outcomes, transparency in algorithm design, regular auditing of system outputs, and inclusive stakeholder input are essential.

Educators must also be trained to interpret and act upon personalized learning data. While algorithms can surface patterns, only humans can provide the nuanced interpretation and relational support required to translate those patterns into transformative learning experiences. Professional development must include data literacy, ethical data use, and human-centered instructional design. Teachers must understand not only what the data indicate but also how to contextualize them within the broader landscape of student development.

The learner's role in personalized systems must also be redefined. Rather than passive recipients of algorithmic instruction, students must become co-designers of their learning journeys. This includes setting personal goals, choosing among content modalities, reflecting on progress, and iterating learning plans based on feedback. Such agency fosters intrinsic motivation and prepares students for the ambiguity and autonomy of real-world problem-solving. To support this shift, schools must cultivate a culture of metacognition, risk-taking, and student voice.

Family engagement is another essential component. Personalized learning systems often extend into the home, especially in hybrid or remote learning environments. Parents must be equipped to interpret learning dashboards, support goal tracking, and co-create learning environments that reinforce school-based goals. Communication between home and school must be continuous, accessible, and two-way. Technology platforms should facilitate this engagement through multilingual interfaces, progress alerts, and contextual explanations of system recommendations.

As these systems mature, the importance of interoperability grows. Personalized learning cannot occur in isolation within a single platform. Learners engage across a range of environments—school, home, extracurricular programs, online communities. To support coherent learning pathways, data systems must communicate, and learning records must follow the learner across settings. This calls for the adoption of universal learning records (ULRs), secure data standards, and learner-controlled data wallets. The infrastructure for such a system must be developed with privacy, portability, and equity at its core.

The long-term societal implications of personalized learning also demand careful consideration. If personalization becomes the dominant mode of education, questions arise about collective identity, shared knowledge, and civic cohesion. Public education has traditionally served as a space where diverse individuals encounter common texts, histories, and norms. Fully individualized learning pathways risk fragmenting these shared experiences. Designers of personalized systems must therefore ensure that while learning is customized, it also includes opportunities for collaboration, discourse, and engagement with diverse perspectives.

An additional consideration arises from the psychological implications of persistent personalization. While algorithmic learning platforms can tailor content to the learner's current performance level, there exists the danger of unintentional stagnation, in which students are continuously offered material at or just above their current ability. This form of incremental progression may neglect the importance of exposure to challenging, unfamiliar, or even uncomfortable content—experiences essential for the development of cognitive flexibility and academic resilience. Personalization must therefore incorporate mechanisms that deliberately stretch the learner's capacity, ensuring that comfort does not come at the cost of growth.

Adaptive systems should embed what is commonly referred to in educational psychology as the "zone of proximal development." This zone represents the sweet spot between what a learner can accomplish independently and what requires guided assistance. Artificial intelligence, when applied thoughtfully, can identify this zone more precisely than traditional static assessments. However, identifying the zone is only the beginning. Educators and system designers must then determine how to provide scaffolding, encouragement, and contextual support to ensure that challenges are met with success rather than frustration.

Moreover, an over-reliance on algorithmic systems can displace the teacher's role as a dynamic facilitator of inquiry. If not carefully managed, this displacement may result in diminished human interaction, which remains vital to learning. Education, fundamentally, is a social process. Dialogues with peers, mentorship from instructors, and interpersonal exchanges form the crucible where meaning is negotiated and internalized. While algorithms can supplement instruction, they cannot replace the relational elements that define transformative educational experiences.

To preserve this human dimension, personalized systems must be designed to augment rather than supplant teacher presence. Educators must have full visibility into how recommendations are made, what decisions are automated, and where professional judgment should override algorithmic output. Interfaces must be intuitive, informative, and configurable, enabling educators to adjust pacing, content emphasis, and group dynamics as needed. This is not a minor design detail but a philosophical stance: intelligent systems must serve pedagogical vision, not dictate it.

The implementation of personalized learning pathways also requires new curricular frameworks. Traditional curricula are linear, standardized, and based on age-grade progression. Personalized curricula, by contrast, are modular, competency-based, and flexible. They allow learners to progress upon mastery, revisit foundational concepts as needed, and accelerate through material they have already demonstrated proficiency in. This restructuring demands a fundamental reorganization of educational institutions—from scheduling models to classroom configurations to assessment protocols.

Competency-based education (CBE) becomes the natural companion to personalized learning. In CBE models, students advance upon demonstration of skill or knowledge, rather than completion of time-based courses. Artificial intelligence facilitates this approach by continuously evaluating performance and updating learner profiles. However, the transition to CBE requires not only technological infrastructure but cultural shifts. Stakeholders must abandon the traditional association between age and grade level, and adopt new metrics for determining progress, graduation, and achievement.

Such shifts may face resistance from both institutional inertia and public perception. Parents, employers, and policymakers are accustomed to diplomas, grade point averages, and standardized test scores. Redesigning educational transcripts to reflect competencies, portfolios, and learning journeys demands broad-based communication strategies and cross-sector collaboration. Universities and industries must be engaged as co-designers in creating credentials that are both meaningful and portable in a post-industrial economy.

The economic model underlying education must also adapt. In traditional systems, schools are funded based on seat time and enrollment. Personalized learning disrupts this model by allowing asynchronous progress, variable pacing, and modular enrollment. New funding structures must account for these dynamics, ensuring that innovation does not disadvantage students from low-income or rural communities. Public investment in high-speed internet, device access, and educator training will be essential to prevent the emergence of a new digital divide.

One area of particular opportunity is the intersection of personalized learning with real-world experience. As students pursue individualized pathways, opportunities arise for integration with internships, apprenticeships, and community-based projects. AI systems can assist in matching students with opportunities aligned to their interests, aptitudes, and career goals. This blending of academic and experiential learning creates richer educational trajectories and strengthens the connection between school and society.

In addition to career alignment, personalized learning must include global awareness. AI systems should expose students to diverse perspectives, cross-cultural content, and international collaborations. In a connected world, education cannot remain provincial. Personalized systems must not only meet learners where they are but also guide them toward understanding where others come from. Inclusion of global competencies—such as cultural empathy, international ethics, and multilingualism—within learning algorithms is essential for nurturing global citizens.

Furthermore, the governance of personalized learning systems must prioritize ethical oversight. Algorithmic decision-making must be transparent, explainable, and auditable. Students and families must have the right to understand how decisions are made, challenge inaccuracies, and request human review. Regulatory bodies should establish standards for algorithmic accountability, including impact assessments, stakeholder consultations, and redress mechanisms. Personalization must not come at the cost of agency or justice.

As personalized learning systems proliferate, the importance of maintaining educational pluralism cannot be overstated. No single platform, algorithm, or framework should dominate the learning landscape. Diversity in pedagogical approach, content source, and instructional philosophy ensures that education remains a space for critical thinking, innovation, and dissent. Monocultures—whether technological or ideological—undermine the democratic purposes of education.

Finally, the long-term impact of personalized learning must be measured not only in terms of academic gains but in the cultivation of whole human beings. Education must prepare individuals to lead purposeful lives, contribute to democratic societies, and steward shared environments. Personalized learning pathways must therefore be evaluated on their ability to foster curiosity, integrity, compassion, and courage. These outcomes, though difficult to quantify, represent the true promise of education in the age of algorithms.

Chapter 6

AI as Teacher, Tutor, and Companion

The integration of artificial intelligence into educational systems marks a definitive departure from the industrial model of instruction. Historically, teaching has been defined by human interaction: the teacher standing at the center of the classroom, orchestrating knowledge delivery and student engagement through direct instruction, Socratic dialogue, and affective presence. This model, while still relevant, is increasingly being supplemented—and in some cases redefined—by intelligent systems capable of performing teaching functions with unprecedented precision, availability, and adaptability. In the context of twenty-first century learning, artificial intelligence is not merely a technological tool; it has begun to function as teacher, tutor, and, more recently, as educational companion.

The concept of AI as teacher is rooted in the automation of content delivery, assessment, and feedback. Intelligent tutoring systems (ITS) have existed for decades in rudimentary forms, offering programmed feedback based on predetermined responses. However, modern AI systems now possess the ability to generate real-time explanations, adjust instructional strategies based on learner behavior, and simulate humanlike interactions. These capabilities enable AI to assume many of the tasks traditionally reserved for classroom instructors, including lecturing, questioning, quizzing, reteaching, and even offering encouragement.

Unlike human teachers, AI systems are not limited by fatigue, scheduling constraints, or subjective bias. They can operate continuously, offering personalized attention to each learner regardless of class size. For students who require repeated exposure to foundational concepts, AI provides an opportunity for unlimited practice without the social pressure of peer observation or the risk of embarrassment. This creates a psychologically safe environment for exploration and error correction—an essential component of effective learning.

However, AI's role as teacher raises significant philosophical and pedagogical questions. If teaching is reduced to information transmission and error correction, then the use of AI is justified by efficiency. Yet if teaching is defined more broadly—as the cultivation of wisdom, character, and civic consciousness—then human educators remain irreplaceable. The most effective educational environments will therefore be hybrid in nature, combining the precision and scalability of AI with the empathy, contextual awareness, and moral reasoning of human instructors.

As a tutor, AI has demonstrated even greater potential. In this capacity, artificial intelligence operates not at the front of the classroom but alongside the learner, offering one-on-one guidance tailored to individual needs. AI-powered tutoring systems analyze students 'real-time responses, identify misconceptions, and provide scaffolding that adjusts dynamically to learner performance. These systems often incorporate natural language processing, enabling them to engage in dialogue, answer open-ended questions, and simulate conversational feedback.

One of the most notable advantages of AI tutoring lies in its capacity to close achievement gaps. Students who struggle to keep pace in traditional classrooms often lack access to individualized support outside of school hours. AI tutors can fill this gap by offering just-in-time assistance, targeted remediation, and opportunities for repeated practice. For students with disabilities, language differences, or interrupted schooling, AI tutors can be customized to accommodate unique learning profiles and ensure accessibility.

Furthermore, AI tutoring systems can serve as diagnostic tools for human educators. By capturing granular data on student engagement, comprehension, and pacing, these systems generate detailed profiles that inform instructional planning. Teachers can use these insights to differentiate instruction, group students more effectively, and intervene early when learning gaps emerge. In this way, AI does not replace the tutor; it enhances the tutor's capacity to provide responsive, data-informed support.

However, ethical concerns must be addressed. AI tutors are only as equitable as the data and algorithms upon which they are built. If training data reflect systemic biases—such as underrepresentation of certain dialects, learning styles, or cultural perspectives—then the system may misinterpret learner responses or provide inaccurate feedback. Transparent algorithm design, diverse data sourcing, and rigorous auditing are necessary to ensure that AI tutors uphold standards of fairness, inclusion, and accuracy.

The most emergent and complex function of AI in education is that of *companion*. In this role, AI moves beyond instructional delivery to provide motivational, emotional, and cognitive support throughout the learning journey. These systems incorporate affective computing—a branch of artificial intelligence that recognizes and responds to human emotions. By analyzing tone of voice, facial expressions, keystroke dynamics, and other behavioral indicators, AI companions can infer emotional states and adjust their responses accordingly.

The AI companion acts not only as a tutor but as a co-learner, coach, and confidant. It encourages persistence during frustration, celebrates achievement, and nudges learners toward goal setting and self-reflection. Some systems are capable of long-term memory retention, enabling them to recall previous conversations, learning goals, or challenges. This continuity of care creates a sense of relational stability that, while artificial, can feel meaningful to the learner.

In particular, AI companions have shown promise in supporting learners who experience social anxiety, trauma, or isolation. For students who struggle with human interaction—whether due to neurodiversity, language barriers, or personal circumstances—AI offers a nonjudgmental, patient presence. While this cannot substitute for human relationships, it can provide a bridge to engagement and confidence-building that later facilitates interpersonal development.

Yet the emotional dimension of AI companionship is fraught with ethical ambiguity. Developers and educators must ask whether children should form attachments to non-human entities and how such relationships might affect their social-emotional growth. There is a risk of displacing human intimacy with artificial simulation, potentially impairing empathy, critical thinking, or authentic connection. Designers must tread carefully, ensuring that AI companions are framed not as substitutes for human presence but as supplements that reinforce human values and promote relational skills.

The legal implications of AI companionship also require attention. If an AI system retains memory across sessions, stores emotional responses, or engages in psychologically suggestive dialogue, what responsibilities do developers and educators bear for the outcomes? Clear consent protocols, data protection standards, and parental oversight mechanisms must be embedded in any AI system that interacts with minors on an emotional or relational level. The line between support and surveillance is thin, and it must be guarded with transparency and accountability.

From a technical standpoint, the architecture of AI-as-companion systems necessitates complex integration. These platforms must combine language generation, sentiment analysis, adaptive learning, and user modeling within a unified interface. They must function across devices, support accessibility features, and deliver consistent performance in diverse settings. Moreover, they must provide interfaces for educators and parents to monitor engagement, intervene when necessary, and ensure alignment with pedagogical objectives.

As these systems evolve, the nature of the learning environment itself changes. Classrooms may no longer be structured around a single teacher delivering content but around dynamic constellations of human and artificial agents interacting in real time. Students may move fluidly between peer discussion, AI coaching, project-based exploration, and self-directed learning. The boundaries between physical and digital space, school and home, teacher and machine become increasingly porous. Educational design must adapt accordingly.

This reconceptualization of the learning space introduces new demands on infrastructure. High-speed connectivity, secure cloud platforms, device availability, and user-centered design become foundational to educational equity. Schools must invest not only in hardware and software but in the policies, training, and culture shifts required to support AI integration. Professional development must address not only technical fluency but pedagogical adaptation—how to co-teach with AI, when to override algorithmic suggestions, and how to preserve human judgment in a hybrid learning ecosystem.

The expanding role of AI in education also reshapes how students develop their understanding of knowledge, authority, and trust. Traditionally, the teacher has been perceived as a primary source of truth—an expert and moral guide within the classroom. However, the introduction of intelligent systems capable of providing real-time answers, personalized instruction, and emotionally responsive feedback complicates this perception. Students may begin to view AI as equally authoritative or, in some cases, more reliable than human instructors due to the precision and consistency of machine-generated responses.

This shift in epistemological trust has serious implications for critical thinking and digital literacy. Students must be taught not only how to use AI tools but how to interrogate their outputs. Questions such as: *What data is this AI drawing from? How does it determine accuracy? Who designed this system and with what values?* must become integral components of modern pedagogy. Instruction in AI literacy should include an understanding of algorithmic bias, limitations of training data, ethical design, and the human decisions that shape machine behavior.

Equipping students with this literacy ensures that the AI companion does not become an unquestioned authority but rather a tool subject to scrutiny and thoughtful interaction. In this context, the educator's role evolves into that of a mentor in digital discernment—modeling how to challenge sources, compare perspectives, and evaluate claims, whether they originate from humans or machines. The classroom becomes a training ground for digital citizenship in an AI-augmented world.

Parallel to this instructional shift is the transformation of assessment practices. AI systems can perform real-time evaluation, track longitudinal growth, and generate personalized feedback loops. While this enhances responsiveness and supports formative learning, it also raises questions about the validity and purpose of assessment. If students are evaluated continuously by invisible systems, how do they understand their own progress? Are they empowered by this data or overwhelmed by it?

To address this concern, assessment must be made transparent and participatory. Students should have access to their data, understand the criteria by which they are evaluated, and be given agency in shaping their learning goals. This transparency reinforces student autonomy and fosters intrinsic motivation. AI systems should be designed to support—not supplant—student reflection, self-assessment, and goal setting. Feedback must be framed not only in terms of correctness but in terms of growth, process, and future potential.

As AI becomes embedded across educational settings, a new set of ethical responsibilities emerges for designers, educators, and institutions. These include data privacy, informed consent, algorithmic accountability, and equity of access. Policies must ensure that student data is not exploited for commercial purposes, that AI systems do not entrench existing inequalities, and that users are protected from manipulation or harm. Educational institutions should establish ethical review boards and adopt AI governance frameworks to guide procurement, deployment, and oversight.

The role of AI as a long-term companion also intersects with emotional development. While AI can simulate empathy, it does not possess consciousness, intentionality, or genuine moral agency. Its ability to recognize emotion is limited to pattern detection; its expressions of care are programmed outputs. Students must be taught to understand this distinction, to recognize the difference between simulation and sincerity. This awareness is not meant to devalue AI, but to preserve the essential humanity of authentic relationships.

For younger students especially, there exists the potential for attachment to AI systems that appear nurturing, responsive, and present. While such interactions can support learning, they must be contextualized within a broader framework of human connection. Educators and caregivers must ensure that time spent with AI does not displace time spent with peers, mentors, and family. Social learning, cooperative tasks, and interpersonal problem-solving remain irreplaceable elements of holistic development.

Moreover, the emotional design of AI systems must avoid infantilization or coercion. Some platforms adopt overly animated interfaces, gamification techniques, or persuasive prompts that can distort student motivation. If learning becomes overly dependent on external stimuli or emotional triggers, students may struggle to develop self-regulation and intrinsic engagement. Designers must prioritize authenticity, developmental appropriateness, and pedagogical alignment in the affective design of AI companions.

Another critical consideration is cultural responsiveness. AI systems must reflect the diversity of learners 'backgrounds, languages, and worldviews. This includes not only content representation but also communication styles, contextual examples, and value frameworks. A culturally homogeneous AI system risks alienating or misinterpreting learners from underrepresented communities. Localization, multilingual support, and community co-design are necessary to ensure that AI companions serve all students equitably.

The potential of AI as a lifelong learning companion also merits attention. As educational pathways become more nonlinear, individuals will require guidance not only during their school years but throughout their careers. AI companions that evolve with the learner, maintaining a portfolio of experiences, preferences, and goals, could support continuous reskilling, career planning, and personal development. However, such continuity also intensifies concerns about data retention, surveillance, and autonomy. Learners must have control over their data, the ability to reset or delete their history, and the right to opt out of persistent profiling.

This vision of AI as an enduring companion underscores the need for educational systems to articulate the moral purpose of learning. The ultimate aim of education is not simply knowledge acquisition or workforce preparation, but the cultivation of wisdom, justice, and human flourishing. AI can support this mission only to the extent that its design, deployment, and governance are aligned with humanistic values.

In conclusion, the emergence of AI as teacher, tutor, and companion represents a profound redefinition of the educational experience. These roles expand the capacity of schools to offer personalized, responsive, and accessible learning while simultaneously introducing new ethical, pedagogical, and philosophical challenges. The integration of AI into the teaching process demands a rigorous commitment to transparency, equity, human agency, and relational integrity. As these systems become more sophisticated, the responsibility of educators and policymakers increases—not only to manage technology, but to reimagine education in light of what it means to be human in an age of intelligent machines.

Chapter 7

The AI Curriculum – What Every Child Must Now Learn

The rapid acceleration of artificial intelligence across industries, services, and daily life requires a fundamental rethinking of educational content. The traditional curriculum, built largely for the industrial and early information eras, must evolve into a new paradigm—one that prepares learners not only to use AI, but to understand, critique, and co-create it. The future of education will not simply involve teaching about artificial intelligence as a subject; rather, it will involve embedding AI-related competencies, literacies, and ethical frameworks across all areas of learning. This integrated approach is the foundation of what can now be defined as the *AI Curriculum*—a holistic, multi-disciplinary, and ethically grounded learning framework that every child must be equipped with in order to thrive.

The AI Curriculum is not a single subject. It is an overarching pedagogical transformation that touches language, mathematics, science, social studies, the arts, and physical development. Just as literacy and numeracy once served as the bedrock for participation in modern economies, AI literacy now constitutes a core competency for both personal and civic life. At its essence, the AI Curriculum teaches students to become responsible agents in an intelligent world: to understand algorithms, to question machine output, to work symbiotically with digital systems, and to retain their moral compass amidst exponential technological change.

The development of such a curriculum begins with defining its core pillars. These pillars include: (1) computational thinking and logic, (2) data and algorithmic literacy, (3) systems design and machine learning concepts, (4) ethical reasoning and digital philosophy, and (5) human-AI collaboration. Each of these elements is not merely technical; they represent cognitive tools that shape how students see and influence the world around them.

Computational Thinking and Logic

At the foundation of the AI Curriculum lies computational thinking. This is not equivalent to programming or coding, though it often includes both. Rather, it involves the structured mental habits that enable individuals to approach problems with clarity, abstraction, and precision. It involves skills such as decomposition (breaking problems into parts), pattern recognition, algorithmic design, and evaluation of outcomes.

Introducing computational thinking at early educational stages builds the scaffolding for later understanding of algorithms and systems. Activities may include puzzle solving, logical sequencing, flowchart creation, and simple game design. These skills prepare learners not just for computer science, but for structured problem solving across all domains—from writing a persuasive essay to engineering a science experiment. As students advance through the stages of education, computational thinking should be integrated into every subject area, including history (e.g., evaluating cause and effect), art (e.g., pattern-based design), and mathematics (e.g., algorithmic strategies).

Data and Algorithmic Literacy

The second pillar involves fluency in data and algorithms. In a world increasingly governed by data-driven systems, students must understand what data is, how it is collected, who controls it, and how it is interpreted. They must also learn how algorithms function—not only how they compute but how they influence outcomes and shape decisions. This includes understanding training data, models, accuracy, error, and bias.

In practical terms, this means teaching students how to interpret data visualizations, conduct basic data analyses, and question data sources. It also means examining case studies where algorithmic systems have produced unintended or harmful outcomes—such as discriminatory facial recognition software, flawed predictive policing, or biased hiring tools. These examples ground abstract concepts in real-world relevance and teach learners to apply skepticism and ethical reflection.

By middle school and high school levels, students should be able to create simple algorithms, evaluate their effectiveness, and understand the difference between deterministic and probabilistic systems. They should also be introduced to key terms such as neural networks, regression, classification, and reinforcement learning—not necessarily to master the mathematics, but to develop conceptual fluency.

Systems Design and Machine Learning Concepts

Building on algorithmic understanding, the AI Curriculum should introduce learners to the design and function of machine learning systems. This includes how inputs are structured, how models are trained, how outputs are evaluated, and how feedback loops are created. Students should experiment with creating basic AI models using visual interfaces or sandbox environments that demystify the process.

Design thinking should be emphasized alongside technical knowledge. Learners must be taught to define user needs, anticipate unintended consequences, and iterate responsibly. In collaborative projects, students might design chatbots, recommenders, or virtual agents for educational or social use cases. These experiences reinforce not only the mechanics of AI, but the importance of context, empathy, and user-centered design.

Additionally, the curriculum must include instruction on the infrastructure behind AI: cloud computing, sensor networks, application programming interfaces (APIs), and cybersecurity. Even if students do not become engineers, they must understand the systems that mediate their lives—just as they understand the civic infrastructure of governments or the financial systems of economies.

Ethical Reasoning and Digital Philosophy

Perhaps the most urgent and distinctive component of the AI Curriculum is its emphasis on ethical reasoning. Students must not only understand what AI can do, but what it should do—and what it must never do. Ethical dilemmas in AI often involve trade-offs: privacy versus convenience, automation versus employment, personalization versus manipulation, or autonomy versus surveillance.

Students should be taught moral frameworks (such as consequentialism, deontology, and virtue ethics) and apply them to case studies involving AI. They should debate questions such as: *Should AI be allowed to make medical decisions? Can machines have rights? Who is responsible when an autonomous system causes harm?* These inquiries develop critical consciousness and moral imagination.

Digital philosophy should accompany this ethical work. Students must explore what it means to be human in an age of intelligent machines. They must question assumptions about consciousness, creativity, and free will. The AI Curriculum should encourage reflection on identity, memory, social media, and the future of labor in a world where machines participate in thought, language, and decision-making.

Human-AI Collaboration and Emotional Intelligence

The final pillar of the AI Curriculum emphasizes the practical and philosophical skills needed for effective collaboration with intelligent systems. This involves more than interface familiarity; it requires an understanding of how to co-create, co-think, and co-decide with algorithms and machine agents. In the same way that teamwork, leadership, and negotiation are taught for human collaboration, so too must students be trained to communicate, oversee, and complement AI systems in joint tasks.

Students must be taught the concept of "human-in-the-loop" systems, where decisions are enhanced—not replaced—by AI. This training encourages students to act as supervisors, validators, and partners, preserving human agency while leveraging machine capabilities. For instance, a student working with an AI writing assistant should learn when to accept suggestions, when to override them, and when to refine them further based on contextual understanding.

This collaborative training must also prioritize emotional intelligence. Machines do not possess feelings, but they increasingly interpret, respond to, and simulate emotions. Students must therefore learn to manage their own emotional responses to machine behavior—avoiding both anthropomorphism and technophobia. They must understand that while machines can support mental health, offer companionship, or simulate empathy, such interactions are fundamentally artificial and must be situated within broader social-emotional development guided by real human relationships.

Subject Integration and Cross-Disciplinary Relevance

An effective AI Curriculum is not isolated from the rest of the school experience. Rather, it is designed to integrate seamlessly with all major subject areas. In language arts, students may analyze how AI systems generate and translate text, raising questions about authorship and authenticity. In mathematics, students can use data science projects to explore real-world datasets, applying statistics to uncover patterns or build basic prediction models. In science, students might investigate genetic algorithms, swarm intelligence, or the ethical limits of AI in biology and medicine.

In the arts, AI becomes a co-creator. Students can collaborate with generative models to produce music, visual art, and design prototypes—sparking reflection on the nature of creativity and the boundaries between human and machine expression. In physical education and health, AI might be used to track performance metrics, analyze movement, or simulate real-time coaching. These cross-curricular applications show that AI is not a narrow specialization but a universal literacy.

Moreover, the AI Curriculum supports global education goals, including the United Nations Sustainable Development Goals (SDGs). Students can explore how AI supports climate modeling, disaster prediction, disease tracking, and poverty reduction—linking technical knowledge with civic responsibility. Education for sustainable development, when paired with AI fluency, equips students to be ethical innovators and global problem solvers.

Curricular Staging: From Early Childhood to Graduation

To implement the AI Curriculum effectively, a staged developmental progression must be defined. Beginning in early childhood, students are introduced to foundational computational thinking through physical play, storytelling, and age-appropriate logic puzzles. Concepts like "sequence," "if-then," and "repeat" are explored using physical manipulatives, programmable robots, or visual programming environments such as ScratchJr.

In primary school, students begin to engage with more abstract data representation, understand the concept of fairness in algorithms, and use guided coding environments to design games or solve basic problems. They also begin exploring digital citizenship and are introduced to the idea that not all data is neutral.

Middle school serves as a critical transition point, where students are exposed to real-world data sets, basic machine learning models, and early exposure to AI ethics. This is also the stage for collaborative projects, interdisciplinary learning, and identity exploration through digital platforms. By high school, students should be capable of building and evaluating AI models, leading ethical debates, and conducting independent inquiry projects that showcase innovation and critical reflection.

Graduating students should possess the ability to:

1. Understand and explain core AI concepts.
2. Apply algorithmic and data reasoning to solve authentic problems.
3. Critically evaluate the social impact of AI systems.
4. Collaborate with AI tools across multiple disciplines.
5. Uphold ethical and human-centered values in AI design and usage.

Teacher Training and Institutional Preparedness

A curriculum is only as strong as the educators who bring it to life. Preparing teachers for the AI Curriculum requires comprehensive professional development, institutional support, and cross-sector partnerships. Many current educators lack formal training in AI or data science, and professional development must go beyond workshops to include credentialing pathways, mentorship networks, and access to real-time co-teaching AI tools.

Schools must also update their digital infrastructure. This includes secure access to cloud platforms, availability of devices for each learner, robust cybersecurity measures, and ethical data collection protocols. Curricular success also depends on school leadership, parental engagement, and community partnerships. Institutions must communicate clearly about the goals and safeguards of the AI Curriculum, especially when it comes to data privacy and student well-being.

Collaboration with industry and academia can provide students with exposure to real-world problems, mentorship from AI professionals, and access to state-of-the-art platforms. Public-private partnerships must be transparent and guided by educational ethics, not just technological enthusiasm.

Assessment and Certification

Traditional tests cannot adequately measure AI literacy. Instead, assessment must include performance-based tasks, reflective journals, project-based evaluations, and portfolio development. Students should demonstrate not only technical understanding but ethical reasoning, creativity, and collaboration. Credentialing systems might include micro-certifications, digital badges, or AI portfolios that evolve over time—portable evidence of learning that students can use in university applications or employment.

These credentials must be recognized across institutions, ideally supported by standardized frameworks that align with national and global educational benchmarks. This will ensure portability, consistency, and equity. Moreover, assessment systems must themselves be subject to ethical scrutiny, with safeguards against algorithmic bias, student surveillance, or overly reductive scoring systems.

Toward a Just and Intelligent Future

The AI Curriculum is not a luxury or an elective. It is a foundational requirement for participation in a world reshaped by intelligent systems. It ensures that students are not passive consumers of technology, but active, ethical agents who shape the tools and narratives of the future. More importantly, it secures the role of education not as a technical pipeline, but as a humanistic institution dedicated to dignity, justice, and wisdom in an age of machines.

Every child, regardless of geography, background, or ability, deserves access to this curriculum. And every educator, institution, and policymaker bears responsibility for ensuring that the AI Curriculum is delivered with care, rigor, and a commitment to equity. The future will not wait. The curriculum must now lead.

Chapter 8

The Collapse of the Age-Based Grade System

For over a century, formal education has operated on an age-based grading structure. This model, wherein students are grouped by chronological age and progress annually through standardized grade levels, has served as the scaffolding for curriculum design, teacher assignment, assessment pacing, and institutional governance. It originated during the industrial revolution, when efficiency, uniformity, and scalability were prioritized in the design of mass education. At the time, it made sense to streamline instruction by delivering the same material to children of similar ages, assuming relatively equal readiness and cognitive development.

However, in an era defined by personalized learning, artificial intelligence, and global interconnectivity, this structure has become increasingly obsolete. Age-based grading no longer aligns with the needs of learners, the nature of knowledge, or the capabilities of emerging technologies. It fails to accommodate the profound differences in learning pace, prior knowledge, socio-emotional development, and cognitive diversity that exist among students of the same age. The system penalizes both acceleration and remediation, often stigmatizing learners who do not conform to the artificial standard of grade-level performance.

The collapse of the age-based grade system is neither a speculative future nor a distant reform agenda. It is a present necessity, unfolding incrementally through innovations in competency-based education, mastery learning models, and AI-enabled personalized pathways. Artificial intelligence has rendered the logic of the traditional grade structure inefficient and, in many cases, educationally harmful. In the post-industrial learning ecosystem, flexibility, individualization, and progression based on demonstrated competence rather than age are not just possible—they are imperative.

The foundational flaw of the age-based model lies in its assumption of homogeneity. Chronological age is a poor proxy for readiness, aptitude, or interest. Neuroscience has confirmed that children develop at vastly different rates, influenced by genetic, environmental, cultural, and psychological factors. A nine-year-old who excels in mathematical reasoning may lag in reading comprehension. A thirteen-year-old with executive functioning challenges may master scientific content but struggle with written expression. The existing structure does not accommodate such asymmetry.

Moreover, this model imposes arbitrary ceilings and floors on learning. Advanced students are forced to wait for their peers, resulting in disengagement, underachievement, or boredom. Struggling students are pushed forward without mastery, accumulating gaps that become insurmountable by adolescence. In both cases, the age-based system impedes natural learning rhythms and reinforces inequity. The one-size-fits-all pace punishes difference, rather than designing for it.

Artificial intelligence has made it possible to transcend these limitations. Through adaptive learning platforms, AI systems can monitor student progress in real time, adjust instructional content based on performance, and provide immediate feedback and scaffolded support. These systems do not rely on chronological age. They operate based on demonstrated understanding, engagement data, error patterns, and individualized learning trajectories. As a result, a student can be simultaneously working at an advanced level in one domain and receiving foundational support in another—without stigma or administrative disruption.

This shift reorients the function of educational time. Rather than structuring learning around fixed schedules and annual benchmarks, schools must begin to view time as a variable that adjusts to support mastery. Mastery becomes the constant; time becomes flexible. Students move forward when they are ready, not when the calendar dictates. This competency-based progression is already being piloted in various districts and international systems, often with promising results. These models prioritize deep understanding over superficial coverage, reducing the need for remediation and repetition while increasing learner agency and motivation.

Transitioning to a post-grade system requires a reimagining of curriculum architecture. Instead of organizing content into grade-specific silos, educators must design learning progressions that reflect conceptual pathways and developmental readiness. A mathematics curriculum, for example, would be structured around strands of number theory, algebra, geometry, statistics, and modeling, with defined competencies and micro-certifications within each. Students would progress through these strands based on mastery, not age. The same logic would apply to language arts, sciences, social studies, and digital literacies.

Assessment practices must also evolve. Traditional grade-level assessments are designed to sort, rank, and pace students according to normative expectations. They measure performance against age-based standards, often ignoring where students actually are in their learning journeys. In contrast, competency-based assessment evaluates specific skills or understandings, providing granular feedback on what a student knows and can do. These assessments are often formative, project-based, and embedded in the learning process itself. They prioritize growth, reflection, and application over test-taking performance.

Educators, in this model, shift from deliverers of age-batched content to facilitators of individualized pathways. Their role becomes that of coach, mentor, and designer of learning experiences that adapt to student needs. This professional shift requires substantial training in differentiated instruction, data literacy, emotional intelligence, and learning design. Teachers must be empowered to use AI analytics ethically and creatively, recognizing when to intervene, when to personalize, and when to let students struggle productively.

The dismantling of age-based grades also disrupts school architecture. Classrooms can no longer be defined by static rosters of same-aged peers. Instead, learning pods, cross-age collaborations, and thematic groupings become the norm. Students may work in multi-age teams on interdisciplinary projects, guided by shared interests or common goals. The school schedule becomes modular and flexible, supporting asynchronous progress and personalized pacing.

Furthermore, graduation itself must be redefined. If students progress at their own pace, the concept of "finishing school" at age eighteen becomes arbitrary. Some students may complete core competencies by sixteen and pursue internships, college courses, or entrepreneurial ventures. Others may require more time and support, extending their formal education to twenty or beyond. This fluidity reflects the reality of human development and the growing diversity of post-secondary pathways.

The collapse of the age-based grade system also challenges longstanding notions of academic identity and social belonging. For generations, students have formed their identities around grade levels: friendships, extracurricular activities, and even social hierarchies have been shaped by grade-based grouping. The transition to a non-graded system raises critical questions about peer interaction, mentorship dynamics, and student well-being.

While it may appear disruptive, the elimination of rigid grade levels actually opens space for more authentic and diverse social relationships. Rather than forming bonds solely based on age, students may connect through shared interests, competencies, or project affiliations. Mixed-age learning environments foster mentoring relationships, collaborative problem-solving, and empathy across developmental stages. Younger students gain aspirational models, while older students reinforce their learning through peer instruction.

Educational research supports this approach. Studies in Montessori and other mixed-age environments consistently show benefits in leadership development, academic responsibility, and social maturity. Moreover, when students are allowed to pursue learning at their natural pace, self-esteem is often enhanced. Learners are no longer labeled "behind" or "gifted" based on arbitrary benchmarks. They are simply progressing along their own continuum, supported by data-driven insights and human-centered guidance.

Still, this shift requires thoughtful scaffolding. Students need support in navigating more open-ended structures. Teachers must be trained in developmental psychology, conflict resolution, and facilitation strategies for diverse age groups. Schools must implement systems for tracking progress, celebrating milestones, and ensuring every student is seen, supported, and challenged. Digital dashboards, learner profiles, and AI-generated reports can assist in monitoring holistic development, but they must be complemented by robust human relationships.

The role of families in this transition is pivotal. Parents and guardians have been conditioned to interpret grade levels as proxies for progress. They often rely on traditional report cards, honor rolls, and grade promotion as indicators of success. The new model must offer clear, comprehensible alternatives that provide insight into student growth, strengths, and goals. Parent dashboards, student-led conferences, and digital portfolios can serve as transparent and engaging tools for communication.

Additionally, higher education institutions must adapt. Colleges and universities have historically relied on transcripts and grade point averages for admissions decisions. The competency-based model challenges this paradigm. Institutions of higher learning will need to adopt more holistic, evidence-based admissions processes that recognize authentic learning, project work, and demonstrated mastery. Some leading universities have already begun to accept portfolios, digital badges, and capstone experiences in lieu of traditional grades. This trend must be accelerated and standardized to support systemic change.

Globally, several educational systems are experimenting with or transitioning toward post-grade structures. In Finland, age-based grouping has become more flexible, with students advancing based on readiness rather than age. In New Zealand, schools are increasingly adopting learning progressions that allow for individualized pacing. In the United States, districts in New Hampshire, Colorado, and Utah have piloted competency-based models, supported by state legislation and federal innovation grants. These models emphasize performance over seat time, reflection over ranking, and learning over labeling.

The policy landscape must evolve to support these reforms. State and national education departments must redefine standards, graduation requirements, and accountability metrics. Funding formulas must reward growth, not attendance. Accreditation bodies must revise criteria to accommodate flexible pacing and mastery-based certification.

Assessment consortia must develop new tools that align with personalized, non-graded learning models. Without policy alignment, schools may face barriers to innovation, constrained by legacy regulations and outdated compliance structures.

Technology, particularly artificial intelligence, plays a crucial role in enabling this transformation. AI systems can track progress across multiple dimensions—academic, behavioral, and social-emotional—offering educators real-time insight into student needs. These tools can generate personalized learning paths, adaptive assessments, and tailored interventions. More importantly, they can provide students with agency. Through dashboards, nudges, and visualizations, learners gain awareness of their own trajectories and can make informed decisions about their next steps.

However, this reliance on AI demands vigilance. Issues of data privacy, algorithmic bias, and digital equity must be addressed with urgency. Schools must adopt transparent data governance policies, ensure parental consent, and provide equitable access to devices and connectivity. AI systems must be designed with inclusivity, explainability, and human oversight. The goal is not to automate education, but to humanize it through precision, personalization, and empowerment.

The collapse of the age-based grade system also intersects with labor market transformations. Employers increasingly value skills, portfolios, and problem-solving capacity over degrees and transcripts. The workforce of the future will be dynamic, interdisciplinary, and lifelong. Education systems must prepare students not for a single graduation, but for continual reinvention. A flexible, mastery-based system aligns more closely with this reality than a rigid, age-locked progression.

Finally, this transformation reaffirms the philosophical purpose of education. The ultimate goal is not to sort students into ranks, but to cultivate agency, curiosity, and capability. A post-grade system honors the uniqueness of each learner, embracing the messiness of growth and the variability of human development. It restores trust in learners 'capacity to direct their own journeys, supported by caring mentors and intelligent tools.

In conclusion, the age-based grade system, while historically functional, is incompatible with the demands and possibilities of twenty-first-century education. Artificial intelligence has rendered its inefficiencies and inequities untenable. A new model—grounded in mastery, flexibility, and human flourishing—is emerging. Its realization depends on courageous leadership, thoughtful design, and an unwavering commitment to equity. The time to dismantle the grade-level orthodoxy has arrived. What replaces it must be more just, more adaptive, and more worthy of the children it serves.

Chapter 9

Redesigning School Infrastructure for the AI Age

The emergence of artificial intelligence as a foundational force across every sector demands more than curricular reform. It necessitates a rethinking of the physical and digital architecture in which learning occurs. The traditional school building, with its rigid hallways, time-locked schedules, and compartmentalized classrooms, was designed for industrial-era efficiency. It prioritized order, supervision, and content delivery. However, in the age of AI, learning must become fluid, personalized, and deeply interconnected. As pedagogy evolves toward adaptability and mastery, the built environment must mirror these principles.

This chapter explores how school infrastructure must be redesigned to accommodate the realities and opportunities of an AI-integrated education system. It examines physical design, digital infrastructure, safety protocols, learning ecosystems, and policy implications—establishing a blueprint for the future-ready school.

The Limits of the Traditional School Layout

Conventional schools have long been organized around fixed schedules, age-based classrooms, and centralized control. Most buildings follow a standardized template: rectangular classrooms aligned along corridors, each housing a teacher responsible for delivering subject-specific content to students of the same age group. The design reflects a broadcast model of education, where information is delivered to passive recipients in a uniform sequence.

This spatial model reinforces the very structures that are becoming obsolete: teacher-centered instruction, age-graded classrooms, time-based progression, and subject silos. The inflexibility of physical space often limits pedagogical innovation. For example, it is difficult to facilitate cross-age collaboration, interdisciplinary projects, or personalized pacing when classroom assignments are based strictly on time and age.

Moreover, many school facilities are aging, underfunded, and technologically unprepared for AI integration. The lack of robust connectivity, flexible workspaces, and secure digital access creates a structural barrier to transformation. Thus, the redesign of school infrastructure is not a matter of aesthetic improvement but of systemic necessity.

Principles of AI-Era Learning Environments

To support AI-enhanced education, school infrastructure must embody the following principles: adaptability, connectivity, inclusivity, sustainability, and security. These principles are not only architectural but philosophical. They reflect the values of a learning ecosystem that recognizes diversity, empowers agency, and prepares students for a dynamic, data-driven world.

1. **Adaptability**
   AI-powered education demands environments that accommodate varying group sizes, multiple instructional modes, and shifting schedules. Spaces must be reconfigurable—allowing for rapid transformation from individual workstations to group project zones, from seminar-style arrangements to studio-based explorations. Movable furniture, modular walls, and embedded technology enable such flexibility.
2. **Connectivity**
   High-speed internet, cloud-based platforms, and intelligent classroom technologies are essential. Infrastructure must support seamless integration of AI tools, including adaptive learning systems, augmented reality platforms, biometric feedback devices, and real-time data dashboards. Devices must be accessible, and digital equity must be ensured for every student.
3. **Inclusivity**
   Spaces must be designed for universal access. This includes not only compliance with physical accessibility standards but

the creation of environments that support neurodiverse learners, mental health needs, and cultural representation. Sensory-friendly zones, multilingual displays, and identity-affirming art contribute to an inclusive infrastructure.

4. **Sustainability**
   Future-ready schools must be environmentally conscious. AI systems can support energy efficiency, predictive maintenance, and ecological monitoring. Infrastructure should incorporate green materials, renewable energy sources, and natural lighting—promoting both environmental stewardship and student well-being.
5. **Security**
   In an AI-driven environment, digital security is paramount. Schools must implement robust cybersecurity protocols, encrypted data systems, and AI-powered monitoring tools that protect student privacy. Physical security must also evolve, with intelligent surveillance, biometric access control, and crisis response integration.

Flexible Learning Zones

One of the most visible changes in AI-era schools is the replacement of traditional classrooms with flexible learning zones. These zones are not fixed rooms but fluid spaces designated for different types of learning activity. Examples include:

- **Exploration Labs**: Spaces equipped with robotics kits, 3D printers, AI programming tools, and AR/VR stations. Students use these labs for experimentation, prototyping, and applied STEM learning.
- **Collaboration Studios**: Modular spaces designed for project-based learning. These areas include writable walls, digital screens, mobile furniture, and breakout zones for team discussion.
- **Reflection Hubs**: Quiet zones where students can reflect, journal, meditate, or receive individual coaching. AI systems may track emotional well-being through non-invasive indicators, prompting timely support from educators.
- **Community Forums**: Multipurpose spaces that host town halls, exhibitions, peer showcases, and cross-generational

learning events. These forums reinforce the school's role as a civic hub.

Each zone is equipped with AI-compatible infrastructure: voice-activated assistants, smart boards, real-time analytics displays, and learning management system integration. Students carry personal devices that sync with these systems, allowing them to pick up their progress anywhere, anytime.

Digital Architecture and the Rise of the Hybrid School

The infrastructure of schools in the AI era extends beyond walls and physical space. Digital architecture now plays an equally central role in shaping learning experiences. The rise of hybrid and fully online learning models—accelerated by global disruptions and technological advancements—demands robust, scalable, and intelligent digital environments.

A future-ready school is not defined solely by its campus but by its cloud. Learning management systems (LMS), student data dashboards, adaptive content platforms, and AI-driven tutoring agents form the digital backbone of a hybrid educational infrastructure. These systems must be interoperable, secure, and user-centered, enabling continuous learning regardless of physical location.

In a well-designed hybrid model, physical attendance is no longer synonymous with engagement. Students may attend school onsite three days a week and work remotely the other two, depending on project demands, individual pacing, or health considerations. Digital spaces mirror physical ones—featuring virtual collaboration zones, AI-monitored discussion boards, and interactive simulations. Physical infrastructure, therefore, must be designed to complement—not compete with—this digital expansion.

Redefining Time, Schedules, and Spatial Ownership

As learning becomes more personalized and asynchronous, school schedules must become less rigid. Time blocks designed for mass instruction—such as 45-minute class periods—are being replaced by flexible modules that adapt to learning goals and student readiness. Schools may implement dynamic scheduling tools powered by AI, which optimize resource allocation, teacher availability, and learner engagement in real time.

In this model, spatial ownership also changes. Students no longer "belong" to a single classroom. They move through zones based on activity, need, or interest. Teachers become mobile facilitators, meeting learners in physical or virtual spaces and using AI dashboards to monitor progress, assign interventions, and offer real-time feedback. Instead of assigning homerooms, schools may create "learning hubs" where small communities of students meet regularly for mentorship, peer reflection, and collective goal setting.

Teacher Workspaces and AI-Enhanced Facilitation

Teacher infrastructure must also evolve. The conventional teacher desk—fixed in front of the class—is no longer the epicenter of learning. Educators require agile workspaces equipped with dual-monitor setups, live analytics dashboards, curriculum design tools, and real-time student support interfaces. These environments must facilitate collaboration with other educators, interaction with AI teaching assistants, and continuous professional learning.

AI can assist teachers by generating custom lesson plans, identifying learning gaps, analyzing student behavior, and suggesting targeted resources. However, this support requires spatial and digital infrastructure that empowers, rather than replaces, human judgment. Teacher preparation spaces must therefore be treated as high-performance zones, no less important than laboratories or studios.

Community Integration and Interdisciplinary Design

Redesigning school infrastructure also means reconnecting schools to their communities. AI-era learning demands authentic, real-world engagement. Schools should be designed as open platforms that host community events, business partnerships, maker fairs, and policy dialogues. Classrooms may be co-located with local libraries, museums, science parks, or entrepreneurship incubators.

Such integration encourages interdisciplinary learning and blurs the boundary between academic content and civic life. Architecture should support permeability—physical and ideological—between the school and the world. This may involve open-plan community lobbies, co-working spaces for visiting mentors, or exhibition zones for student-led initiatives addressing real social challenges.

Policy and Funding Implications

The redesign of infrastructure cannot succeed without structural support from policy and funding agencies. School building codes, capital investment plans, maintenance protocols, and funding formulas must evolve to prioritize innovation, flexibility, and inclusion. Policy must incentivize modular design, universal broadband access, energy-efficient systems, and teacher-centered technology planning.

At the national level, governments must establish standards for AI readiness in educational facilities. This includes minimum digital access specifications, security protocols for student data, and guidelines for equitable distribution of resources. International aid organizations and private foundations can play a critical role in supporting low-income regions, ensuring that innovation is not limited to affluent districts or developed nations.

Ethical Infrastructure and Student Rights

The infrastructure of AI-integrated education must reflect not only functional efficiency but ethical intentionality. Every technological upgrade must be assessed through the lens of student dignity, safety, and consent. Biometric entry systems, AI-based behavior monitors, and predictive analytics must be implemented with transparency and accountability.

Students should have agency over their data and voice in how technology is used in their learning environments. Schools must adopt participatory design models, where students, families, and community members contribute to decision-making about the spaces and systems that shape their educational experiences.

Conclusion: The Architecture of Possibility

Redesigning school infrastructure for the AI age is not a cosmetic endeavor. It is a redefinition of the learning experience. The walls of a school communicate values; the layout suggests priorities; the technologies embedded in daily routines shape how students learn, interact, and imagine their futures. As AI transforms what is possible in education, the environments in which education unfolds must evolve in tandem.

This is not a call for futuristic novelty. It is a mandate for relevance, equity, and opportunity. The school building must now be a platform—physical, digital, ethical—on which learners stand not to be contained, but to be launched. Those who design these platforms shape not only the next generation of students but the very society they will inherit and rebuild.

Chapter 10

Preparing Educators for an AI-Powered Classroom

Introduction

The integration of artificial intelligence into education has introduced a profound transformation not only in how students learn but in how educators must teach. The role of the teacher is undergoing a fundamental evolution—from content deliverer to cognitive coach, from sole instructor to collaborative facilitator, from curriculum implementer to AI-powered learning designer. In this context, the preparation of educators becomes the fulcrum upon which the success of the AI-augmented classroom will pivot. Without intentional, systemic, and visionary preparation, even the most advanced technologies will fail to produce meaningful learning outcomes.

This chapter provides a comprehensive examination of how educators must be prepared to thrive in classrooms shaped by artificial intelligence. It outlines the new competencies required, the shifts in pedagogical approach, the ethical considerations involved, and the institutional changes needed to support teacher transformation at scale. More than a technical upgrade, preparing educators for AI integration represents a cultural shift—a redefinition of the profession in alignment with a new era of human-machine collaboration in education.

The Changing Role of the Educator

Traditionally, educators have been seen as the primary source of knowledge within the classroom. Instruction has followed a linear path: teachers lecture, students listen, assessments follow. With the advent of AI, this model becomes increasingly outdated. Intelligent tutoring systems, automated assessments, adaptive platforms, and content-generating algorithms now perform many of the functions once handled manually by educators. However, rather than rendering teachers obsolete, these tools elevate the human dimension of education.

In an AI-powered classroom, the educator becomes an orchestrator of learning environments, a mentor for critical thinking, a guide for ethical reasoning, and a designer of interdisciplinary projects. This role requires not only technological fluency but a deep understanding of pedagogy, psychology, and social-emotional development. Teachers must know when to leverage AI and when to override it. They must interpret algorithmic insights without becoming beholden to them. They must use data to empower learners, not to label them.

Essential Competencies for the AI-Era Educator

To fulfill these expanded responsibilities, educators must acquire a new set of professional competencies that extend beyond traditional teacher training frameworks. These include:

1. **AI Literacy**
   Educators must possess a foundational understanding of what artificial intelligence is, how it works, and what its capabilities and limitations are within an educational context. This includes knowledge of algorithms, data training processes, machine learning, and bias in AI outputs. Importantly, teachers must be able to explain these concepts to students in age-appropriate language.
2. **Data Interpretation and Learning Analytics**
   Modern AI platforms generate real-time data on student engagement, performance, behavior, and progression. Teachers must know how to read this data, draw actionable conclusions, and design responsive interventions. This competency also involves distinguishing between correlation and causation, identifying anomalies, and contextualizing quantitative insights with qualitative observation.
3. **Ethical and Inclusive Technology Use**
   Teachers must be trained to implement AI tools ethically. This includes awareness of student privacy rights, equitable access, algorithmic bias, and the potential for surveillance misuse. Educators must learn to challenge inequities ampli-

fied by AI and to foster culturally responsive uses of technology.

4. **Pedagogical Design with AI Tools**
   Teachers must gain fluency in using AI to personalize instruction, differentiate learning paths, and design interdisciplinary projects. They should understand how to integrate AI-enhanced simulations, natural language processing tools, intelligent tutoring systems, and generative AI into the learning cycle to enhance—not replace—human interaction.
5. **Facilitation of Higher-Order Thinking**
   Since AI can automate low-level tasks such as content recall and grammar correction, educators must focus on cultivating skills that AI cannot replicate easily. This includes critical thinking, ethical reasoning, creativity, empathy, and systems thinking. Teachers must design experiences that stretch students beyond what AI can deliver.
6. **Continuous Professional Learning and Adaptability**
   Given the rapid pace of technological change, educators must embrace a growth mindset and commit to lifelong professional development. This involves not only learning new tools but reflecting on their impact, adapting to evolving platforms, and co-designing solutions with students, colleagues, and AI systems.

Institutional Support and Professional Development Models

Effective preparation of educators for the AI era requires a systemic, multi-layered approach. Isolated workshops or voluntary certifications are insufficient. Institutions must embed AI literacy and adaptive pedagogy into all levels of teacher training—from pre-service programs to ongoing in-service development. Universities, school districts, ministries of education, and private education providers must align around a shared vision of educator transformation.

Pre-Service Preparation

Teacher training programs must be redesigned to include comprehensive coursework in educational technology, data science basics, digital ethics, and AI systems. Trainee educators should experience classrooms where AI tools are used not only as instructional aids but as pedagogical frameworks. Practicums must include exposure to adaptive learning platforms, digital content creation, and analytics dashboards.

Curricula should encourage cross-disciplinary learning, drawing on cognitive psychology, systems design, and sociology of technology. Pre-service teachers must be taught to reflect critically on the social implications of AI in the classroom, the risks of over-reliance, and the need for human judgment in high-stakes decision-making. Pedagogical theories must be updated to reflect the affordances and constraints of human-AI partnerships.

In-Service Development

For practicing educators, professional development must shift from traditional, top-down formats toward collaborative, embedded learning experiences. Peer learning communities, AI co-design workshops, and reflective inquiry models should replace one-off seminars. Teachers need sustained opportunities to experiment, iterate, and share their experiences with AI tools in context.

Districts can support this shift by creating roles for instructional technology coaches, allocating professional learning time within the school schedule, and providing microcredential pathways in AI-integrated instruction. Leadership must prioritize teacher agency in technology adoption and protect space for experimentation without punitive evaluation.

Leadership and School Culture

School leadership plays a decisive role in shaping how teachers perceive and engage with AI. Principals, department heads, and instructional coordinators must themselves be trained in AI literacy and change management. They must model a culture of curiosity, courage, and inquiry. Where leadership treats AI integration as surveillance or cost-cutting, teachers respond with resistance or compliance. Where it is framed as empowerment and creativity, teachers respond with initiative and innovation.

School culture must honor the complexity of teaching. AI systems cannot capture the full scope of emotional labor, ethical dilemmas, and intuitive decision-making that educators perform daily. A culture of trust, dialogue, and professional respect is essential to ensure that AI enhances rather than undermines the human dimension of education.

Addressing Teacher Concerns and Resistance

Many educators approach AI with anxiety or skepticism. Fears of replacement, loss of autonomy, surveillance, and technocratic control are legitimate. Effective preparation programs must address these fears directly. Teachers should be invited into conversations about the purpose, scope, and limits of AI in education. They should participate in tool selection, policy development, and classroom implementation planning.

Resistance often arises not from unwillingness but from unacknowledged tensions. Teachers who feel unheard or overburdened are less likely to engage creatively with new demands. Preparation efforts must therefore begin with listening, empathizing, and co-creating. Professional development should be framed not as training for compliance but as an invitation to leadership in shaping the future of education.

Ethical Stewardship and Human Flourishing

Ultimately, the preparation of educators for an AI-powered classroom is not a technical project. It is an ethical commitment. Teachers are stewards of human development. They must prepare students not only to use AI tools but to live with them, question them, and shape their evolution. Educators must cultivate habits of mind that sustain democratic societies: skepticism, compassion, discernment, and courage.

This requires a profound re-centering of human purpose in education. Teachers must see themselves not as intermediaries between students and content, but as architects of learning environments where human potential is amplified by, not subordinated to, technology. In such environments, AI serves to free teachers from repetitive tasks so they may focus on what matters most: building relationships, inspiring inquiry, and fostering transformation.

Conclusion: Reclaiming the Art and Future of Teaching

The preparation of educators for AI-powered classrooms is among the most urgent and complex challenges of the current educational era. It demands vision, humility, and collaboration across every level of the system. It also demands faith in the profession of teaching—not as a fading tradition, but as a rising craft redefined by new tools and timeless purpose.

Educators who embrace AI thoughtfully and ethically are not abandoning their calling. They are reclaiming it. They are refusing to be reduced to content dispensers or algorithmic monitors. They are becoming guides for a generation that must navigate not only knowledge but power, possibility, and peril in an AI-defined world. With the right preparation, they will not only survive this transformation—they will lead it.

Chapter 11

The Family–School Partnership in an AI World

The rise of artificial intelligence in education represents not merely a technological transformation but a profound reordering of the ecosystem in which children grow, learn, and develop. While institutions adapt and educators evolve, families remain the foundational context in which a child's learning is first shaped and continuously reinforced. In this AI-powered age, the relationship between home and school is no longer peripheral—it is central. The integration of AI into learning environments compels a new framework for the family-school partnership: one built on transparency, trust, digital literacy, and shared accountability for ethical and developmental outcomes.

This chapter explores the evolving role of families in the context of AI-enhanced education. It analyzes how parents and caregivers must be prepared, included, and empowered to participate in this transformation. It also outlines the responsibilities that schools hold in guiding, informing, and collaborating with families to ensure that AI technologies are used ethically, equitably, and developmentally appropriately. The family-school partnership, once rooted in logistical coordination and academic support, must now be reimagined as a co-governance structure for raising AI-ready children in a rapidly shifting world.

Redefining the Home as a Learning Hub

The traditional division between the domains of home and school has become increasingly blurred. Digital learning environments, accelerated by AI systems, now extend the school experience into the household in ways previously unimaginable. Homework platforms track engagement, intelligent tutors provide personalized feedback, and learning analytics notify families of progress in real time. These capabilities reposition the home as a continuous learning hub, where education does not pause when the school day ends.

This transformation requires that families possess the skills, tools, and understanding necessary to support and interpret AI-driven learning. Parents must be equipped to monitor their child's digital learning platforms, contextualize algorithmic feedback, and advocate when automated systems misrepresent or misdiagnose their child's needs. Furthermore, they must create physical and emotional spaces within the home that support sustained focus, critical inquiry, and safe exploration within digital ecosystems.

In this new paradigm, the concept of parental involvement expands. It is no longer sufficient to attend parent-teacher conferences or supervise homework completion. Instead, parents are asked to become co-navigators of personalized learning journeys—interpreting dashboards, asking questions of predictive reports, and fostering digital resilience. Such a shift is not intuitive and cannot be assumed. It must be explicitly cultivated by schools, communities, and policymakers.

Family Digital Literacy: The Cornerstone of AI Collaboration

At the heart of a productive family-school partnership in the AI era lies digital literacy. Parents and caregivers must possess baseline knowledge about AI: how it functions, where it is used in the classroom, and what implications it has for data privacy, learning equity, and student identity. Without this knowledge, families may misinterpret AI outputs, become disengaged from learning processes, or unwittingly endorse systems that perpetuate harm.

Digital literacy for families should include the following core components:

1. **Understanding AI-Powered Tools**
   Families must be familiarized with the specific AI platforms used by the school. This includes knowledge of adaptive learning systems, intelligent tutoring platforms, voice assistants, predictive grading systems, and digital portfolios. Schools must provide accessible orientation materials and multilingual support.
2. **Navigating Learning Analytics**
   Families must be trained to read and interpret the dashboards and analytics shared by schools. This includes recognizing

patterns, understanding scoring logic, and distinguishing between raw metrics and holistic indicators of learning. Training sessions or parent academies can demystify these systems.

3. **Protecting Data and Privacy**
   Parents must understand how their child's data is collected, stored, and used. They should be aware of the rights they hold under local, national, or international laws and be empowered to opt out, challenge inaccuracies, or demand transparency. This understanding must be supported by clear school policies and ethical vendor agreements.
4. **Modeling Healthy Tech Behavior**
   Children observe and internalize family attitudes toward technology. Parents must model balanced, intentional, and critical engagement with digital tools. This includes setting screen time boundaries, promoting ethical use of AI assistants, and encouraging offline exploration and creativity.

When families are digitally literate, they become empowered participants in educational transformation. They can ask informed questions, hold institutions accountable, and support their children in becoming thoughtful, empowered learners in an AI-saturated world.

Ethical Alignment Between Schools and Families

In a landscape shaped by artificial intelligence, ethical alignment between schools and families is essential. AI systems embedded in education—such as predictive performance algorithms, facial recognition tools, sentiment analysis software, or biometric trackers—have the power to influence a child's self-perception, access to resources, and future opportunities. When decisions are made about how such tools are deployed, families must not be treated as passive observers but as equal stakeholders.

To achieve this alignment, schools must engage families in transparent, inclusive dialogue around the purposes, limits, and safeguards of AI in learning. This may take the form of:

- **Community Listening Sessions**: Regular forums where school leaders, technologists, and parents discuss planned AI implementations, surface concerns, and co-create ethical guidelines.

- **Consent and Opt-In Mechanisms**: Clear, multilingual documentation and workflows that allow families to opt in to AI usage, rather than automatic enrollment without meaningful understanding.
- **Ethics Councils**: Joint school-family committees that review AI tools, analyze data use practices, and develop ongoing ethical oversight mechanisms, including student representation.

These practices foster mutual trust. They acknowledge that while schools are responsible for pedagogical innovation, families are responsible for a child's broader development. Both must be at the table when technology reshapes what, how, and why a child learns.

Rebuilding Trust in the Age of Automation

As AI becomes more embedded in the classroom, many families express concern that their children are being reduced to data points or managed by machines. These fears—though sometimes shaped by misinformation—are grounded in legitimate worries about depersonalization, algorithmic bias, surveillance, and loss of human connection. In marginalized communities, these concerns are amplified by historical experiences with institutional inequities and technological exploitation.

Rebuilding trust requires not only better communication but deeper transformation. Schools must demonstrate that AI does not replace human relationships but strengthens them. Educators must show how they use AI insights not to control learners, but to support them. Families must see that their feedback is not only heard but integrated into institutional practices.

Trust also depends on consistency. When schools claim to personalize learning through AI but deliver one-size-fits-all content, families disengage. When predictive systems are introduced without explanation or recourse, families resist. To foster partnership, schools must act with transparency, humility, and responsiveness—acknowledging that the journey toward ethical, effective AI in education is shared and ongoing.

Building Inclusive, AI-Literate School Communities

Strong family-school partnerships require more than individualized communication; they require shared cultural shifts. Schools must become hubs of community learning, where families gain digital literacy alongside students, and where intergenerational knowledge flows in both directions. This may involve:

- **Parent-Child AI Workshops**: Events where families and students explore AI tools together, building mutual understanding and trust.
- **Community Tech Labs**: On-campus or mobile labs where families without home internet access can explore educational platforms, receive training, and access school resources.
- **Peer Family Mentors**: Trained parents from the community who support others in navigating school technologies, offering culturally responsive guidance and eliminating barriers.
- **Public Exhibitions of Student AI Work**: Showcases where families experience firsthand how students are using AI to create, inquire, and solve real-world problems.

Such initiatives transform schools into living ecosystems of learning—where families do not simply consume institutional decisions but shape them.

Policy and Infrastructure for Sustained Partnership

To support long-term, AI-era family-school partnerships, policy must evolve. Education ministries and local governments must allocate funding for digital literacy programming, family engagement coordinators, multilingual communication systems, and accessible broadband infrastructure. School boards must mandate inclusive consultation processes before AI tools are adopted. Regulatory bodies must enforce standards for transparency and consent.

Technology vendors must be held accountable not only for performance but for inclusion. Platforms should be co-designed with parent input, feature plain-language interfaces, and embed features for family engagement. Vendors who fail to support ethical, inclusive partnership should be removed from procurement lists.

In parallel, research institutions should expand the study of family engagement in AI-enhanced education—developing evidence-based frameworks for equity, effectiveness, and scalability.

Conclusion: Co-Raising AI-Empowered Citizens

The future of education will not be defined by technology alone. It will be shaped by the quality of relationships surrounding the learner. In an age when machines can adapt instruction, predict outcomes, and manage learning flows, the human roles of support, care, and ethical anchoring become even more critical.

The family-school partnership must now evolve into a co-governance alliance. Schools and families must work side by side to ensure that AI serves children's development—not as an engine of efficiency, but as a catalyst for equity, creativity, and agency. When families are respected as partners and equipped as leaders, they not only support their own children—they help redesign the entire system.

In this shared journey, every school becomes a node of human dignity in a digital world. And every family becomes a co-architect of the future.

Chapter 12

New Metrics and Assessments in an AI-Centered Education System

The integration of artificial intelligence into educational ecosystems has introduced a transformative moment in the domain of student assessment. Historically tethered to standardized formats and rigid timelines, educational evaluation has functioned more as a gatekeeper of opportunity than as a catalyst for learning. However, as artificial intelligence redefines pedagogical processes, the need to recalibrate the metrics and modalities of assessment has become urgent, both practically and philosophically.

In the AI-centered classroom, learning is no longer a static act of content acquisition but a dynamic interplay of problem-solving, adaptive reasoning, creative synthesis, and collaborative engagement. These complex skills, essential to future success, demand assessment systems capable of capturing cognitive nuance, personal growth, and interdisciplinary application. Traditional tests—multiple-choice formats, timed essays, and end-of-term examinations—are ill-suited for this task. They offer snapshots where streams are needed, rankings where reflection is required, and standardization where personalization is more appropriate.

Artificial intelligence introduces not only tools for instructional adaptation but also frameworks for real-time, multimodal, and competency-based assessment. Machine learning models can analyze patterns in student behavior, identify strengths and gaps with precision, and offer continuous feedback loops that support the growth of the whole learner. These capabilities, however, do not simply enhance assessment; they necessitate its reinvention.

The purpose of this chapter is to chart a comprehensive vision for this reinvention. It argues for a paradigm shift from high-stakes testing to holistic, AI-augmented evaluation grounded in transparency, equity, and developmental integrity. It examines the historical context of educational assessment, the limitations of legacy systems, the affordances of artificial intelligence, and the ethical and practical imperatives for change. Through this lens, assessment emerges not as a final judgment but as a formative dialogue—a mirror of learning's depth, complexity, and humanity.

The Historical Foundations of Educational Assessment

The current practices of educational assessment are rooted in a legacy shaped by the industrial revolution, colonial administration, and the rise of bureaucratic state systems. These origins reflect specific societal goals: standardization, stratification, and efficiency. The emergence of mass education in the nineteenth and early twentieth centuries brought with it the need for scalable methods of evaluating large student populations. Consequently, assessments were designed less to cultivate individual potential and more to sort learners into predefined tracks based on perceived ability, often linked to socio-economic class, race, and geography.

The model adopted by most modern educational systems emerged from psychometric traditions. Influenced by the work of early psychologists such as Alfred Binet and Lewis Terman, the intelligence quotient (IQ) and standardized testing frameworks became embedded as default mechanisms for determining aptitude and academic progression. These tools were premised on the belief that intelligence was measurable, static, and distributable across a bell curve. Accordingly, school assessments mirrored these assumptions, emphasizing rote memorization, time constraints, and norm-referenced scoring.

Throughout the twentieth century, high-stakes assessments—national exams, entrance tests, and grade-level benchmarks—gained prominence as gatekeepers of opportunity. Institutions such as the College Board and testing organizations proliferated. Governments employed test scores as tools of accountability and control, linking them to funding, teacher evaluation, and school rankings. These systems created powerful incentives to teach to the test and marginalize forms of learning that did not fit neatly within quantifiable outcomes.

However, this historical trajectory also reveals the structural inequities embedded in assessment. Students from marginalized communities often faced cultural, linguistic, and socio-economic barriers that skewed test performance. The underlying assumption that all learners begin from the same starting line and progress at the same rate failed to acknowledge the rich diversity of human development. Moreover, the content and format of standardized assessments often reflected dominant cultural norms, reinforcing a narrow definition of intelligence and achievement.

As artificial intelligence now introduces the possibility of individualized learning paths, real-time feedback, and contextual evaluation, it is essential to interrogate this history. One cannot simply layer AI on top of outdated assumptions. The reinvention of assessment must begin with an understanding of its past, recognizing that measurement has never been neutral, and that tools of evaluation can either replicate injustice or catalyze transformation.

The next sections will explore how this historical inheritance collides with contemporary educational demands—and how AI, when guided by ethical frameworks and inclusive design, may enable a departure from antiquated paradigms.

Section 3: The Crisis of Standardized Testing in the 21st Century

The twenty-first century has witnessed an escalating crisis in standardized testing—a system once designed to bring order and objectivity to education is now increasingly viewed as a mechanism of exclusion, distortion, and systemic failure. Across educational systems globally, educators, students, parents, and policymakers have raised fundamental concerns about the validity, fairness, and relevance of high-stakes testing in a world transformed by globalization, digitization, and artificial intelligence.

The crisis manifests in several critical dimensions. First, standardized testing fails to measure the full range of competencies that define readiness in the contemporary world. Literacy and numeracy remain essential, but so too are critical thinking, collaboration, emotional intelligence, cross-cultural communication, digital fluency, and ethical reasoning. These latter capabilities do not lend themselves easily to multiple-choice questions or time-limited essays. By prioritizing what is easily scored, standardized tests diminish what is most essential.

Second, these assessments continue to disproportionately disadvantage students from historically marginalized backgrounds. Research consistently demonstrates that test scores correlate more closely with socio-economic status than with academic potential. Cultural bias in test language, access to preparatory resources, differences in home learning environments, and structural inequities in schools all contribute to outcome disparities. The result is a system that perpetuates privilege and penalizes diversity under the guise of meritocracy.

Third, standardized testing exerts a distorting effect on teaching and learning. Curricula become narrowed to align with test content, with less emphasis on inquiry, experimentation, and holistic development. Teachers face pressure to "teach to the test," and learners experience heightened anxiety, burnout, and disengagement. In some jurisdictions, entire school years are organized around testing cycles, reducing education to a procedural exercise rather than a formative experience.

Moreover, the reliance on single-point-in-time assessments is increasingly misaligned with how learning actually unfolds. Knowledge construction is iterative, contextual, and social. Learners build understanding through exploration, failure, and revision—processes poorly captured by one-off exams. As a result, standardized testing often measures compliance rather than competence, speed rather than depth, and memorization rather than meaning.

The crisis has been further amplified by the rise of artificial intelligence and emerging models of knowledge access. In an era where generative AI can instantly provide answers to factual questions, the value of recalling information has diminished. What matters more is the ability to evaluate, synthesize, apply, and ethically deploy knowledge in real contexts. Yet standardized assessments remain anchored in the retrieval-based logic of a pre-digital world.

The COVID-19 pandemic served as an accelerant for this crisis. As schools moved online, many nations suspended or modified traditional examinations. This disruption exposed the fragility and inflexibility of the standardized system and sparked renewed conversations about alternative forms of assessment. Some institutions permanently eliminated standardized entrance exams; others shifted toward portfolio reviews, teacher assessments, and performance tasks. These transitions, while uneven, demonstrated that change is possible—and perhaps overdue.

In sum, the crisis of standardized testing is not simply a technical problem but a philosophical reckoning. What does society choose to measure, and why? Whose abilities are validated, and whose are ignored? What kind of learner—and citizen—is this system designed to produce? As artificial intelligence enables more nuanced, inclusive, and personalized assessment models, these questions must no longer be deferred. They must become central to the design of an educational future that honors all learners.

Artificial Intelligence as a Disruptive Force in Evaluation

The emergence of artificial intelligence (AI) has fundamentally disrupted traditional paradigms of educational assessment. No longer confined to static measurement tools, educators and institutions are now equipped with dynamic, intelligent systems capable of evaluating learning as an ongoing process, rather than a terminal event. This shift carries profound implications for how society defines knowledge, tracks progress, and distributes opportunity.

At its core, AI introduces three major disruptions to the assessment domain: the integration of continuous feedback mechanisms, the capacity to personalize assessment pathways, and the ability to analyze vast amounts of complex learning data in real time. These affordances redefine what assessment is, what it measures, and how its outputs are used.

The first major disruption lies in the transformation of feedback from episodic to continuous. In traditional educational models, students complete an assignment or take an exam, await a grade, and move on. Feedback is delayed, often sparse, and focused on outcome rather than process. AI-powered systems invert this model. Through real-time monitoring and adaptive analytics, learners receive immediate, actionable feedback that helps refine their understanding and correct misconceptions during the learning experience. This supports a culture of formative development rather than summative finality.

Secondly, AI enables unprecedented personalization of the assessment process. Algorithms can tailor tasks to the learner's proficiency level, preferred modality (visual, auditory, kinesthetic), pacing needs, and cognitive profile. A single concept—such as mathematical problem-solving—may be assessed through varied entry points: interactive simulations, spoken explanations, or real-world case applications. This modularity honors neurodiversity and mitigates the cultural and linguistic biases embedded in standardized formats.

Thirdly, AI's ability to synthesize massive and multidimensional data streams allows for richer diagnostic insights. Machine learning systems can analyze not only correct or incorrect responses, but also patterns of error, time-on-task, help-seeking behavior, collaboration quality, and emotional engagement. These indicators provide a deeper understanding of how a student learns, not just what they know. For instance, two students may reach the same answer, but their pathways—one linear and confident, the other iterative and uncertain—offer different instructional implications.

Yet disruption also raises critical tensions. The same algorithms that empower personalization can, if poorly designed, replicate existing inequalities. Predictive models risk penalizing students with nontraditional learning trajectories or masking systemic barriers as individual deficits. Furthermore, an overreliance on automation may reduce complex human development to decontextualized data points, eroding the relational and interpretive dimensions of education.

To ensure that AI's disruption becomes a force for equity and excellence, several conditions must be met. Assessment systems must be developed collaboratively with educators, ethicists, and learners. Data must be transparent, interpretable, and used to support, not sort. And algorithms must be continuously audited for bias, fairness, and cultural responsiveness.

When responsibly deployed, AI becomes not a replacement for educators, but an extension of their insight. It allows teachers to shift from score-giving to meaning-making, from gatekeeping to coaching. In doing so, AI reclaims assessment as a space not of exclusion but of empowerment—where every learner is seen, supported, and understood.

Real-Time and Embedded Assessments: Redefining Timeliness

In the architecture of traditional education, assessment has often been constructed as an interruption—an externally imposed checkpoint that halts learning to evaluate its progression. This model, reliant on scheduled tests and end-point evaluations, isolates assessment from the natural flow of inquiry and development. Artificial intelligence challenges this separation by introducing real-time and embedded assessments—continuous, context-aware processes that are interwoven into the learning experience itself.

Real-time assessment refers to the capacity of AI systems to evaluate learner behavior and performance instantaneously. Whether a student is working through a complex math problem, engaging with a science simulation, or composing a written response, AI can analyze inputs as they occur. The system identifies misconceptions, patterns of hesitation, and inconsistencies in reasoning, offering immediate feedback tailored to the learner's unique trajectory. This shift from delayed feedback to instantaneous correction supports metacognitive development and fosters a growth mindset.

Embedded assessment, by contrast, integrates evaluation seamlessly within the learning task. Rather than pausing to test knowledge separately, the learning activity itself becomes the vehicle for assessment. For example, as a student navigates a virtual lab environment, the AI tracks decision-making processes, data interpretation, and experimentation strategies—all of which provide evidence of scientific reasoning. In this model, assessment is no longer an external audit but a formative companion to exploration and discovery.

The pedagogical implications of real-time and embedded assessments are profound. First, they support differentiated instruction at scale. Educators can receive dashboards summarizing learner progress across multiple dimensions—conceptual mastery, engagement levels, social collaboration—allowing for targeted interventions that are responsive, not reactive.

Second, these systems reduce the anxiety and artificiality associated with traditional testing. When assessment is integrated into authentic learning tasks, students are less likely to experience performance pressure or test-specific preparation behaviors. The focus shifts from test-taking to meaning-making, enhancing intrinsic motivation and deeper cognitive engagement.

Third, embedded assessments allow for more holistic evaluation. Rather than fixating on correctness alone, AI systems can examine how students approach problems, whether they persist through difficulty, how they respond to feedback, and how they transfer knowledge across contexts. This approach recognizes that learning is not a binary outcome but a multi-dimensional process shaped by cognitive, emotional, and social factors.

However, the deployment of real-time and embedded assessment systems requires careful design. The granularity of data collected raises legitimate concerns about student privacy, surveillance, and consent. Additionally, educators must be equipped to interpret and act upon the insights generated by these systems. Without proper training and institutional support, the promise of real-time assessment may translate into data overload or misapplication.

There is also a risk that continuous evaluation may lead to a sense of constant monitoring, undermining student autonomy and well-being. To mitigate this, assessment tools must be designed with ethical constraints and human-centered principles, ensuring that learners remain active participants in their evaluation journey rather than passive subjects of algorithmic scrutiny.

In conclusion, real-time and embedded assessments redefine the concept of timeliness in education. They shift the locus of assessment from the endpoint to the process, from judgment to guidance, and from interruption to integration. As such, they serve as a cornerstone of AI-centered education—one that aligns evaluation with the rhythms of authentic learning and the aspirations of human development.

Adaptive Assessment Engines and Personalized Learning Paths

Adaptive assessment represents one of the most significant shifts in modern educational evaluation. Unlike static assessments that present identical content to all learners, adaptive assessment engines adjust in real time to the learner's performance, interests, and needs. These systems, empowered by artificial intelligence, challenge the very notion of a fixed curriculum or universal standard. Instead, they offer an individualized journey where each assessment dynamically responds to the learner's evolving context.

The foundation of adaptive assessment lies in machine learning algorithms trained to identify patterns in student input—correct and incorrect answers, hesitation times, help requests, content engagement levels—and subsequently calibrate the complexity and format of subsequent tasks. A student who demonstrates mastery of foundational concepts may be directed toward higher-order thinking problems. Conversely, if a learner struggles, the system may adjust downward, revisiting prerequisite skills or presenting content through alternative modalities such as visuals, audio explanations, or scaffolded prompts.

This feedback loop creates a personalized learning path, where assessment and instruction are indistinguishable. Every question becomes both a diagnostic and a learning opportunity. Over time, the AI engine builds a detailed learner profile, capturing not only content knowledge but also metacognitive traits such as perseverance, risk-taking, and responsiveness to feedback.

Such personalization offers numerous pedagogical advantages. First, it prevents boredom and frustration by ensuring that learners operate within their optimal zone of development—challenged but not overwhelmed. Second, it honors the diversity of cognitive styles and cultural backgrounds. Learners may demonstrate understanding through a range of inputs, whether written, spoken, visual, or kinetic. Adaptive engines can accommodate these preferences, reducing the linguistic and cultural biases often embedded in standardized tests.

Third, adaptive assessments provide educators with fine-grained insights into learner trajectories. Rather than a single score, teachers receive multidimensional dashboards that reveal conceptual understanding, procedural fluency, and learning habits. These tools enable timely intervention and informed instructional planning, particularly in inclusive or mixed-ability classrooms.

However, the deployment of adaptive assessment engines also introduces complex challenges. One primary concern is algorithmic transparency. Educators and students must understand how decisions are made—what criteria are used to adjust difficulty, how learner data is interpreted, and what constitutes mastery. Black-box algorithms, while efficient, risk eroding trust and agency if their logic remains opaque.

Another concern involves content integrity and alignment. If adaptive systems introduce material dynamically, they must still ensure coherence with curriculum standards, grade-level expectations, and developmental appropriateness. Poorly designed engines may lead to fragmented learning experiences or misaligned instruction.

Moreover, while personalization enhances engagement, it may inadvertently isolate learners from shared learning experiences. Education is not solely an individual pursuit; it is also a communal process. Therefore, adaptive assessment must be balanced with opportunities for collaboration, dialogue, and shared inquiry.

Equity considerations are also paramount. Not all schools or learners have equal access to the technological infrastructure required for adaptive systems. Without proactive policy and resource allocation, the adoption of AI-enhanced assessments may deepen existing divides rather than close them.

Finally, the ethical use of learner data remains a foundational concern. Adaptive engines generate and rely upon extensive personal information—academic histories, behavioral trends, engagement metrics—that must be protected through robust data governance, encryption protocols, and consent mechanisms. Students should retain ownership of their data and be informed participants in how it is used.

In essence, adaptive assessment engines are not merely technological upgrades; they represent a philosophical realignment of education—from standardization to personalization, from competition to growth. When designed with ethical foresight and educational integrity, they offer a powerful tool for nurturing each learner's potential, respecting their uniqueness, and guiding them along a path of meaningful and continuous development.

Multimodal Assessments and AI Interpretation

The growing complexity of knowledge production, communication, and problem-solving in the twenty-first century has necessitated a departure from text-dominant models of assessment. While traditional exams rely heavily on written and numerical inputs, modern learners operate in a world saturated with multimedia, digital interaction, and multimodal expression. In this context, multimodal assessments—evaluations that capture learning across various formats such as speech, gesture, drawing, coding, modeling, and simulation—have emerged as essential tools for comprehensive evaluation. Artificial intelligence plays a critical role in enabling these assessments to be analyzed at scale, with depth, and in real time.

Multimodal assessment recognizes that learners think, process, and express ideas in diverse ways. A student might articulate their understanding of ecological systems through a video documentary, a digital infographic, a coding simulation, or an interactive presentation. These formats are not merely alternative representations; they are complex cognitive artifacts that demand planning, synthesis, and audience awareness. As such, they offer richer evidence of learning than a single written response could provide.

The implementation of multimodal assessments has historically been constrained by human limitations in scoring and interpretation. Evaluating a multimedia presentation or creative simulation requires time, expertise, and subjective judgment. AI resolves many of these barriers. Using technologies such as natural language processing, computer vision, speech recognition, and sentiment analysis, AI systems can evaluate diverse artifacts in structured and scalable ways. These systems can detect conceptual accuracy, coherence, originality, engagement, and emotional tone—offering a multidimensional picture of student performance.

For example, an AI-driven language assessment platform might evaluate spoken responses for fluency, pronunciation, vocabulary diversity, syntactic complexity, and even emotional confidence. A system assessing digital art submissions could analyze use of color, composition, symbolism, and relation to a central theme. In mathematics, gesture recognition can be used to analyze problem-solving strategies expressed on a digital whiteboard. These capabilities bring once-unmeasurable competencies into the evaluative domain.

The use of multimodal assessment also benefits learners with diverse needs. Students with dyslexia, speech impairments, or neurodiverse processing styles may struggle in written-only evaluations but excel in visual, verbal, or kinesthetic formats. By expanding the modes of assessment, AI-inclusive systems foster greater equity and inclusivity.

Nonetheless, this approach presents several challenges. First, ensuring validity and reliability across modalities is complex. What constitutes "quality" in a podcast may differ significantly from that in a visual essay. Without clearly defined rubrics, assessment risks becoming inconsistent or overly subjective. AI models must be trained on diverse, representative datasets to minimize bias and ensure fairness.

Second, there is a tension between creativity and conformity. If AI systems prioritize certain patterns—syntax, vocabulary, structure—they may inadvertently reward conventionality and penalize innovation. Learners who push boundaries or adopt non-standard forms of expression may find themselves disadvantaged unless the system is explicitly designed to accommodate such variation.

Third, data privacy concerns intensify in multimodal contexts. Video, audio, geolocation, and behavioral cues introduce biometric and personal data into the assessment process. Safeguards must be rigorous and transparent, with strict consent protocols and ethical review standards.

Teachers also face a significant learning curve. Interpreting AI-generated analysis of multimodal work requires new forms of pedagogical literacy. Professional development must evolve to equip educators with the skills needed to engage critically and constructively with AI feedback, and to translate it into meaningful support for students.

Lastly, infrastructure disparities must not be overlooked. Access to high-quality devices, high-speed internet, and digital creation tools is uneven across regions and populations. Multimodal assessment should not become a new barrier to opportunity. Equity must guide design and implementation, ensuring that students from all backgrounds can participate and benefit.

Multimodal assessment, interpreted and supported by AI, reflects the pluralism and complexity of real-world problem-solving. It encourages learners to communicate meaningfully, demonstrate understanding authentically, and engage creatively. If embraced thoughtfully, this approach will not only improve the quality of evaluation, but also align assessment with the rich, multimodal world in which today's students will live, work, and lead.

The Rise of Competency-Based Education and AI Support

Competency-based education (CBE) marks a transformative departure from the traditional time-based model of schooling, which ties academic progression to age, grade level, and hours spent in instruction. Instead, CBE anchors educational advancement in the demonstrated mastery of specific knowledge, skills, and dispositions. In this framework, students move forward only when they have achieved clear and measurable competencies—regardless of the time it takes. As educational systems embrace this philosophy, artificial intelligence emerges as an essential enabler, facilitating scalable, accurate, and personalized assessment of learner competencies across diverse domains.

The fundamental premise of CBE is that learning is not a race against the calendar, but a journey toward mastery. It prioritizes depth over pace and understanding over performance. This model aligns closely with real-world demands, where individuals are evaluated not by the seat time spent in training but by their ability to apply knowledge and perform tasks effectively. As economies shift toward skills-based hiring and as lifelong learning becomes imperative, CBE offers a more meaningful and relevant educational experience.

Artificial intelligence significantly enhances the feasibility and fidelity of CBE implementation. First, AI systems can continuously track learner progress across a spectrum of micro-competencies, generating dynamic learner profiles that reflect not only what has been mastered but also how and under what conditions. These profiles become the basis for personalized learning plans, adaptive interventions, and targeted support.

Second, AI can operationalize the assessment of complex competencies that traditional tests struggle to measure. For example, evaluating a student's ability to collaborate, lead a project, or resolve a conflict requires multidimensional observation. AI-enabled platforms can analyze communication logs, group dynamics, reflection journals, and peer evaluations to form a holistic picture of such competencies.

Third, AI systems can automate and scale the delivery of performance tasks and simulations. In a CBE framework, students must often demonstrate mastery through real-world application—solving problems, building models, producing media, or coding solutions. AI can generate personalized scenarios, provide formative feedback during task execution, and assess the final product against a rubric. This supports authenticity without sacrificing efficiency.

Moreover, AI can help standardize and validate the assessment of competencies across institutions. Shared ontologies and AI-driven scoring models allow for consistency in how competencies are defined and measured, supporting portability of credentials and interoperability between learning environments. This is especially relevant for digital badges, micro-credentials, and skills transcripts—new forms of certification that are gaining traction in both academic and employment sectors.

However, the integration of AI into CBE also introduces critical design and ethical considerations. The definition of competencies must be inclusive, culturally responsive, and future-oriented. If AI systems are trained on narrow or biased conceptions of success, they may reinforce systemic inequities rather than disrupt them.

Additionally, while CBE aims to empower learners through autonomy and mastery, algorithmic systems must not undermine that autonomy through excessive monitoring or prescriptive learning paths. Learners must retain agency over their educational journeys, with AI serving as a guide rather than a governor.

Teacher roles must also evolve. In a CBE environment supported by AI, educators shift from content deliverers to learning architects, coaches, and evaluators of complex human skills. This requires significant professional development, trust in AI tools, and collaboration between educators and technologists.

Furthermore, stakeholders—including parents, employers, and policymakers—must be educated about the implications of CBE and the nature of AI-validated credentials. Public trust in non-traditional assessments will depend on the transparency, rigor, and demonstrable value of these new systems.

In conclusion, the rise of competency-based education, amplified by artificial intelligence, represents a powerful realignment of educational priorities. It shifts the focus from compliance to capability, from time-spent to skills-demonstrated, and from standardized evaluation to personalized mastery. If implemented thoughtfully, this model will not only enhance learning outcomes but also prepare students to thrive in an uncertain, rapidly evolving world where adaptability, problem-solving, and ethical judgment are paramount.

Ethical Challenges in AI-Based Assessment

As artificial intelligence becomes increasingly integrated into educational assessment systems, questions of ethics move from the periphery to the center of design, implementation, and policy-making. The power of AI to process vast quantities of data, personalize assessments, and adaptively evaluate learner progress offers transformative potential. However, with that power comes the responsibility to ensure that such systems are fair, transparent, accountable, and respectful of human dignity. Ethical considerations must not be retrofitted into AI-based assessments; they must be foundational.

The first major ethical concern pertains to bias. AI systems, including those used in educational contexts, are trained on historical data sets that may reflect existing social inequalities and prejudices. If not carefully curated and constantly audited, these systems risk perpetuating or even amplifying disparities. For example, natural language processing models trained on predominately English-centric, Western-centric, or male-centric data may misinterpret or undervalue the inputs of learners from diverse linguistic, cultural, or gendered backgrounds. This creates a feedback loop in which marginalized students receive inaccurate evaluations, reinforcing systemic disadvantage under the guise of objectivity.

Transparency is the second pillar of ethical AI. In traditional assessments, grading criteria and scoring methods are generally accessible and explainable. In contrast, AI-based assessments often function as "black boxes," making decisions through opaque algorithmic processes that neither educators nor learners fully understand. This opacity undermines trust and accountability. For AI to serve as a legitimate evaluator, it must be accompanied by interpretable models, clear documentation, and mechanisms for explanation and challenge.

Another critical issue is data privacy. AI assessment systems collect and analyze an immense volume of personal information—academic performance, behavior patterns, facial expressions, eye movement, voice inflection, and even emotional states. Without stringent safeguards, this data can be vulnerable to misuse, breaches, or commercial exploitation. Learners must be informed about what data is collected, how it is stored, who has access, and for what purposes it is used. Consent must be meaningful, not buried in lengthy legal disclaimers. Furthermore, the principle of data minimization should guide system design—collecting only what is necessary and retaining it only as long as required.

Agency and autonomy must also be preserved. AI assessment systems should empower, not control. There is a risk that algorithmic recommendations could become mandates—dictating what students learn, how they learn, and at what pace. This mechanistic approach can reduce education to compliance and strip learners of their role as active agents in their own development. Ethical AI systems must be designed to support human judgment, not supplant it. They should offer choices, encourage reflection, and respect learner individuality.

Accountability mechanisms are equally essential. When an AI system produces an incorrect, biased, or harmful evaluation, who is responsible? The developer, the educator, the institution, or the platform provider? Ethical governance requires that roles and responsibilities be clearly defined, that systems undergo regular external auditing, and that learners have access to recourse if they are unfairly assessed The introduction of AI must not weaken existing protections or blur lines of responsibility.

The psychological impact of continuous, AI-mediated evaluation also warrants attention. Learners may feel surveilled, judged, or reduced to a set of metrics. This can erode motivation, creativity, and emotional safety—especially for younger or more vulnerable populations.

Ethical systems must consider not only what is technically feasible but what is educationally desirable and developmentally appropriate.

Moreover, there is a broader concern about the commodification of education. As private technology firms increasingly supply AI tools for assessment, the risk of commercialization intensifies. Student data becomes a valuable asset, and assessment tools may prioritize scalability and profitability over pedagogical soundness. Public institutions must retain control over core educational functions, and policies should guard against the privatization of educational sovereignty.

Finally, inclusivity must be a design imperative. AI systems should be co-developed with input from diverse stakeholders—educators, students, parents, ethicists, and communities. This participatory approach ensures that systems reflect shared values and serve all learners, not just a privileged subset.

In sum, the ethical challenges of AI-based assessment are not secondary concerns—they are existential. The legitimacy, efficacy, and sustainability of these systems hinge on their ability to uphold the principles of justice, transparency, autonomy, and human flourishing. If these challenges are met with rigor and resolve, AI can become a tool not only of innovation but of integrity.

The Role of Human Educators in AI-Assisted Assessment Systems

As artificial intelligence assumes an increasingly prominent role in educational assessment, the question arises: what is the role of the human educator in this new evaluative landscape? Far from rendering teachers obsolete, AI-based assessment systems elevate the significance of human judgment, empathy, and pedagogical expertise. Rather than replacing educators, artificial intelligence reconfigures their function—transforming them from test administrators and scorers into learning designers, data interpreters, and developmental mentors.

One of the most immediate roles that educators retain is the interpretation of AI-generated data. While AI systems can efficiently evaluate performance indicators, identify patterns, and suggest intervention points, they lack the contextual awareness and relational insight that human teachers bring. A sudden drop in a student's engagement score may be flagged by an algorithm, but only a teacher, familiar with the student's home situation or emotional state, can interpret that data accurately and empathetically. In this capacity, the educator becomes the bridge between quantitative signals and qualitative understanding.

Educators also play a critical role in validating the outputs of AI assessments. While algorithmic scoring may achieve consistency and speed, it is not immune to error or bias. Teachers must review AI-generated assessments—particularly in subjective domains such as writing, artistic production, or group collaboration—to ensure that evaluations align with pedagogical goals and human values. This function is essential not only for fairness but also for maintaining trust in technology-assisted evaluation systems.

Moreover, teachers are instrumental in framing assessment as a constructive and empowering process. AI systems may offer real-time feedback, but it is the educator who contextualizes that feedback, translates it into actionable strategies, and supports the learner emotionally and intellectually as they process it. Feedback alone is not formative; it becomes formative when delivered with insight, encouragement, and developmental intent.

Another indispensable role of educators lies in instructional design. AI assessment systems are most effective when integrated seamlessly with learning activities. Educators, with their deep understanding of curriculum, student diversity, and classroom dynamics, are uniquely positioned to design learning environments where assessment is embedded, authentic, and aligned with instructional objectives. They decide how, when, and why AI tools are used, ensuring that these systems enhance rather than distort the educational experience.

The ethical oversight of AI tools is also a teacher's responsibility. Educators must be vigilant about how student data is collected, interpreted, and acted upon. They must advocate for transparency, challenge questionable outputs, and protect students from surveillance or undue stress. In this sense, teachers function as stewards of both educational integrity and student welfare.

In collaborative learning environments, teachers facilitate interpersonal dynamics that AI cannot replicate. Assessment in such contexts often involves negotiation, reflection, and social interaction. While

AI might monitor participation or sentiment, it cannot foster community, resolve conflict, or nurture the interpersonal skills that are essential for teamwork and leadership. The teacher remains the architect of these human dimensions of assessment.

Educators also act as cultural and moral interpreters. As AI tools increasingly shape what is valued and measured in education, teachers help students critically examine those values. They can encourage students to question algorithmic authority, reflect on the ethics of technology, and assert their agency in a data-driven world. In this role, the teacher is not only a facilitator of learning but also a guide in digital citizenship and ethical reasoning.

Finally, teachers are irreplaceable mentors in the development of identity and purpose. While AI can track learning paths, it cannot inspire passion, model resilience, or ignite curiosity in the same way a human can. Assessment, at its best, is not merely about evaluating what a student knows but helping them discover who they are. This process is deeply relational and inherently human.

In conclusion, the rise of AI-assisted assessment does not diminish the educator's role—it expands and elevates it. Teachers are no longer limited to mechanical grading or administrative tasks; they become the interpreters, designers, mentors, and ethical stewards of a more personalized and humane educational system. The synergy between artificial intelligence and human educators holds the promise of a future where assessment becomes not a judgment imposed, but a journey shared.

Toward a Global Framework for AI-Enhanced Assessment Standards

The global adoption of artificial intelligence in education necessitates the establishment of shared frameworks that define, regulate, and align AI-enhanced assessment practices. While national education systems vary in structure, curriculum, and policy orientation, the digital tools that power AI-driven assessments often transcend borders. Without coordinated standards, the rapid proliferation of AI in assessment risks exacerbating educational inequalities, enabling unchecked commercial influence, and undermining public trust. A global framework is, therefore, not only a matter of policy coherence but a prerequisite for ethical, inclusive, and scalable implementation.

The first objective of such a framework must be **definitional clarity**. At present, the terminology surrounding AI-enhanced assessment remains inconsistent across countries and even within regions. Terms such as "adaptive assessment," "automated feedback," "learning analytics," and "AI evaluation engines" are used variably, often conflated or misunderstood. A global framework should establish a taxonomy of AI assessment modalities, delineating their scope, functionality, and pedagogical applications. This shared vocabulary facilitates international research, collaboration, and policymaking.

A second imperative is the **standardization of ethical principles** governing AI use in assessment. This includes universal commitments to transparency, data protection, equity, and human oversight. These principles must be codified in international agreements and operationalized through local policy instruments. For example, all AI systems used in educational assessment should be required to disclose their data sources, algorithmic logic (where feasible), and known limitations. Learners and educators should retain agency, with the right to opt out or appeal algorithmic evaluations.

Equity remains a central concern in the formulation of global standards. Disparities in technological infrastructure, language representation, and cultural relevance mean that AI systems may perform well in some contexts and poorly in others. A truly global framework must mandate **cross-cultural validation** of AI assessment tools and require inclusive design practices that engage underrepresented regions, dialects, and learner profiles. Failure to do so risks embedding Western-centric norms and reinforcing global educational hierarchies.

Another dimension involves **interoperability and credentialing**. As AI assessment systems generate personalized learning data and micro-credentials, these records must be portable and recognized across educational institutions and national borders. A global framework can establish protocols for the verification, formatting, and transferability of AI-generated learning evidence. This will support student mobility, cross-border higher education, and transnational skills recognition.

The role of **international organizations** such as UNESCO, the OECD, and the World Bank is pivotal in shaping and promoting such standards. These bodies possess both the convening power and the policy experience to coordinate multi-stakeholder dialogues, develop benchmarking tools, and facilitate regional implementation plans. Collaborative projects such as the UNESCO "AI and the Futures of Learning" initiative already signal growing momentum toward a shared vision.

Importantly, the framework must include **mechanisms for local adaptation and feedback**. While overarching principles provide coherence, they must be flexible enough to accommodate the cultural, linguistic, and pedagogical specificities of individual systems. Local educators, researchers, and communities must be active participants in shaping how global standards are interpreted and applied.

The **commercial sector** also requires guidance under this framework. As private firms play a growing role in supplying AI assessment tools, standards must address issues such as profit incentives, intellectual property, and competitive fairness. Public-private partnerships must be structured around mutual accountability, with strong regulatory oversight to prevent exploitation, data monetization, or educational dependency on proprietary technologies.

To ensure sustainability, the framework must be **future-proofed**—capable of evolving alongside advances in machine learning, natural language processing, and cognitive computing. A periodic review process, informed by empirical evidence and stakeholder input, should be institutionalized. This allows for the iterative refinement of standards and fosters resilience in the face of rapid technological change.

Lastly, the global framework must serve as a **platform for shared innovation**. By setting a common foundation, it enables collaboration across borders—shared AI training datasets, co-designed tools, multilingual interface development, and open-source software contributions. This spirit of collective progress ensures that AI-enhanced assessment becomes not a privilege of the wealthy few but a public good for learners everywhere.

In conclusion, the rise of AI in educational assessment presents both a challenge and an opportunity for global governance. Without a shared framework, the field risks fragmentation, inequity, and ethical lapse. With one, it can usher in a new era of high-quality, personalized, and inclusive learning evaluation—anchored in human rights, pedagogical integrity, and international solidarity.

Rethinking Accreditation and Graduation in the AI Age

The longstanding traditions of academic accreditation and graduation are undergoing unprecedented scrutiny in the wake of artificial intelligence's integration into education. Historically, diplomas and certificates have served as proxies for competence, signaling that a learner has fulfilled predetermined requirements within a fixed educational structure. However, as artificial intelligence enables granular, real-time, and multimodal assessment of learning outcomes, these traditional models are increasingly misaligned with the realities of student achievement, workforce readiness, and lifelong learning. Rethinking accreditation and graduation in the AI age is not a matter of institutional preference—it is an urgent necessity.

Traditional accreditation systems are often built on inputs rather than outcomes. Course credits, seat time, and instructor credentials are used as markers of educational quality. In contrast, AI-enhanced systems are capable of validating learning through continuous demonstration of competencies—regardless of how, where, or when they are acquired. A student who learns advanced calculus through a MOOC, builds machine learning models in an after-school club, and contributes to open-source software projects may demonstrate more capability than peers who followed conventional coursework. Yet, under current systems, such a student may receive no formal recognition. This disconnect demands a radical rethinking of how learning is accredited.

Artificial intelligence allows for **the development of dynamic learner profiles** that track mastery across hundreds of micro-competencies. These profiles, visualized through dashboards and validated through AI-driven assessments, can serve as living transcripts. Unlike static grades, they provide a multidimensional view of learner growth, including soft skills such as critical thinking, collaboration, creativity, and resilience. They can also showcase real-world outputs—portfolios, code repositories, design prototypes—authenticated and timestamped through blockchain or digital credentialing systems. In this model, graduation becomes less of a ceremonial endpoint and more of a flexible transition point—based on readiness, not time.

This approach has profound implications for **educational equity and mobility**. Learners from non-traditional backgrounds—homeschooled students, refugees, incarcerated youth, or those engaged in informal learning—can demonstrate their qualifications without having to navigate rigid institutional gatekeeping. Competency-based credentials, backed by AI-validated evidence, allow for personalized pacing and multiple pathways to success. This flexibility supports equity without sacrificing rigor.

Rethinking accreditation also demands **redefinition of institutional roles**. Schools and universities must shift from being sole certifiers of learning to becoming facilitators, verifiers, and platforms for lifelong learning. They may issue credentials in partnership with global AI systems, community-based learning networks, or professional guilds. The focus moves from curriculum completion to capability demonstration.

Workforce alignment is a key driver in this shift. Employers increasingly prioritize demonstrable skills over formal degrees. AI-enhanced credentials, linked to real-world simulations, project-based learning, and authentic performance data, offer a more reliable indicator of job readiness than transcripts alone. As AI tools become standard in hiring—analyzing portfolios, coding samples, or recorded interviews—educational credentials must evolve to remain relevant.

Yet, this transformation also introduces **significant challenges**. First, the legitimacy of AI-verified credentials must be established across industries, regions, and cultures. Employers, universities, and governments need assurance that these credentials are reliable, comparable, and tamper-proof. This requires standardized frameworks, cross-institutional agreements, and robust data governance.

Second, the **psychosocial and cultural importance of graduation**

rituals must not be underestimated. For many communities, graduation is a rite of passage—a celebration of perseverance, identity, and family achievement. A shift to fluid transitions and modular credentials must find ways to preserve the dignity and meaning of educational milestones. New rituals and forms of recognition may need to be designed.

Third, **ethical oversight is paramount**. If AI determines when and how a student is ready to graduate, the algorithms must be transparent, fair, and regularly audited. Students must retain the right to challenge evaluations, seek human review, and access support if unjustly delayed or denied graduation. Accreditation systems must be inclusive, not discriminatory.

Furthermore, **teacher and counselor roles must be redefined**. In the AI age, educators become guides in helping students curate their learning paths, build digital portfolios, and navigate credentialing ecosystems. This requires significant upskilling, institutional support, and reimagined professional development.

Lastly, **policy frameworks must evolve** to enable flexible accreditation. Governments must allow for alternative credentialing models, digital transcripts, and AI-authenticated portfolios to serve as valid indicators for college entry, job applications, and professional licensing. Accreditation agencies must adapt their evaluation criteria to accommodate non-linear, AI-supported learning experiences.

In summary, the integration of artificial intelligence into education renders the traditional models of accreditation and graduation increasingly obsolete. The future demands systems that are flexible, evidence-based, inclusive, and aligned with the complex realities of lifelong learning. Graduation, in the AI age, is not a conclusion—it is a dynamic declaration of readiness, capability, and continuous growth.

Policy Recommendations for Equitable AI-Integrated Assessment Systems

The promise of AI-enhanced assessment lies not merely in technological sophistication, but in its capacity to make education more equitable, inclusive, and responsive to the full spectrum of human potential. However, without careful governance, artificial intelligence may reproduce or exacerbate existing disparities in educational access, outcomes, and opportunity. For policymakers, the task is to proactively shape the use of AI in assessment through clear, enforceable, and equity-centered strategies. The following recommendations offer a blueprint for designing policies that uphold educational justice in the age of intelligent systems.

1. Establish a National AI-in-Education Policy Framework.
Governments should develop comprehensive policy frameworks that define the scope, standards, and safeguards for the use of AI in educational assessment. These frameworks must articulate clear goals—such as inclusion, transparency, and accountability—and establish the legal basis for data protection, algorithmic auditing, and stakeholder rights. This ensures that AI is deployed with deliberate oversight rather than fragmented experimentation.

2. Mandate Equity Audits for All AI Assessment Tools.
Before any AI system is approved for classroom use, it should undergo rigorous equity audits to assess for bias, fairness, and cultural responsiveness. These audits should test how the tool performs across different races, languages, socioeconomic backgrounds, gender identities, and learning styles. Ongoing audits must be conducted periodically, with publicly available reports.

3. Require Explainability and Transparency.
AI systems used in assessment must meet minimum standards for explainability. Educators, students, and parents should be able to understand how decisions are made and what data is used. This includes access to decision logic, training data summaries, and the ability to appeal or override algorithmic outputs. Black-box models should be discouraged in high-stakes contexts.

4. Protect Learner Data and Limit Commercial Use.
Student data must be protected under updated and enforceable data privacy laws. These laws should require informed consent, limit data retention periods, and restrict third-party access—particularly by commercial vendors. Selling or repurposing assessment data for advertising, surveillance, or non-educational analytics must be prohibited.

5. Fund Educator Training and Capacity-Building.
Professional development programs must be established to train teachers and school leaders in the use of AI-driven assessment tools. This includes technical fluency, ethical oversight, data interpretation, and integration with instructional design. Educators must not be passive recipients of AI tools—they must be co-designers and critical evaluators.

6. Promote Inclusive Design Through Participatory Development.
Policies should require that AI assessment tools be co-developed with input from students, teachers, families, and communities—especially those historically marginalized in education. Participatory design ensures that systems reflect lived realities, local needs, and cultural contexts. It also builds trust and buy-in from end-users.

7. Support Open-Source and Public Sector Innovation.
Governments should invest in the development of public AI tools for assessment, ensuring that innovation is not monopolized by private corporations. Open-source platforms allow for transparency, collaboration, and adaptation to diverse educational settings. They also reduce dependency on costly proprietary software.

8. Create Certification Standards and Independent Evaluation Bodies.
A national or international certification process should be established for AI assessment tools, with independent bodies tasked with evaluating systems for technical quality, educational relevance, and ethical compliance. Only certified tools should be permitted for public use, particularly in compulsory education.

9. Provide Legal Recourse and Student Rights Protections.
Students and families must have access to legal mechanisms if harmed by AI-based evaluations—whether through misclassification, data breaches, or algorithmic discrimination. The right to human review, correction, and explanation must be enshrined in policy. AI must never function as an unaccountable authority.

10. Align AI Assessment Policies with Broader Educational Goals.
Finally, policymakers must ensure that AI assessment systems reinforce, rather than distort, the goals of education. These include holistic development, critical thinking, civic engagement, and personal growth—not merely efficiency or standardization. AI policies must be guided by pedagogical principles, not market logic.

In conclusion, the ethical and equitable use of AI in assessment is not a technological issue alone—it is a matter of governance, values, and public will. The right policies, developed collaboratively and enforced rigorously, can ensure that AI becomes a force for empowerment rather than exclusion. Policymakers must act with urgency and foresight to design a future of assessment that honors every learner's humanity.

From Standardization to Personalization

The shift toward AI-centered assessment necessitates a movement away from standardization as the primary goal of evaluation. Instead of expecting all learners to reach identical benchmarks at the same time, assessment in an AI-powered ecosystem can honor individual progressions, diverse talents, and personalized learning pathways.

Personalized assessment does not imply a lack of rigor or coherence. Rather, it requires robust frameworks that define competencies, establish mastery thresholds, and respect learner variability. These may include:

1. **Competency-Based Assessment Models**
   Learners are assessed based on mastery of specific skills or knowledge areas, regardless of age or grade level. Progression is tied to demonstrated understanding rather than seat time or test dates.
2. **Performance-Based Tasks**
   Students complete authentic tasks that require application of skills in real-world or simulated contexts. AI can evaluate these performances using rubrics aligned with human-scored exemplars and refine scoring algorithms through transparent calibration.

3. **Portfolio Assessment Systems**
   AI tools can support the curation and analysis of digital portfolios containing artifacts of learning over time—videos, projects, code samples, research papers, design documents, and reflections.
4. **Self and Peer Assessment Integration**
   With the aid of AI-facilitated reflection prompts and evaluation frameworks, students can become assessors of their own work and that of peers—developing metacognitive skills and community accountability.

Ethical Considerations in AI-Based Assessment

While the capabilities of AI offer transformative potential, their use in assessment raises complex ethical considerations. Without careful design and oversight, these systems risk amplifying biases, invading privacy, or reducing learners to algorithmic predictions.

Core ethical issues include:

1. **Bias and Fairness**
   AI models are trained on existing data, which may reflect systemic inequities. Predictive algorithms risk reinforcing stereotypes or misjudging learners from underrepresented communities.
2. **Transparency and Explainability**
   Students, families, and educators must understand how AI systems evaluate work, what criteria are used, and how decisions are made. Black-box scoring undermines trust and agency.
3. **Consent and Data Ownership**
   Learners must retain control over their assessment data. Systems must be designed to allow users to access, audit, and contest AI-generated evaluations.
4. **Human Oversight and Interpretation**
   AI assessments should augment, not replace, human judgment. Educators must retain the authority to contextualize scores, consider extenuating circumstances, and exercise professional discretion.

To address these challenges, assessment systems must be governed by clear ethical guidelines, developed in consultation with educators, students, families, ethicists, and technologists. Ethical review boards, transparent audit trails, and open-source scoring frameworks can strengthen accountability and public trust.

A Vision for the Future – Human-Centered Intelligence in Education

As artificial intelligence becomes embedded in the fabric of education, the question that must guide all design, policy, and pedagogical choices is not simply "What can AI do?" but "What should AI do in service of human learning and flourishing?" The future of assessment—and education more broadly—must be grounded in a vision that places human-centered intelligence at its core. This vision is not about accelerating automation or achieving algorithmic perfection. It is about ensuring that technology amplifies, rather than diminishes, the purpose, dignity, and diversity of human development.

A human-centered intelligence model reframes the role of assessment from judgment to growth. Instead of ranking learners by comparative performance on standardized exams, future assessments will illuminate individual learning journeys—highlighting strengths, identifying areas for support, and mapping personalized development over time. Artificial intelligence can facilitate this by processing rich, real-time learning data across modalities—text, speech, behavior, and emotion—and transforming it into meaningful insights. But those insights must serve the learner's sense of agency, not reduce them to a digital profile.

In this future, students are not passive recipients of scores but active participants in their own evaluation. They will reflect on their progress, co-construct goals with teachers, and engage in peer-to-peer feedback empowered by AI tools. Assessment becomes dialogic, iterative, and relational—deeply embedded in the learning process rather than detached from it. Artificial intelligence will scaffold this process, but the dialogue must remain grounded in human interaction.

Educators, far from being displaced, will rise in stature as interpreters, mentors, and ethical stewards. Their role will be to curate learning experiences, design equitable assessment systems, and mediate between machine-generated insights and human development. They will draw on AI tools not to mechanize their labor but to deepen their professional judgment, support diverse learners, and unlock new pedagogical possibilities.

Assessment will also extend beyond cognitive domains to include social-emotional learning, civic competence, creativity, and ethical reasoning. These domains, often overlooked by traditional tests, are essential to navigating a world shaped by complexity, interdependence, and rapid change. AI-enabled assessment can support their development, but only if guided by clear frameworks that value the full humanity of each learner.

This vision also includes structural transformation. Schools and systems will adopt flexible models of credentialing—recognizing learning wherever it occurs, validating skills in real time, and supporting multiple pathways to graduation and lifelong learning. AI-verified microcredentials, digital portfolios, and blockchain-authenticated evidence will enable learners to move fluidly between educational, professional, and civic spaces. Learning will no longer be confined by age, geography, or institutional boundary.

Yet this future cannot be realized without deliberate, inclusive governance. A human-centered intelligence paradigm requires policy frameworks that embed rights, equity, and participation at every level. It demands rigorous ethical standards, public accountability, and meaningful representation of marginalized voices. It calls for a global effort to democratize the development and distribution of AI systems—ensuring that education remains a public good and not a privatized commodity.

Most importantly, this vision affirms that intelligence is not just what machines do—it is what humans are capable of becoming. Artificial intelligence may analyze data at scale, but it cannot feel wonder, wrestle with moral dilemmas, or dream of a more just world. Education, therefore, must nurture those uniquely human capacities—curiosity, empathy, resilience, imagination—that machines cannot replicate. AI should be designed to serve those goals, not to define them.

In conclusion, the future of assessment in an AI-driven education system is not preordained—it is a choice. That choice must reflect a commitment to human dignity, learning equity, and developmental integrity. It must balance innovation with wisdom, speed with care, and automation with humanity. If done right, AI can help create an education system that is more personalized, inclusive, and transformative than ever before. But only if it remains anchored in the intelligence that truly matters: the human kind.

Chapter 13

Redesigning the Learning Environment – AI- Optimized Classrooms and Digital Infrastructure

The convergence of artificial intelligence and education necessitates a fundamental reconfiguration of the physical, digital, and conceptual environments in which learning occurs. Traditional classrooms, designed in an era marked by industrial standardization and analog instruction, no longer reflect the demands of a digitally dynamic, cognitively diverse, and technologically mediated society. The limitations of fixed infrastructure, generalized pedagogy, and inflexible timetables reveal a growing incongruence between existing educational architectures and the fluid, responsive nature of intelligent systems. As artificial intelligence integrates into instructional delivery, assessment mechanisms, and administrative processes, the spatial and systemic design of learning environments must evolve to harness this transformation.

The integration of artificial intelligence into learning environments extends beyond the mere inclusion of devices or software. It redefines spatial logic, reorders pedagogical priorities, and reconfigures the relationship between learners, instructors, and the content they engage with. Artificial intelligence not only individualizes learning trajectories but also reconstructs the logistical and epistemological frameworks through which knowledge is accessed and constructed. Classrooms of the future, guided by intelligent systems, will not be constrained by rigid seating arrangements, blackboards, or synchronous instructional delivery. Rather, they will embody flexibility, adaptivity, and inclusivity—principles that align with both the technological affordances and the evolving understanding of how learning occurs.

Moreover, the emergence of AI-powered instructional models introduces new infrastructural imperatives. These imperatives involve both tangible resources, such as broadband connectivity, energy-efficient hardware, and interactive surfaces, and intangible frameworks, such as interoperable data systems, cybersecurity protocols, and algorithmic transparency standards. Educational systems must respond to this multifaceted transformation with strategic planning, equitable resource allocation, and evidence-based policy reform. Without a deliberate redesign of the environments in which students engage, the pedagogical advantages of artificial intelligence risk being diminished by logistical constraints or inequitable access.

This chapter presents a comprehensive examination of the necessary transformation of learning environments in response to artificial intelligence. The analysis begins with the spatial reorganization of physical classrooms, including furniture design, environmental sensors, and immersive technologies. It then explores the construction of digital ecosystems capable of supporting personalized learning, adaptive scheduling, and real-time feedback. The chapter proceeds to assess the infrastructural requirements that underpin AI integration, including data architectures, hardware specifications, and cloud-based platforms. Further sections address the ethical and policy implications of such redesign, with particular attention to equity, accessibility, and cultural responsiveness. The discussion concludes with a forward-looking synthesis of design principles for the AI-optimized school and recommendations for scalable implementation across diverse educational contexts.

Throughout the chapter, the analysis maintains an evidence-driven and critical perspective, recognizing both the transformative potential and the embedded risks of intelligent systems in educational settings. Emphasis is placed on ensuring that technology serves pedagogical and developmental priorities, rather than dictating them. By anchoring the redesign of learning environments in human-centered design, inclusive practice, and systemic coherence, educational institutions can position themselves to navigate the future of instruction with intentionality, equity, and effectiveness.

The Historical Logic of Classroom Design and Its Incompatibility with AI Learning Models

The architecture of the modern classroom has remained largely unchanged since the onset of mass public education in the late nineteenth and early twentieth centuries. This design—characterized by fixed seating, teacher-centered instruction, standardized materials, and synchronized schedules—was not developed to optimize cognitive growth, emotional development, or personalized learning. Instead, it was constructed to mirror the logic of the industrial age, prioritizing efficiency, conformity, and top-down control. The teacher functioned as the primary source of information, the classroom served as a containment space, and the curriculum followed a linear progression regulated by age and grade level.

This model, although effective for delivering uniform content to large groups, exhibits structural and pedagogical misalignment with the affordances and principles of artificial intelligence-based learning systems. Traditional classrooms presume that all learners must proceed at the same pace, receive the same information in the same format, and demonstrate mastery through uniform assessments. Artificial intelligence, by contrast, operates on the logic of individualization, adaptivity, and real-time feedback. These principles are fundamentally incompatible with physical environments and instructional rhythms designed for mass uniformity.

Furthermore, the physical layout of conventional classrooms inhibits the dynamic data flows and multimodal interactions that AI systems rely upon. Rows of desks facing a chalkboard or digital projector do not facilitate collaborative learning, interactive feedback loops, or diversified content delivery. AI-enabled learning requires spaces where learners can transition fluidly between individual tasks, peer collaboration, instructor interaction, and immersive digital experiences. Rigid spatial configurations impede this fluidity and restrict the deployment of intelligent instructional tools.

The temporal structure of traditional schooling also conflicts with the temporal logic of AI systems. Standardized schedules—often segmented into rigid blocks—fail to accommodate individual learning rhythms, cognitive fatigue patterns, or differentiated pacing. AI systems, equipped with real-time analytics and behavioral data, can recommend when a learner should take a break, revisit material, or accelerate through content. However, these insights are rendered inert within environments that lack the flexibility to adapt to such recommendations.

Additionally, legacy classroom designs are often technologically fragmented or under-resourced. In many schools, digital tools are retrofitted into existing infrastructures without redesigning the spatial and operational context. This leads to superficial adoption of AI capabilities—where intelligent systems are added as supplements rather than integrated as core elements of the learning environment. Without intentional redesign, artificial intelligence remains constrained by outdated pedagogical assumptions and logistical bottlenecks.

Moreover, the teacher's role in traditional classrooms centers on content delivery and behavioral management. This paradigm overlooks the potential for educators to function as data-informed mentors, learning architects, and cognitive coaches—roles that align with AI-augmented instruction. When the classroom environment restricts mobility, limits data visualization, or isolates the teacher from real-time analytics, the pedagogical possibilities of artificial intelligence are diminished.

The incompatibility between historical classroom logic and AI-enabled instruction is not a minor technical issue; it is a foundational misalignment that must be addressed through comprehensive design reform. Classrooms must be reconceptualized not as fixed spaces but as responsive ecosystems—spaces where data, human interaction, and adaptive technologies coalesce to support the full diversity of learners. The next section will explore how spatial redesign, informed by human-centered design principles and AI integration, can create environments that not only accommodate but amplify the potential of intelligent education.

The Architecture of Adaptive Learning Environments

The emergence of adaptive learning environments marks a radical departure from the standardized, linear, and fixed educational spaces of the past. At the heart of this shift lies the principle that learning spaces must be responsive—both to real-time data inputs and to the unique cognitive, emotional, and social needs of individual learners. Adaptive environments incorporate dynamic layouts, embedded technologies, and intelligent feedback mechanisms that reconfigure space, content delivery, and instructional flow according to constantly evolving learner profiles.

Architecturally, adaptive classrooms emphasize modularity. Unlike traditional classrooms that rely on immovable desks and static focal points, adaptive spaces employ mobile furniture, multi-use zones, and reconfigurable workstations. This modularity enables spontaneous collaboration, peer-to-peer instruction, and individualized task execution without spatial conflict. Such flexibility is not merely aesthetic—it is integral to supporting differentiated instruction and fluid learning pathways, both of which are central to artificial intelligence-based pedagogical models.

Integrated into these environments are embedded sensors and Internet-of-Things (IoT) devices that continuously gather contextual data. These inputs include lighting preferences, acoustic feedback, ambient temperature, air quality, motion tracking, eye-gaze analysis, and biometric stress indicators (collected only under ethical safeguards). This data informs environmental adjustments in real time, enabling the classroom to modulate conditions for optimal cognitive performance and emotional regulation. For example, dimming lights or reducing noise in response to signs of sensory overload enhances focus and supports neurodiverse learners.

In AI-optimized environments, walls are no longer passive barriers. Instead, they serve as intelligent display surfaces capable of rendering personalized dashboards, collaborative whiteboards, or immersive visualizations based on lesson context. These surfaces may integrate gesture recognition, multilingual translation layers, and dynamic touch-based interfaces that accommodate diverse learning styles. Floorspace is also leveraged through the use of augmented reality overlays and spatial computing, allowing learners to navigate content three-dimensionally or simulate environments beyond the classroom.

A critical feature of adaptive environments is their capacity to host multimodal content delivery systems. Learners interact with information not just through text and images but through sound, haptics, motion, and simulation. This multisensory integration is especially valuable in disciplines that benefit from experiential learning—such as science, engineering, and the arts. Artificial intelligence systems select and modify these modes based on individual preferences, cultural backgrounds, and demonstrated engagement levels, ensuring that content delivery remains inclusive and cognitively congruent.

The teacher's role within such environments evolves accordingly. Rather than being confined to the front of the room or tied to a singular instructional mode, educators operate as mobile facilitators and diagnostic interpreters. Equipped with wearable or tablet-based dashboards, instructors receive real-time insights into student engagement, emotional state, performance trends, and group dynamics. These analytics empower educators to adjust instructional strategies on the fly, initiate targeted interventions, or organize adaptive groupings based on complementary learning patterns.

In addition to enhancing instruction, adaptive environments foster greater learner agency. Students are empowered to navigate content independently, set learning goals, and choose the tools or modalities that best support their comprehension. Personal AI agents embedded into learning platforms act as guides—offering hints, summarizing progress, and suggesting relevant resources. These agents also interact with the environment, adjusting lighting, workstation preferences, or even background music in accordance with learner profiles. This seamless orchestration of space, technology, and pedagogy supports a holistic learning experience that prioritizes both autonomy and support.

Importantly, adaptive environments extend beyond the classroom to virtual and hybrid contexts. In online or blended models, adaptive design principles manifest through interface personalization, intelligent content sequencing, and spatial simulations delivered through extended reality (XR) platforms. These environments replicate the dynamic responsiveness of physical spaces while expanding access and scalability across geographies.

The architecture of adaptive learning environments thus represents a blueprint for educational spaces in the era of intelligent systems. It integrates spatial flexibility, environmental sensitivity, real-time data utilization, and multimodal interaction to create a learning ecosystem that continuously aligns with student needs. However, such transformation requires intentional design, substantial investment, and a commitment to equity, all of which will be explored in subsequent sections.

Intelligent Interfaces and Personalized Learning Stations

Central to the functionality of an AI-optimized classroom is the interface through which learners interact with both content and intelligent systems. Intelligent interfaces represent more than technological upgrades; they serve as cognitive extensions that bridge the gap between human intent and machine capability. These interfaces must support diverse learning profiles, accommodate multiple forms of input, and enable seamless interaction across physical and digital domains. Personalized learning stations, designed with these interfaces at their core, function as the operational nucleus for student engagement in AI-enhanced educational environments.

A personalized learning station refers to a workstation—whether a physical desk, a digital device, or a hybrid configuration—equipped with adaptive technologies, biometric feedback tools, and content delivery systems tailored to the learner's developmental profile. These stations integrate hardware such as tablets, haptic keyboards, eye-tracking monitors, and speech recognition modules with AI-driven software platforms capable of modifying instructional sequences, pace, and complexity in real time. The objective is to create a learning cockpit in which the student interacts with content, assessments, and collaborators through a responsive and individualized interface.

One of the defining characteristics of intelligent interfaces is their ability to process multimodal input. Learners may engage through voice commands, stylus annotations, tactile gestures, or facial expressions, depending on their preferences and needs. The system analyzes these inputs not only to navigate interfaces but also to assess engagement, comprehension, and emotional state. For example, hesitation in voice tone or repeated erasures in digital writing may signal cognitive struggle, prompting the AI system to offer clarification or suggest a review module. By interpreting these signals with contextual awareness, intelligent interfaces transform passive observation into proactive support.

Additionally, these systems facilitate content personalization through machine learning algorithms trained on longitudinal student data. The platform constructs and continuously updates a learner profile incorporating cognitive strengths, preferred learning styles, prior performance, and metacognitive behaviors. Using this profile, the system dynamically selects resources—textual, visual, auditory, or kinesthetic—that align with the learner's profile and current zone of proximal development. The content delivery becomes neither too simplistic to disengage nor too advanced to frustrate, thereby maintaining optimal cognitive challenge.

Intelligent interfaces also serve as mediators between the student and other actors within the educational ecosystem. Communication modules embedded in the platform enable the sharing of annotated work, reflection logs, and inquiry threads with instructors, peers, or even external mentors. Feedback, when delivered through these systems, is immediate, context-sensitive, and often visualized through progress graphs or performance heatmaps. These visualizations help learners understand their trajectory, recognize patterns, and develop metacognitive strategies.

Equity considerations must guide the design and deployment of intelligent learning stations. Each interface must accommodate accessibility needs, including screen readers, alternative text descriptions, speech-to-text functions, and customizable visual layouts. Multilingual support is essential in diverse learning environments, particularly in global classrooms that serve students from varied linguistic and cultural backgrounds. The integration of these features ensures that intelligent interfaces empower all learners, not just those already fluent in digital literacies.

The personalization enabled by AI does not occur in isolation. Intelligent interfaces are connected to broader classroom systems, enabling real-time communication between student stations, instructor dashboards, and school-wide learning management systems. This integration allows for dynamic reconfiguration of peer groupings, alerts to educators regarding disengaged students, and synchronization with broader curricular goals. For example, if a student demonstrates mastery of a mathematics concept ahead of schedule, the system may suggest peer tutoring roles or advanced extension activities, all coordinated through the interface.

From a pedagogical standpoint, intelligent interfaces redefine the role of the student as an active co-constructor of learning. The agency provided by personalized systems encourages learners to set goals, select tasks, and engage in reflection—all within a scaffolded environment that supports risk-taking and iterative improvement. By decentralizing content access and instructional control, intelligent interfaces cultivate learner autonomy while maintaining consistent instructional quality through AI oversight.

Security, privacy, and ethical considerations remain paramount. Personalized learning stations collect sensitive behavioral and biometric data that must be encrypted, anonymized, and regulated through strict governance policies. Students and guardians must be granted transparent access to data use policies, control over data retention, and the ability to opt out of specific features. Ethical interface design ensures not only legal compliance but also the cultivation of trust in AI systems.

In conclusion, intelligent interfaces and personalized learning stations constitute a critical infrastructural pillar in the transformation of education through artificial intelligence. By providing responsive, inclusive, and empowering platforms for student engagement, these systems enable a level of precision, adaptability, and insight previously unattainable in traditional learning environments. As these tools become more ubiquitous, their design, governance, and pedagogical alignment will determine whether AI fulfills its promise as a democratizing force in education or reinforces existing inequities.

The Role of Teacher Dashboards and AI-Augmented Pedagogy

In AI-optimized classrooms, educators occupy a role that transcends traditional instruction. They are no longer limited to disseminating information, administering standardized assessments, or maintaining order through routine. Instead, they operate as strategic orchestrators of personalized learning ecosystems, leveraging real-time insights, predictive analytics, and intelligent resource management. The central instrument through which this transformation is actualized is the teacher dashboard—a digital interface that aggregates data, interprets patterns, and recommends pedagogical actions grounded in artificial intelligence.

Teacher dashboards serve as the command center for AI-augmented pedagogy. These platforms integrate inputs from multiple sources—student learning stations, biometric sensors, content progression modules, and behavioral monitoring systems—to present instructors with a coherent and actionable overview of class dynamics. Rather than requiring educators to manually track academic progress, behavioral shifts, or emotional fluctuations, the dashboard automates data synthesis, highlights anomalies, and suggests interventions. This capacity enhances instructional precision and situational awareness.

At the core of AI-augmented pedagogy lies the principle of differentiated instruction. Through the dashboard, teachers receive individualized profiles for each learner, including mastery levels across competencies, preferred modalities, pacing metrics, and engagement trends. These profiles are continuously updated as students interact with learning materials, complete assessments, and respond to feedback. Consequently, instructors can assign tailored tasks, form strategic peer groups, or modify content delivery—all with evidence-based justification.

Furthermore, the teacher dashboard supports the curation of instructional resources. AI algorithms scan repositories of vetted educational content—videos, texts, simulations, games—and recommend materials aligned to both curriculum standards and learner needs. This intelligent recommendation system reduces the cognitive and administrative burden on educators, allowing them to focus on instructional design and relational support. Importantly, these suggestions remain non-prescriptive; teachers maintain agency in accepting, modifying, or rejecting them based on their professional judgment.

One of the most valuable functions of the dashboard is real-time alerting. If a student's performance declines sharply, emotional indicators suggest distress, or a pattern of disengagement emerges, the system flags the issue immediately. Alerts are often accompanied by explanatory diagnostics, suggesting potential causes and corresponding strategies. For example, if a student demonstrates cognitive fatigue in late sessions, the dashboard may propose schedule adjustments or breaks. These features enable proactive rather than reactive teaching, minimizing learning gaps and promoting timely intervention.

AI-augmented pedagogy also extends to formative assessment. Dashboards visualize data through performance graphs, heat maps, and growth trajectories, helping instructors evaluate both short-term progress and long-term development. This continuous feedback loop supports mastery-based learning, where advancement is contingent upon demonstrated competency rather than seat time. Teachers can reassign practice modules, customize scaffolding, or revise pacing with immediate impact, guided by system-generated evidence.

Moreover, the dashboard facilitates collaboration between educators. In team-taught environments or departmental settings, dashboards can be linked to enable cross-classroom insights. Teachers share intervention strategies, monitor comparative analytics, and co-design interdisciplinary projects informed by a shared understanding of learner profiles. These collaborative features foster instructional consistency, pedagogical innovation, and professional learning communities grounded in data.

Despite these advantages, the use of teacher dashboards must be governed by ethical considerations. Data overload, surveillance concerns, and algorithmic bias can undermine the pedagogical value of AI systems if left unregulated. Educators must be trained not only in the operational use of dashboards but also in critical data literacy—understanding what the data represent, how it is generated, and where its limitations lie. Institutional policies must delineate boundaries around data access, consent protocols, and retention periods to prevent misuse and uphold student dignity.

Additionally, the transition to AI-augmented pedagogy requires a redefinition of teacher preparation and professional development. Educators must be equipped with interdisciplinary competencies, including data interpretation, systems thinking, digital ethics, and adaptive instruction. These skills are not peripheral; they are central to the effective utilization of AI in learning environments. Institutions must provide sustained support, mentorship networks, and iterative training opportunities to scaffold this transition.

In summary, teacher dashboards and AI-augmented pedagogy represent a paradigm shift in instructional design and delivery. They reposition educators as empowered facilitators of personalized, data-informed, and ethically grounded learning experiences. While technology enables precision and scale, it is the pedagogical insight, emotional intelligence, and ethical stewardship of educators that ultimately determines the success of AI integration in the classroom. As AI continues to evolve, so too must the tools and frameworks that support those who guide learners through its potential.

Intelligent Scheduling and Learning Flow Optimization

In traditional educational systems, time operates as a fixed scaffold—determining when subjects are taught, how long instructional blocks last, and the order in which content is delivered. This rigid scheduling model emerged from industrial-era constraints that prioritized standardization, institutional convenience, and administrative simplicity. However, such models often fail to account for the cognitive rhythms, emotional variability, and learning preferences of individual students. The integration of artificial intelligence into the scheduling domain offers an opportunity to redesign temporal structures in education, enabling intelligent scheduling systems that optimize learning flow in alignment with personalized developmental trajectories.

Intelligent scheduling refers to the dynamic allocation of instructional time, learning activities, and environmental conditions based on real-time data analysis and predictive modeling. Rather than enforcing uniform schedules across heterogeneous learner populations, AI systems identify optimal timeframes for different types of learning—such as cognitive-intensive tasks, creative exploration, physical activity, or reflective practice—according to individual or cohort-specific patterns. These insights are derived from continuous monitoring of attention levels, task completion rates, emotional indicators, and cognitive fatigue metrics.

At the individual level, intelligent scheduling systems personalize daily routines to maximize learning efficiency and well-being. For example, a student who demonstrates peak focus in the mid-morning may be assigned high-cognitive-load subjects such as mathematics or science during that window, while lower-load or creative subjects are scheduled later. The system may also recommend breaks, mindfulness sessions, or physical movement intervals when indicators suggest cognitive depletion or emotional dysregulation. By aligning instructional flow with neurobiological rhythms, these schedules promote sustained engagement, deeper retention, and reduced burnout.

In collaborative settings, intelligent scheduling facilitates dynamic group formation based on real-time readiness, complementary learning profiles, and shared project goals. AI systems can synchronize availability across multiple learners and educators, schedule group tasks at optimal convergence points, and ensure balanced participation by rotating roles and time allocations. This scheduling flexibility supports interdisciplinary learning, project-based instruction, and equitable collaboration across diverse learning populations.

At the institutional level, intelligent scheduling systems enable administrative efficiency and pedagogical adaptability. AI models analyze facility usage, teacher workload, resource availability, and curricular requirements to generate optimized timetables that minimize conflicts and maximize instructional quality. These models are capable of simulating thousands of schedule permutations in real time, selecting configurations that balance educational goals with logistical constraints. In times of disruption—such as weather events, health emergencies, or infrastructural failures—these systems rapidly reconfigure schedules to ensure continuity of learning.

Intelligent scheduling also plays a critical role in supporting mastery-based progression. Unlike traditional systems, where all students advance simultaneously regardless of proficiency, AI-enabled scheduling adapts instructional timing to match demonstrated mastery. Learners who require additional support receive extended time, iterative instruction, or alternative pacing, while those who master content early are advanced to enrichment modules or mentorship roles. The resulting learning flow is nonlinear, responsive, and anchored in competency rather than chronology.

Technologically, intelligent scheduling systems require integration across multiple platforms—student learning profiles, teacher dashboards, facility management systems, and institutional calendars. They operate through centralized data hubs, often cloud-based, with embedded machine learning algorithms that evolve over time. These systems must prioritize interoperability, allowing seamless communication between disparate databases and user interfaces. Security and privacy considerations must be embedded into the system architecture, ensuring that scheduling decisions are informed by ethical data practices.

From a pedagogical perspective, intelligent scheduling empowers educators to transcend traditional time constraints. Teachers gain flexibility in how they sequence instruction, manage classroom dynamics, and intervene when necessary. They can coordinate across subjects to create thematic units, align with learners 'curiosity trajectories, and accommodate real-world events or cultural observances. The resulting instructional model is not only more humane and inclusive but also more rigorous, as it aligns learning intensity with learner readiness.

Equity remains a central concern in intelligent scheduling design. The algorithms must be calibrated to recognize and counteract systemic biases that may affect scheduling outcomes. For instance, students from marginalized communities must not be disproportionately scheduled into remedial tracks or excluded from enrichment opportunities due to algorithmic misclassification. Transparency in scheduling logic, audit trails, and stakeholder feedback loops are essential to maintaining trust and fairness in automated decision-making.

In conclusion, intelligent scheduling and learning flow optimization redefine the role of time in education. Through real-time data analytics, predictive modeling, and dynamic reconfiguration, these systems replace rigid temporal structures with flexible, responsive, and learner-centric models. As AI becomes more deeply embedded in educational infrastructure, the capacity to align instructional time with individual developmental rhythms will emerge as a cornerstone of effective and equitable learning environments.

Infrastructure Requirements and the Role of Cloud-Based Systems

The full realization of AI-optimized classrooms depends not solely on pedagogical shifts or user interfaces but on a robust and scalable infrastructure capable of supporting complex data flows, interoperability, and real-time processing. The educational ecosystem of the future will require architecture that mirrors the computational intensity, security rigor, and adaptability of modern enterprise environments. At the core of this transformation lies cloud-based infrastructure—a foundational enabler of distributed, intelligent, and resilient learning systems.

Cloud-based infrastructure refers to a network of remote servers that store, process, and manage data and applications via the internet, removing reliance on localized computing power. In the context of AI-enabled education, cloud platforms facilitate access to intelligent learning environments regardless of device type, physical location, or institutional boundaries. They serve as the digital backbone for personalized learning systems, teacher dashboards, biometric sensors, content repositories, and AI algorithms—ensuring seamless synchronization across devices and user roles.

One of the primary advantages of cloud infrastructure is **scalability**. As educational systems generate increasing volumes of data—from behavioral analytics to cognitive modeling—the ability to dynamically expand storage, bandwidth, and computational resources becomes indispensable. Cloud platforms accommodate this growth without requiring institutions to invest in costly physical hardware or dedicated IT staff. Instead, usage-based pricing models allow schools and districts to scale services proportionally to their needs, democratizing access to powerful technologies.

Real-time processing is another critical requirement. AI-driven instruction relies on continuous data inputs—such as eye tracking, speech patterns, keystroke dynamics, and performance metrics—to deliver personalized interventions. Cloud computing allows these inputs to be analyzed instantaneously, ensuring that instructional modifications, feedback loops, and emotional support mechanisms occur without delay. Low-latency connectivity is essential, particularly in hybrid or remote settings where learners engage from varied geographies and network conditions.

Data interoperability is central to system coherence. AI-optimized classrooms involve multiple applications—student information systems, learning management systems, assessment tools, content libraries, and external platforms. Cloud-based solutions utilize APIs (Application Programming Interfaces) and standardized data protocols to enable seamless integration. This interoperability ensures that learner data flows fluidly between tools, preserving continuity and enabling holistic analytics. Without this, instructional fragmentation and data silos diminish the impact of personalization.

Security and privacy are non-negotiable in educational cloud systems. Student data, particularly when enriched with biometric and behavioral inputs, is highly sensitive. Cloud platforms must incorporate end-to-end encryption, multi-factor authentication, compliance with data protection laws (e.g., FERPA, GDPR), and robust access control protocols. Additionally, administrators must implement transparent data governance policies outlining who has access to what information, for what purpose, and for how long. Ethical safeguards are not peripheral—they are infrastructural imperatives.

Cloud infrastructure also supports **content democratization**. Centralized storage enables schools to access extensive libraries of learning resources—open educational resources (OER), licensed materials, simulations, and AI-generated content—without maintaining local servers. These repositories are updated in real time, reducing administrative burdens and ensuring alignment with evolving curricular standards. Content delivery can be adjusted automatically based on learner profiles, linguistic preferences, and cultural contexts, creating truly inclusive learning experiences.

In addition, cloud platforms facilitate **disaster recovery and instructional continuity**. In the event of natural disasters, pandemics, cyberattacks, or infrastructure failures, cloud systems maintain uptime through geographically redundant data centers and automatic failover mechanisms. This resilience ensures that learning continues uninterrupted, safeguarding educational equity during times of crisis. Offline capabilities with local caching and delayed synchronization further enhance accessibility for underserved or rural communities.

The **role of edge computing**, a complement to cloud infrastructure, is also growing in educational contexts. Edge computing involves processing data near the source of generation—such as a student's device or a classroom hub—rather than in centralized data centers. This approach reduces latency, preserves bandwidth, and enhances privacy by performing certain analyses locally before transmitting results to the cloud. In AI classrooms, edge devices can process sensitive biometric data on-site, minimizing exposure and supporting real-time responsiveness.

For institutional leaders, transitioning to cloud-based infrastructure requires strategic planning. Legacy systems must be audited for compatibility, migration roadmaps must be developed, and stakeholder training must accompany deployment. Investment in broadband expansion, device accessibility, and IT support services is essential, especially in public education systems where equity remains a core mandate. Cloud adoption is not merely a technical upgrade; it is a systemic transformation that touches every layer of educational operations.

In summary, the infrastructure of AI-optimized classrooms must be cloud-enabled, secure, scalable, and interoperable. Cloud computing does not simply support AI—it operationalizes it at scale, transforming isolated innovations into system-wide capacity. As education enters a new era defined by intelligence, responsiveness, and personalization, the underlying infrastructure must evolve accordingly. The future of learning will be powered by the clouds—but grounded in intentional design, ethical governance, and universal access.

Biometric Feedback Loops and Environmental Modulation

As educational spaces evolve toward dynamic and intelligent systems, the inclusion of biometric data introduces a transformative layer to the classroom environment. Biometric feedback loops represent the real-time physiological data cycles collected from students to inform adjustments in instruction, pacing, and environmental stimuli. When harnessed ethically and responsibly, this information can optimize cognitive performance, enhance emotional regulation, and support inclusive education for neurodiverse populations. Environmental modulation—driven by biometric insight—refers to the dynamic adjustment of classroom variables such as lighting, temperature, sound, and spatial configuration based on learner-specific biometric responses.

Biometric data in educational settings commonly includes heart rate variability (HRV), galvanic skin response (GSR), pupil dilation, eye movement patterns, respiratory rate, facial expression recognition, voice tone analysis, and posture monitoring. These indicators offer a window into the learner's affective and cognitive states, including stress, confusion, fatigue, engagement, or focus. Such signals, once processed through artificial intelligence systems, enable the learning environment to react accordingly—offering real-time, data-informed interventions.

The **feedback loop** is the mechanism through which this process occurs. For example, a student struggling with a complex math problem may exhibit increased heart rate and reduced eye fixation. In response, the system might suggest a calming interface, provide a guided solution breakdown, or introduce a motivational prompt via the student's interface. Simultaneously, lighting around the workstation may dim to reduce visual strain, and ambient noise levels may adjust automatically to create a quieter space conducive to focus. These modifications form a continuous loop: biometric input → environmental response → behavioral change → updated biometric input.

Environmental modulation systems function as the responsive "nervous system" of the AI-optimized classroom. Smart lighting adjusts its intensity and color temperature based on pupil dilation and screen interaction. HVAC systems regulate airflow and temperature according to student comfort metrics. Soundscaping tools employ AI-generated audio environments to modulate stress levels, using tones, white noise, or nature sounds as needed. Even furniture, including ergonomic desks and chairs, may dynamically adjust to maintain optimal posture and physical comfort, especially during extended periods of cognitive engagement.

For neurodiverse learners, such modulation is particularly critical.

Students with sensory processing sensitivities benefit from environments that recognize early indicators of sensory overload and adjust accordingly. Sudden brightness, repetitive sounds, or prolonged static sitting can trigger stress responses. AI-enabled modulation can create sensory havens—personalized micro-environments within the classroom—without isolating students or requiring manual intervention by instructors. This promotes autonomy, dignity, and uninterrupted engagement.

Additionally, biometric feedback can inform instructional decisions. If a group of students exhibits synchronized signs of confusion or cognitive fatigue, the system may prompt the instructor to introduce a discussion break, realign the instructional pace, or pose a formative question to recalibrate attention. These insights support a more empathetic, responsive form of teaching that respects the fluctuating nature of human cognition and emotion.

The integration of biometric loops also extends into **self-regulated learning**. Dashboards provided to students may include visualizations of their own biometric trends—heart rate during tests, concentration patterns during reading, or stress levels during collaborative projects. These metrics, when framed constructively, help learners develop metacognitive awareness and emotional intelligence. Students begin to recognize when they are most productive, what triggers cognitive overload, and how to engage in self-care practices like mindfulness, breathing exercises, or strategic breaks.

While the benefits are extensive, the **ethical considerations** surrounding biometric data are equally profound. Informed consent, data minimization, anonymization protocols, and opt-in models are essential. No learner should be compelled to participate in biometric monitoring, and all data must be treated with the highest levels of confidentiality. Furthermore, systems must be transparent in their decision-making, and educators must retain the ability to override automated responses when contextual knowledge warrants human judgment.

From a technological standpoint, biometric systems require **low-latency processing, localized edge computing capabilities**, and highly secure data storage. Sensitive data must be analyzed in real time but retained only briefly unless specific educational value justifies longitudinal storage. Hardware components—including wearables, eye-tracking cameras, and skin-contact sensors—must be ergonomically designed, non-invasive, and culturally appropriate. Maintenance of these systems requires collaboration between IT professionals, educators, bioethicists, and policy makers to ensure sustainable and equitable deployment.

In conclusion, biometric feedback loops and environmental modulation represent one of the most sophisticated layers of the AI-enhanced classroom. By making invisible signals visible—and actionable—these systems empower learning environments to become responsive ecosystems attuned to the complex interplay of cognition, emotion, and physiology. When ethically implemented, they offer a new paradigm of education: one in which the classroom not only sees and hears the learner but feels with them, adapting in real time to support success and well-being.

Governance, Maintenance, and Ethical Oversight of AI Infrastructure

As artificial intelligence becomes deeply embedded in the educational ecosystem, the need for comprehensive governance and ethical oversight intensifies. The intelligent infrastructure that powers AI-optimized classrooms—encompassing real-time data collection, predictive analytics, environmental modulation, and biometric feedback—demands vigilant management to ensure functionality, fairness, and integrity. Without a structured governance framework, the risks of data misuse, technological malfunction, institutional dependency, and ethical breaches can undermine the transformative potential of AI-enhanced learning environments.

Governance, in this context, refers to the system of policies, procedures, standards, and oversight mechanisms that define how AI infrastructure is deployed, maintained, monitored, and held accountable. Governance structures must involve cross-functional participation, drawing from educational leaders, technology experts, data privacy officers, legal advisors, and community stakeholders. These bodies are tasked with setting the rules for implementation, evaluating outcomes, resolving conflicts, and adapting to emergent challenges.

Central to effective governance is the **definition of ownership and responsibility**. Institutions must determine who owns the data collected within classrooms, who controls algorithmic decision-making, and who is liable for system failures or harm caused by automation. Clarity in these areas ensures accountability. In many educational systems, data generated by students should remain the intellectual property of the learner and their guardians, with institutions acting as stewards rather than owners.

Maintenance protocols are equally critical. Intelligent classrooms depend on a complex array of hardware (e.g., sensors, displays, wearables), software (e.g., machine learning models, learning management systems), and connectivity infrastructure. These components require continuous updates, security patches, calibration, and functional diagnostics. Maintenance teams—consisting of IT specialists, AI engineers, and support staff—must adhere to preventive schedules, document all interventions, and operate under service-level agreements (SLAs) to minimize downtime.

A crucial element of ongoing oversight is the **monitoring and auditing of AI systems**. Algorithms must be subjected to routine audits that assess fairness, transparency, and accuracy. Educational institutions should implement algorithmic impact assessments (AIAs) before large-scale deployment, analyzing potential bias, access disparities, and unintended consequences. Dashboards used by educators and administrators must include explainability features—tools that clarify how decisions or recommendations were generated—to reduce reliance on opaque "black box" models.

Ethical oversight must guide every phase of AI integration. This involves setting boundaries on the types of data collected, the duration of data storage, and the purposes for which data can be used. Ethics boards or review committees—similar to Institutional Review Boards (IRBs) in academic research—should review new initiatives that involve sensitive technologies or high-stakes decision-making. Ethical principles such as autonomy, beneficence, non-maleficence, and justice must underpin all design and operational decisions.

Transparency and community engagement are also pillars of trustworthy AI governance. Parents, students, and educators must be fully informed about the technologies in use, the nature of data collected, and the rights they retain. Institutions should publish clear privacy statements, user agreements, and grievance procedures. Open forums, feedback channels, and participatory design practices ensure that those most affected by AI systems have a voice in their development and refinement.

A proactive governance model must also address **systemic inequalities and digital divides**. AI systems trained on non-representative data risk reinforcing bias against marginalized populations. Governance structures must include equity audits, disaggregated data reviews, and corrective protocols to ensure inclusive outcomes. Accessibility standards must be embedded into the infrastructure, ensuring compatibility with assistive technologies and accommodation for learners with disabilities.

Cybersecurity and data protection fall within the domain of governance and maintenance. Educational AI infrastructure is a prime target for cyberattacks, data breaches, and exploitation. Institutions must implement encryption standards, intrusion detection systems, role-based access controls, and routine penetration testing. Staff and students should be trained in digital hygiene, phishing awareness, and secure communication protocols to create a culture of cyber-resilience.

Furthermore, governance must anticipate the **evolution of AI technologies**. As models become more autonomous, capable of generating original content or making high-stakes recommendations (e.g., career tracking or intervention referrals), the ethical stakes rise accordingly. Scenario planning, legal foresight, and regulatory alignment are required to prevent future liabilities and preserve public trust. Institutions should also maintain relationships with external auditors, academic researchers, and civil society organizations that can provide independent evaluation and accountability.

Finally, **sustainability** is a long-term governance concern. AI infrastructure consumes energy, relies on complex supply chains, and contributes to electronic waste. Responsible procurement policies, energy-efficient design, and recycling initiatives must be incorporated into institutional practices. Sustainability metrics should be reported alongside academic performance metrics, reinforcing the principle that educational innovation must not come at the cost of environmental stewardship.

In conclusion, governance, maintenance, and ethical oversight form the invisible scaffolding of the AI-optimized classroom. These systems ensure that technology serves pedagogical goals without compromising safety, equity, or integrity. In an era where digital intelligence permeates every aspect of the learning experience, only through robust governance can education maintain its moral compass, uphold public confidence, and fulfill its mission of empowering all learners.

The Future of Educational Architecture and Global Scalability

The reimagination of classroom environments and educational infrastructure in the age of artificial intelligence extends far beyond the scope of individual schools or districts. It requires a paradigm shift in architectural thinking, infrastructural investment, and global policy coordination. As AI-optimized classrooms move from prototype to standard, the architectural design of education itself—its spaces, technologies, governance models, and learning cultures—must scale across geographies, economies, and cultural contexts. The future of educational architecture will not be defined solely by physical buildings or digital tools but by the systemic ability to adapt intelligently to diverse human needs.

Educational architecture, in this expanded sense, encompasses both physical design and systemic organization. It includes classroom layouts, institutional blueprints, national curriculum frameworks, networked learning ecosystems, and digital infrastructures. The infusion of artificial intelligence into this architecture introduces a need for flexibility, modularity, and interoperability. Future classrooms will be conceived not as static structures but as adaptive ecosystems—intelligently configured in real time to respond to changing learner needs, technological evolutions, and environmental constraints.

One emerging design model is the **modular intelligent learning pod**—a self-contained, reconfigurable environment that integrates AI-powered content delivery, biometric sensors, environmental controls, and real-time analytics. These pods can be deployed in varied settings—from rural villages to urban centers—and connected to centralized cloud systems. Their portability, affordability, and energy efficiency make them ideal candidates for global scalability, particularly in regions with limited access to formal educational infrastructure.

Global scalability, however, depends not only on technological feasibility but also on policy alignment and equitable access. Nations and international organizations must work collaboratively to define open standards for educational AI tools, including protocols for data security, language support, accessibility, and ethical use. Interoperability across systems and languages will be critical to ensuring that AI-optimized classrooms do not become exclusive to affluent or technologically advanced regions. Initiatives such as global AI curricula frameworks, shared repositories of open educational resources, and multilingual adaptive content libraries will play pivotal roles.

Economic scalability must also be addressed. While high-income countries may have the resources to deploy cutting-edge learning infrastructure, many lower-income regions struggle with basic connectivity, power supply, and device availability. Scalable solutions must include low-bandwidth AI models, offline-first architectures, and solar-powered devices. Public-private partnerships, philanthropic investment, and multilateral funding initiatives will be essential in bridging the digital divide and creating a foundation for truly global AI-enhanced education.

Cultural adaptability represents another axis of scalability. Educational environments must reflect the cultural values, pedagogical traditions, and societal goals of the communities they serve. AI systems must be trained on culturally relevant datasets, support diverse instructional languages, and respect local knowledge traditions. The future of AI-optimized learning is not one of uniform global standards but of context-aware adaptation. Localization, rather than homogenization, will ensure meaningful educational impact across diverse populations.

Urban planning and national development strategies must also integrate **education as infrastructure**. Just as roads, water systems, and electrical grids are planned at scale, AI-powered learning environments must be considered foundational to economic development and civic resilience. Government ministries, educational institutions, and architectural firms must collaborate on long-term planning that embeds intelligent classrooms into housing developments, community centers, health facilities, and public spaces—creating **learning-centric cities** that foster lifelong education.

The **teacher training ecosystem** will likewise require transformation to meet the demands of scaled AI infrastructure. Global certification programs, open-source training modules, and remote mentoring platforms must prepare educators to operate within intelligent environments, interpret learning analytics, and co-design personalized instruction with AI systems. Professional development must be continuous, equity-focused, and embedded into the technological evolution of educational spaces.

Future classrooms will also serve as **research laboratories**—generating anonymized data to study cognition, behavior, language acquisition, and emotional development across cultural contexts. When ethically governed, these insights can inform global educational policy, neurodevelopmental research, and humanitarian efforts in post-conflict or underserved areas. The classroom thus becomes not just a space of instruction, but a node in a global knowledge-generation network.

The **climate impact** of scalable AI-enhanced education must also be addressed. The infrastructure supporting cloud systems, data storage, and electronic devices has significant carbon implications. Future educational design must integrate green technologies, circular supply chains, and sustainability metrics. Schools can become hubs of environmental education and action—leveraging intelligent infrastructure not only to teach sustainability but to embody it.

In conclusion, the architecture of future learning is not merely digital or spatial—it is ethical, ecological, global, and human-centered. AI-optimized classrooms will succeed at scale only when built upon foundations of equity, adaptability, sustainability, and mutual accountability. The task before educators, technologists, and policy-makers is not only to redesign the classroom—but to rearchitect the very idea of education itself for a new century of learners.

Chapter 14

Rethinking Teacher Roles and Professional Development in an AI-Driven Ecosystem

Introduction

The emergence of artificial intelligence as a central force in education necessitates a profound reevaluation of the teaching profession. While fears of automation often suggest that machines will replace human educators, the evolving reality reflects a far more complex—and promising—transformation. Artificial intelligence will not eliminate the role of the teacher; rather, it will reframe that role within a radically different pedagogical landscape. This transformation requires the reconceptualization of teaching as a hybrid profession: one that merges pedagogical expertise with technological fluency, ethical reasoning, and adaptive leadership.

Teachers, long regarded as content transmitters and classroom managers, will increasingly function as learning architects, data-informed mentors, and ethical stewards of artificial intelligence. Their responsibilities will shift from delivering pre-set curriculum to designing adaptive learning journeys, interpreting real-time analytics, and nurturing the emotional, social, and cognitive development of students within intelligent environments. This evolution requires a systemic overhaul of professional development models, teacher education programs, institutional structures, and labor policies.

The purpose of this chapter is to explore the multi-dimensional transformation of the teaching profession within AI-enhanced classrooms. It examines the redefinition of core competencies, the integration of new professional standards, the restructuring of teacher training, and the ethical implications of human-machine collaboration in education. Through this lens, the teacher emerges not as a figure displaced by technology but as its most critical human complement—essential to the equitable, meaningful, and ethical implementation of AI in learning.

The advent of artificial intelligence has ushered in a transformative era for global education systems. No longer confined to theoretical speculation or pilot programs, intelligent technologies are now embedded within the very fabric of instructional delivery, classroom design, and curriculum architecture. This rapid integration of machine intelligence into learning environments raises a fundamental question: what becomes of the teacher in a world where algorithms can personalize instruction, assess performance, monitor engagement, and even predict learning outcomes?

For centuries, teachers have occupied a central and irreplaceable role within formal education. Traditionally positioned as the primary source of knowledge, disciplinarian, moral guide, and social model, the teacher has borne the responsibility of shaping generations of citizens and professionals. However, as artificial intelligence assumes increasing responsibility for routine, analytical, and even creative educational tasks, the parameters of the teaching profession are undergoing unprecedented disruption. What is emerging is not merely a shift in methodology or tools, but a structural redefinition of the educator's identity, purpose, and function within the ecosystem of learning.

Far from signaling obsolescence, the age of AI has the potential to elevate the teaching profession—provided that educators are equipped with the new literacies, competencies, and institutional supports required to navigate this technological transformation. Teachers will be expected to operate as learning engineers, adept at designing adaptive, student-centered experiences that leverage the analytical power of machines while preserving the irreplaceable human dimensions of empathy, moral reasoning, and social-emotional development. In this reimagined role, educators become co-pilots of learning alongside AI—guiding students through environments where personalized pathways, real-time diagnostics, and intelligent feedback loops redefine how knowledge is acquired, applied, and assessed.

The transformation, however, is not without tension. There exists a growing disconnect between the pace of technological advancement and the preparedness of educational institutions to support teachers through this shift. Existing professional development models, rooted in legacy systems and traditional pedagogy, are often ill-suited to equip teachers with the competencies required to collaborate with intelligent systems. A rethinking of teacher training, credentialing, and in-service learning is not merely beneficial—it is imperative. Educational policy, leadership, and institutional culture must be restructured to recognize the teacher not as a passive recipient of technology, but as an active agent in shaping its ethical use, pedagogical alignment, and cultural adaptation.

Moreover, the redefinition of teaching in the age of AI cannot be viewed in isolation from broader socio-economic and ethical considerations. Issues of equity, labor rights, autonomy, algorithmic bias, and data ethics intersect directly with the evolving responsibilities of educators. Teachers will need to engage not only with machine learning models and learning analytics but with the philosophical and civic questions that accompany their use. They must become critical interpreters of algorithmic decisions, advocates for student agency, and custodians of human-centered values in increasingly automated classrooms.

This chapter seeks to explore these complex dynamics in depth. It will examine the historical trajectory of the teaching profession and how that legacy interfaces with current technological shifts. It will delineate the emerging skill sets and professional standards required for AI-integrated pedagogy. It will analyze the redesign of professional development systems to support ongoing adaptation. It will also assess the labor, legal, and ethical implications of embedding AI within teaching environments. By tracing these threads, this chapter asserts that teachers are not being displaced—they are being redeployed into roles of greater complexity, significance, and influence than ever before.

In this reconceived educational paradigm, the teacher emerges as the anchor of trust, the architect of ethical pedagogy, and the integrator of human insight with artificial intelligence. Ensuring the success of this transformation will depend on deliberate planning, robust support systems, and a reaffirmation of the social contract that positions teachers not as relics of a bygone system, but as pioneers of the next chapter in the human learning story.

The Historical Evolution of the Teaching Profession

The teaching profession has undergone numerous metamorphoses throughout history, each shaped by broader cultural, economic, and technological forces. Understanding the current transformation induced by artificial intelligence requires situating it within the historical continuum of educational change. This historical perspective reveals that the teacher's role has never been static; it has always been an evolving function, responding to the imperatives of the era in which it is embedded.

In **ancient civilizations**, educators were often scholars, philosophers, or religious leaders—tasked with transmitting sacred texts, philosophical doctrines, or cultural norms. Teaching in this period was largely oral, personalized, and elitist. Instruction was restricted to a small, privileged segment of society, and the relationship between teacher and pupil was defined by deference, mentorship, and intellectual apprenticeship. The authority of the teacher stemmed not from institutional credentials but from recognized wisdom and lived experience.

The **medieval and pre-modern periods** witnessed the institutionalization of education through religious schools, guilds, and early universities. Teachers began to occupy more formalized roles, although pedagogy remained largely didactic and teacher-centered. Instructors were seen as gatekeepers of fixed knowledge, and memorization served as the primary instructional technique. As literacy expanded and curricula broadened, the teacher's authority increasingly relied on ecclesiastical or state endorsement, reinforcing the hierarchical structure of the classroom.

The **Industrial Revolution** marked a significant turning point. As societies industrialized, education systems were restructured to meet the demands of a factory-based economy. Schools adopted a standardized, mass-education model, characterized by rigid schedules, age-based cohorts, and a curriculum oriented toward obedience, punctuality, and routine. Teachers were redefined as institutional functionaries—responsible for delivering uniform instruction to large groups and enforcing discipline within bureaucratically governed environments. The factory model of education gave rise to formal teacher training programs, certifications, and national standards, thereby professionalizing teaching but also constraining its creative and relational dimensions.

During the **20th century**, particularly in the post–World War II era, the teaching profession experienced both expansion and diversification. The democratization of education brought new emphasis on inclusivity, differentiated instruction, and child-centered pedagogy. Progressive educational theorists such as John Dewey challenged the authoritarian model, advocating for experiential learning, critical thinking, and democratic classroom participation. In this context, teachers evolved into facilitators of inquiry and agents of social development. However, this shift was not universal. Many systems continued to reinforce traditional models, particularly in under-resourced or politically conservative regions.

The **late 20th and early 21st centuries** witnessed the incursion of digital technology into classrooms. The introduction of computers, the internet, and learning management systems began to alter the way teachers accessed resources, communicated with students, and administered assessments. Nevertheless, these tools often functioned as supplemental, rather than transformative, technologies. Teachers retained primary control over instructional delivery, and digital tools were largely confined to content presentation or administrative efficiency.

What differentiates the current wave of transformation, driven by artificial intelligence, from previous technological shifts is its capacity to automate core instructional functions previously thought to be exclusively human. Adaptive learning systems, generative AI tutors, real-time feedback engines, and predictive analytics are now capable of delivering personalized instruction, diagnosing misconceptions, adjusting pacing, and even generating curriculum content. These developments challenge the foundational assumption that teachers are the sole or primary conveyors of knowledge and assessment.

In response, the teaching profession stands at a historical inflection point. The role of the teacher is no longer defined by knowledge transmission alone, but by the ability to curate, contextualize, interpret, and ethically mediate machine-generated instruction. The profession must transition from the legacy of the factory model and the early digital age into a new paradigm—one in which human and machine collaborate to support the intellectual and emotional growth of learners in complex, dynamic environments.

Thus, the evolution of the teaching profession must be understood as a continuum: from pre-industrial scholar-teachers to industrial-era instructors, from post-industrial facilitators to post-digital learning architects. Artificial intelligence represents the latest—and perhaps most radical—chapter in this trajectory. How educators adapt to this moment will shape not only the future of teaching but the very architecture of education itself.

The Impact of AI on Instructional Delivery and Pedagogical Design

Artificial intelligence is reshaping the pedagogical landscape by transforming the mechanisms through which instruction is delivered and learning is designed. Traditional paradigms of instructional delivery—anchored in lectures, textbooks, and linear curriculum sequences—are giving way to dynamic, data-driven, and learner-responsive models. This transformation challenges educators to reimagine their instructional strategies, pedagogical frameworks, and classroom roles within an AI-augmented environment.

At the core of this transformation is the emergence of **adaptive learning systems**—AI-powered platforms that personalize instruction based on a learner's pace, performance, and preferences. These systems adjust content difficulty in real time, identify conceptual gaps, and provide differentiated feedback tailored to each student's unique learning trajectory. Such technology undermines the one-size-fits-all approach that has long characterized conventional classroom instruction. Instead, it fosters individualized pathways that increase engagement, retention, and mastery.

The use of **natural language processing (NLP)** in educational applications further enhances instructional delivery. AI tutors, powered by advanced NLP models, are capable of answering student queries, generating explanations, and even simulating Socratic dialogue.

These tutors operate on demand, offering round-the-clock support, and can accommodate a range of learning styles and language proficiencies. The teacher's role, in this context, shifts from delivering direct instruction to overseeing, guiding, and contextualizing machine-led interactions—ensuring that students derive meaningful understanding rather than surface-level answers.

AI also enables **real-time learning analytics**, which provide teachers with granular insight into student progress. Dashboards populated with metrics such as time-on-task, concept mastery, error patterns, and emotional engagement allow educators to make informed pedagogical decisions. Instruction can be adjusted on the fly—interventions can be triggered, groupings can be reorganized, and content delivery can be modified to match emerging trends. This data-centric instructional design promotes responsiveness and agility, moving beyond static lesson plans toward iterative learning journeys.

The **automation of formative and summative assessments** further enhances instructional efficiency. AI can grade essays, generate quizzes, assess oral responses, and detect plagiarism with increasing accuracy. While such tools streamline administrative burdens, they also challenge educators to maintain pedagogical integrity. Teachers must critically evaluate the limitations of algorithmic assessment—particularly in detecting nuance, creativity, or cultural context—and ensure that automated evaluations are complemented by human judgment.

Beyond individual classroom applications, AI facilitates **project-based and interdisciplinary learning**. Intelligent platforms can suggest cross-curricular linkages, recommend authentic tasks, and scaffold complex projects with embedded resources and guided feedback. Teachers, in this environment, function as **learning designers**—curating experiences that promote critical thinking, collaboration, and real-world problem-solving. The pedagogical focus shifts from coverage to creation, from information delivery to knowledge construction.

The incorporation of **emotional AI**—technologies that detect affective states through facial expression analysis, voice modulation, or biometric signals—introduces new dimensions to instructional design. These systems can identify disengagement, confusion, or stress, prompting interventions that adjust content delivery or offer motivational support. Teachers must interpret these cues with discernment, balancing technological input with relational awareness to support student well-being.

AI also enables **multimodal learning**, combining text, visuals, simulations, and virtual environments. Instruction can now be delivered through virtual reality field trips, augmented reality labs, and intelligent storytelling platforms that adapt to student interaction. Teachers must gain proficiency in selecting, integrating, and evaluating these tools—not only for their technological appeal but for their pedagogical value and alignment with learning goals.

However, the integration of AI into instructional delivery is not without challenges. The risk of **over-automation** looms large, wherein technology displaces meaningful human interaction. Overreliance on AI can depersonalize the learning experience, reduce critical dialogue, and obscure the relational dynamics that underpin effective education. Teachers must therefore assume the role of **ethical mediators**, ensuring that AI serves as an instrument of empowerment rather than alienation.

Furthermore, pedagogical design in an AI context must remain **culturally responsive and inclusive**. Algorithms trained on biased datasets may inadvertently perpetuate stereotypes, marginalize non-dominant cultures, or reinforce inequities. Educators must be equipped to interrogate these systems, advocate for equity, and adapt instructional content to reflect diverse histories, perspectives, and identities.

In summary, artificial intelligence is redefining how instruction is delivered and how pedagogy is conceptualized. Teachers are no longer mere transmitters of content but orchestrators of personalized, multimodal, and responsive learning experiences. Their role demands a synthesis of technical fluency, pedagogical expertise, and ethical discernment. As AI continues to evolve, the imperative is clear: instruction must remain human-centered, even as it becomes machine-enhanced.

Redefining Core Competencies for 21st-Century Educators

The emergence of artificial intelligence in education has made it imperative to redefine the core competencies required of educators. In the traditional paradigm, effective teaching was often measured by content expertise, classroom management, instructional clarity, and curriculum alignment. While these attributes remain important, they are no longer sufficient. The integration of intelligent systems into the educational ecosystem introduces new pedagogical, technological, ethical, and relational demands that redefine professional expectations.

One of the most foundational competencies in the age of AI is **technological fluency**. This extends beyond basic digital literacy and requires educators to understand the underlying principles of AI tools, their affordances, and their limitations. Teachers must be proficient in navigating adaptive learning platforms, interpreting learning analytics, curating digital content, and integrating intelligent systems into instructional workflows. Technological fluency also entails the ability to critically evaluate software for accuracy, bias, accessibility, and pedagogical relevance.

Closely tied to technological fluency is **data literacy**—the capacity to interpret, analyze, and act upon complex datasets generated by AI systems. Educators must be adept at recognizing patterns in student performance data, identifying anomalies, and deriving actionable insights. They must understand concepts such as algorithmic prediction, learning trajectories, diagnostic assessment, and dashboard interpretation. This competence transforms educators into **data-informed practitioners** who use empirical evidence to tailor instruction, provide timely interventions, and ensure equitable learning outcomes.

Another core competency is **AI-augmented pedagogical design**. Educators must develop the capacity to co-design instructional experiences in collaboration with intelligent systems. This involves selecting appropriate AI tools, sequencing adaptive content, embedding real-time feedback mechanisms, and aligning technological integration with learning objectives. Teachers must also anticipate student interactions with AI and proactively scaffold their engagement to ensure deep understanding rather than superficial automation.

In addition to these technical and design competencies, educators must possess **ethical reasoning and algorithmic awareness**. As stewards of student data and mediators of AI-driven decision-making, teachers must understand the ethical implications of automation. This includes safeguarding student privacy, identifying algorithmic bias, advocating for transparency, and ensuring that AI systems are used in ways that uphold dignity, inclusion, and human rights. Teachers must also be prepared to navigate ethical dilemmas surrounding surveillance technologies, predictive modeling, and automated grading systems.

Equally important is the cultivation of **emotional intelligence and relational pedagogy**. In environments where machines assume certain cognitive functions, the human educator must provide the affective and social dimensions of learning. Educators must build trust, foster empathy, support mental health, and cultivate inclusive classroom cultures. These relational skills become more—not less—important in AI-rich environments, as students seek human connection, moral grounding, and mentorship that cannot be replicated by machines.

Interdisciplinary collaboration is another emerging competency. Teachers must be able to work across disciplinary boundaries, co-teaching with colleagues from other subject areas and collaborating with technologists, data scientists, and instructional designers. This requires fluency in multiple literacies, including digital, media, civic, and computational literacies. Educators must be able to speak the language of multiple domains and synthesize insights that inform holistic learning design.

Furthermore, educators must adopt a **mindset of continuous learning and professional agility**. The pace of technological change necessitates lifelong upskilling and a willingness to adapt. Teachers must engage in ongoing professional development, experiment with new tools, reflect on practice, and iterate instructional approaches based on feedback. Professional agility includes the capacity to navigate uncertainty, embrace innovation, and reframe failure as a catalyst for growth.

Finally, educators must possess **leadership and advocacy skills**. As AI transforms education systems, teachers will increasingly be called upon to shape institutional policies, lead innovation initiatives, mentor peers, and engage with stakeholders. They must advocate for equitable access to technology, represent the voice of educators in policy discussions, and ensure that AI implementation aligns with educational values and social justice principles.

In sum, the core competencies for 21st-century educators in an AI-driven ecosystem are multifaceted and evolving. They encompass technical skills, pedagogical innovation, ethical discernment, emotional intelligence, interdisciplinary collaboration, professional agility, and systemic leadership. Preparing educators to thrive in this environment requires not only redefining these competencies but embedding them into teacher preparation programs, certification standards, and professional development systems at scale.

Reforming Teacher Education and Credentialing Models

The redefinition of educator competencies in the age of artificial intelligence demands a corresponding transformation in the structures that prepare and credential teachers. Legacy models of teacher education—often centered on static curriculum design, limited fieldwork, and periodic credential renewal—are no longer sufficient to prepare professionals for an AI-integrated learning ecosystem. To ensure alignment with the evolving demands of the profession, institutions must fundamentally redesign teacher education programs, certification pathways, and licensure protocols to embed agility, technological literacy, and ethical fluency at their core.

Traditional teacher preparation programs are often structured around discrete courses in pedagogy, content methods, and classroom management. While foundational, this compartmentalized approach rarely integrates the complex realities of modern instructional environments, where teachers must synthesize technological, ethical, and interpersonal skills in real time. Reform efforts must therefore prioritize **interdisciplinary integration**, wherein courses on learning theory are co-taught with AI developers, and ethical reasoning is applied to real-world case studies involving algorithmic decision-making in schools.

One of the most urgent reforms is the **inclusion of AI and data literacy in teacher education curricula**. Prospective educators must receive structured instruction on the principles of machine learning, adaptive technologies, and educational data systems. This instruction should not aim to convert teachers into engineers but rather to cultivate critical understanding of how AI operates, how it is applied in learning contexts, and what implications it carries for equity, privacy, and instructional design. Case-based learning, simulations, and hands-on experimentation with AI platforms should become standard components of the teacher education experience.

Equally important is the incorporation of **design thinking and systems innovation**. Teacher candidates must be trained as learning architects, capable of designing experiences that blend digital and physical modalities, adapt to learner variability, and embed real-time feedback. Institutions should require candidates to complete design practicums, in which they co-create AI-integrated units, analyze implementation data, and iterate based on student outcomes. This iterative, studio-based approach mirrors how innovation is practiced in technology sectors and cultivates the flexibility needed to navigate rapidly changing educational landscapes.

The **clinical experience component** of teacher education must also be reimagined. Traditional student-teaching placements often place candidates in analog classrooms, devoid of meaningful exposure to AI tools. Universities and credentialing agencies must partner with AI-forward schools and innovation hubs to provide immersive practicum settings. In these environments, teacher candidates can gain supervised experience in managing AI-driven instruction, interpreting analytics dashboards, moderating algorithmic feedback, and troubleshooting technical challenges in real time.

Credentialing models must also be reformed to reflect the dynamic nature of educator roles. Static, one-time licensure is increasingly incompatible with a profession that demands **continuous upskilling**. Policymakers should consider modular certification models, whereby teachers earn micro-credentials in areas such as AI literacy, data-informed instruction, ethical technology use, and inclusive digital pedagogy. These stackable credentials can be renewed and updated over time, ensuring that educators remain current with emerging technologies and evolving best practices.

In parallel, **credentialing bodies and accreditation agencies** must update their frameworks to assess teacher readiness in light of AI integration. Evaluation criteria should include the candidate's ability to use adaptive platforms, interpret AI-generated assessments, design inclusive learning environments, and maintain ethical oversight of technology use. Rubrics and performance assessments must evolve beyond traditional teaching demonstrations to include data interpretation exercises, digital lesson audits, and simulated AI interventions.

Reform must also consider the needs of **in-service teachers**. Many experienced educators were trained in analog environments and may feel ill-equipped to engage with AI systems. Targeted professional learning communities, on-demand learning portals, and AI coaching programs must be created to support ongoing development. Districts and ministries of education should incentivize participation through career advancement opportunities, salary differentiation, and recognition of expertise in emerging areas.

To ensure system-wide transformation, **teacher preparation institutions must undergo structural realignment**. This includes hiring faculty with expertise in educational technology and AI ethics, forging partnerships with edtech companies for curriculum co-design, and engaging with research initiatives that explore the impact of AI in education. Institutional leadership must prioritize investment in digital infrastructure, research capacity, and cross-sector collaboration to remain relevant and effective.

In summary, the reformation of teacher education and credentialing systems is not a peripheral adjustment—it is a foundational necessity. Equipping teachers for an AI-driven future requires rigorous, interdisciplinary, and responsive preparation that moves beyond content delivery to cultivate adaptive, ethically grounded, and technologically empowered professionals. Without this transformation, even the most advanced educational technologies will fall short of their potential, constrained by human systems that are not prepared to wield them with wisdom, care, and impact.

Continuous Professional Development in a Rapidly Evolving Technological Landscape

As artificial intelligence technologies accelerate the pace of educational change, continuous professional development (CPD) has become a strategic imperative rather than a peripheral undertaking. In an AI-augmented ecosystem, static certification and episodic in-service training no longer provide sufficient support for educators navigating complex instructional, ethical, and technological terrain. Continuous professional development must be reframed as an integrated, lifelong process that is dynamic, responsive, personalized, and embedded within educators' day-to-day practice.

At the core of effective CPD in an AI-driven context lies the principle of **relevance and contextualization**. Traditional workshop-based training often suffers from generalization and abstraction, failing to address the real-world environments in which teachers operate. Professional learning must shift toward **embedded, job-embedded formats**—including coaching, peer observation, action research, and collaborative problem-solving—where teachers can apply new knowledge in real time and receive iterative feedback on their practices.

The architecture of CPD must also evolve to include **microlearning and modular pathways**. Educators require access to on-demand, bite-sized content that aligns with their immediate needs and professional goals. Microcredentials, digital badges, and modular coursework—focused on discrete competencies such as AI ethics, adaptive assessment interpretation, or learning analytics—enable teachers to pursue self-paced, personalized development. These credentials must be stackable, recognized by licensing bodies, and integrated into career advancement frameworks.

Artificial intelligence itself can serve as a catalyst for personalized CPD. Intelligent recommendation engines can suggest professional learning activities based on classroom data, student performance patterns, and instructional gaps. AI-driven platforms can curate content, deliver feedback on teaching videos, simulate classroom scenarios, and provide adaptive learning modules tailored to an educator's profile. These tools transform professional development into a **continuous learning loop**, responsive to both individual growth and institutional priorities.

Moreover, CPD must emphasize **interdisciplinary and cross-sector collaboration**. The skills required for AI-integrated teaching are not confined to traditional pedagogy; they span computer science, cognitive science, design thinking, and ethics. Professional development programs should facilitate partnerships between educators, technologists, ethicists, and industry leaders, fostering communities of practice that bridge disciplinary silos. These networks enable educators to engage in co-learning, innovation design, and shared inquiry around emerging challenges and opportunities.

Another vital element of CPD in the AI era is the cultivation of **reflective practice and ethical agency**. Teachers must be equipped not only to use AI tools but to interrogate their implications. Professional development must provide space for critical dialogue about algorithmic bias, surveillance concerns, data ownership, and the tension between personalization and standardization. Teachers must emerge from CPD not just as skilled users of AI, but as informed custodians of human-centered education.

Equity in access to CPD is also a significant consideration. Rural, underfunded, or underserved schools often lack the infrastructure or institutional support for robust professional development. National education systems must prioritize equitable distribution of resources, including digital infrastructure, learning platforms, and expert facilitators. Policies must ensure that all educators—regardless of location or socioeconomic context—can access high-quality, AI-relevant professional learning.

Furthermore, the evaluation of CPD effectiveness must be reconceptualized. Rather than relying solely on participation logs or satisfaction surveys, systems must assess impact based on improvements in instructional design, student engagement, ethical implementation of technology, and school-wide innovation culture. Data from AI platforms, peer observations, and instructional artifacts can inform holistic and formative evaluation approaches.

School leaders play a critical role in enabling a culture of continuous professional growth. They must model learning themselves, allocate time for collaborative planning and reflection, and incentivize experimentation and risk-taking. Professional development must be seen not as an add-on, but as an essential component of the educator's role—supported by policy, protected time, and institutional recognition.

In summary, continuous professional development in the age of artificial intelligence must be personalized, embedded, ethically grounded, and equity-focused. It must prepare educators not just to keep pace with technology, but to lead the transformation of learning itself. By reimagining CPD as a lifelong, contextually embedded process, education systems can empower teachers to thrive amid rapid change and ensure that technological progress serves pedagogical and societal progress alike.

Ethical and Labor Implications of Redefining Teaching in an AI World

The redefinition of teaching in the era of artificial intelligence is not merely a matter of skill realignment or professional retraining; it carries profound ethical and labor implications that touch upon the core of educational justice, dignity, and sustainability. As intelligent systems automate instructional, evaluative, and managerial functions, education systems must confront urgent questions about teacher displacement, algorithmic governance, labor equity, and the preservation of human values in AI-mediated environments.

One of the most pressing concerns is the potential for **workforce displacement**. As AI systems increasingly assume tasks traditionally performed by teachers—such as lesson planning, tutoring, grading, and progress monitoring—there arises a risk that policymakers and institutions may view technology as a substitute for human educators rather than as a supplement. In resource-constrained contexts, this perception may drive budget cuts, staff reductions, and the de-professionalization of teaching, under the guise of technological efficiency. Such trends threaten to erode not only employment security but also the relational and cultural dimensions of education that AI cannot replicate.

To counteract this risk, educational leaders must adopt a **human-in-the-loop framework**, wherein AI supports—but does not replace—the professional judgment, empathy, and contextual sensitivity of educators. Policy must affirm that the unique contributions of teachers—particularly in social-emotional development, cultural mediation, and ethical reasoning—remain irreplaceable, even in technologically advanced classrooms. Labor protections must be codified to ensure that automation enhances rather than undermines the teaching profession.

Another ethical dimension concerns the **distribution of technological burden**. As AI systems are integrated into schools, teachers are often expected to adopt new tools without adequate time, training, or support. This results in increased stress, cognitive overload, and inequitable expectations across different schools and districts. Teachers in underfunded or understaffed institutions may face disproportionate implementation demands, exacerbating professional burnout and widening disparities in teaching conditions.

To mitigate these burdens, institutions must provide structured implementation plans, phased rollouts, and compensatory support mechanisms. These may include paid training periods, technical support teams, collaborative implementation cycles, and mental health resources. Furthermore, teachers must be included in the **design and governance of AI systems**, ensuring that technological adoption reflects pedagogical needs and classroom realities rather than corporate priorities or top-down mandates.

The ethical use of teacher data also warrants close scrutiny. As educators interact with AI systems, their decisions, performance metrics, and behavioral data are increasingly tracked and analyzed. While such data can inform professional growth and instructional design, it also raises concerns about surveillance, autonomy, and misuse. Teachers must be granted full transparency into how their data is collected, interpreted, and applied. Privacy policies must be clear, consent-based, and compliant with robust data protection standards.

Equally important are the **gendered and racialized dynamics of AI**

implementation. Historical inequities in the teaching profession may be amplified if AI systems replicate or exacerbate bias. For example, algorithmic tools used in hiring, evaluation, or classroom observation may unintentionally penalize teachers from marginalized communities if they are trained on biased datasets. Professional development opportunities, access to high-quality AI tools, and recognition systems must be designed to prevent the reproduction of systemic discrimination.

There is also a need to address the **ethical obligation to redefine success** in teaching beyond measurable efficiency. The rise of AI systems that emphasize quantifiable outputs—test scores, engagement metrics, or pacing benchmarks—may create pressure to conform to algorithmic standards of "effectiveness" at the expense of creativity, critical inquiry, and relational pedagogy. Institutions must reaffirm the intrinsic, non-instrumental purposes of education: cultivating human potential, fostering democratic citizenship, and nurturing empathy, resilience, and imagination.

From a labor policy standpoint, teacher unions, professional organizations, and advocacy groups must proactively engage in the AI discourse. Collective bargaining agreements should be updated to include clauses related to technological integration, workload adjustment, data governance, and ethical oversight. Unions must also advocate for **technological literacy as a protected professional right**, ensuring that all teachers are equipped to engage critically and constructively with the tools that shape their work.

Finally, the global dimension of labor implications must be considered. In many low- and middle-income countries, the promise of AI in education is often coupled with donor-driven agendas and proprietary technologies. If not carefully governed, this can lead to **neo-colonial educational models**, where local pedagogical practices are displaced by imported, automated systems developed in cultural contexts disconnected from learners 'realities. A decolonial approach to AI in education must prioritize local agency, context-sensitive design, and equitable global knowledge production.

In conclusion, the redefinition of teaching in the AI era is a profoundly ethical and labor-sensitive process. It requires a collective commitment to protecting the professional rights, dignity, and well-being of educators while harnessing the potential of intelligent technologies to enhance human flourishing. By centering ethical foresight, equity, and teacher voice in the AI integration process, education systems can build a future where technological advancement and labor justice advance hand in hand.

Global Implications and Policy Recommendations for Redefining Teaching in the Age of AI

The transformation of teacher roles in the context of artificial intelligence is not confined to individual classrooms or national borders. It is a global phenomenon that carries far-reaching implications for educational policy, labor markets, cultural systems, and equity in knowledge creation. As intelligent technologies proliferate across regions and school systems, policymakers must anticipate and address the systemic shifts that accompany AI adoption. The imperative is not only to modernize instruction but to do so in a way that safeguards educational justice, cultural integrity, and long-term societal wellbeing.

One of the most significant global implications is the **emergence of new educational inequalities** driven by uneven access to AI infrastructure, training, and institutional capacity. High-income nations, endowed with robust digital ecosystems and innovation hubs, are better positioned to pilot and scale AI-enabled education reforms. In contrast, low- and middle-income countries may struggle to procure adequate devices, ensure internet connectivity, or train teachers in AI-integrated pedagogies. Without coordinated international action, the digital divide may deepen into an **AI divide**, reinforcing global hierarchies in educational opportunity and technological literacy.

To address this challenge, multilateral organizations, such as UNESCO, the OECD, and the World Bank, must prioritize **equitable AI capacity-building** as a core element of their educational development agendas. This includes funding for digital infrastructure, curriculum localization, teacher training, and open-source platforms that reduce dependency on proprietary software. Collaborative partnerships between governments, universities, and industry must support context-sensitive innovation that amplifies local knowledge and pedagogical traditions rather than displacing them.

At the national level, policymakers must implement comprehensive **AI-in-education frameworks** that articulate the roles of teachers, the boundaries of automation, and the conditions for ethical technology use. Such frameworks should include clear guidelines on data privacy, algorithmic transparency, teacher agency, and learner protection. Regulatory bodies must ensure that AI deployment aligns with national curriculum standards, cultural values, and legal protections for educators.

A critical policy focus must be the **reinvention of teacher preparation and credentialing systems**, as discussed in earlier sections. Ministries of education should embed AI literacy, data ethics, and digital pedagogy into pre-service curricula, licensure requirements, and in-service training mandates. Investments in teacher education should be viewed as a national security priority—essential for ensuring a future workforce capable of navigating, adapting to, and critically engaging with intelligent systems.

Governments must also protect teachers 'rights amid technological transformation. This includes updating labor codes to define fair working conditions in AI-rich environments, establishing professional standards for tech-enabled teaching, and safeguarding teachers from algorithmic overreach in performance evaluations. Policymakers must affirm that **human educators are not replaceable commodities**, but civic actors entrusted with shaping democratic, inclusive, and humane societies.

To support innovation, governments should incentivize **school-level experimentation and teacher-led design** of AI-enhanced learning models. Funding programs, innovation fellowships, and incubator initiatives can empower educators to prototype new instructional frameworks, test open-source AI tools, and disseminate best practices. These bottom-up approaches ensure that AI integration is grounded in classroom realities and informed by teacher expertise rather than dictated solely by top-down mandates or commercial interests.

International benchmarking and knowledge-sharing mechanisms are also essential. Global platforms that document and compare teacher role transformations across countries can provide valuable insight into successful strategies, contextual challenges, and cross-cultural innovations. Transnational teacher exchange programs, research collaboratives, and digital learning observatories can foster mutual learning and solidarity among educators navigating the AI transition.

Additionally, **cross-sector policy alignment** is vital. Educational reforms must be synchronized with workforce development, cybersecurity, human rights, and national AI strategies. For example, if national AI roadmaps emphasize ethical and inclusive innovation, then teacher training programs must embed the corresponding principles into professional development content. Inter-ministerial collaboration is needed to ensure coherence between education policy, technology regulation, and labor law.

Finally, policy responses must reflect a **philosophical commitment to human-centered education**. In a world increasingly shaped by machines, it is the teacher who upholds the human dimensions of learning: empathy, ethical discernment, cultural continuity, and transformative imagination. Policies must reinforce—not marginalize—these humanistic elements by valuing educator expertise, recognizing professional complexity, and investing in teaching as a long-term public good.

In conclusion, the global implications of AI in education necessitate a bold, coordinated, and equity-driven policy agenda. Redefining the role of teachers must not be reduced to technical implementation; it must be approached as a structural redesign of education systems in service of social progress. By crafting forward-thinking policies that empower educators and protect their role in shaping the future, societies can ensure that the age of artificial intelligence becomes not a threat to teaching, but a renaissance of its possibilities.

The Educator as a Moral Architect in the Age of Intelligence

The advent of artificial intelligence in education marks not only a technological milestone but a civilizational inflection point. It forces a reckoning with the fundamental question of what it means to educate—and by extension, what it means to be human—in an era of intelligent machines. While algorithms may simulate aspects of teaching, it remains the human educator who must interpret, adapt, contextualize, and ultimately humanize the learning process. In this regard, the teacher is no longer merely a content expert or instructional facilitator, but a moral architect charged with constructing the ethical and cultural scaffolding of AI-enhanced learning environments.

This expanded role demands not just technical proficiency, but moral clarity, pedagogical adaptability, and epistemic humility. As intelligent systems automate routine instructional tasks and deliver personalized content, the value of the teacher increasingly resides in those domains machines cannot replicate: the fostering of trust, the cultivation of judgment, and the capacity to mentor young people through ambiguity, complexity, and moral dilemma. The teacher is tasked not only with preparing students to navigate a digitized world but with helping them imagine and construct a more just, humane, and sustainable future within it.

To fulfill this role, teachers must be empowered with the tools, training, and institutional supports required to thrive in complexity. Professional development must extend beyond technical skill acquisition to include deep ethical inquiry, cross-disciplinary synthesis, and design-based problem-solving. Teacher education programs must prepare candidates to serve as stewards of human agency in a digital age, capable of interpreting data without surrendering to it, and of collaborating with machines without relinquishing professional or moral judgment.

In policy terms, the teacher must be recognized not as a passive recipient of AI reform but as a co-creator of it. Systems that exclude teacher voice from the design, deployment, and governance of educational technologies risk not only alienating the profession but compromising the equity and integrity of AI implementation. Teachers must be seated at the table where algorithmic decisions are debated, curricular frameworks are reimagined, and ethical guidelines are codified. Their lived experience in the classroom is an essential epistemic resource—one that must be mobilized to guide systems through this period of epistemological upheaval.

Furthermore, the labor implications of AI integration must not be reduced to questions of efficiency or cost-effectiveness. The dignity of teaching as a profession must be reaffirmed and protected. This includes ensuring fair compensation, professional autonomy, and meaningful career pathways in AI-augmented environments. It also requires resisting the commodification of teaching through techno-solutionist narratives that frame educators as outdated or obsolete. The educator of the AI age is not diminished by technology; rather, the educator becomes its ethical compass and pedagogical translator.

The global dimension of this transformation cannot be overstated. In every society, teachers carry the cultural codes, historical memories, and civic responsibilities that anchor education to its highest purposes. As AI systems gain prominence worldwide, the risk of cultural homogenization and pedagogical monoculture increases. Teachers must be entrusted to preserve local epistemologies, challenge imported biases, and adapt intelligent tools to the needs and values of their communities. Their role is not only instructional but custodial—safeguarding the diversity, equity, and meaning of education in an increasingly automated world.

In conclusion, the redefinition of the teaching profession in the age of artificial intelligence is not a peripheral adjustment to modernity—it is a central challenge of educational and ethical significance. It demands a rearticulation of what teachers are, what they do, and why they matter. It requires systems to recognize educators not as employees in a knowledge economy, but as moral architects in an age of intelligent uncertainty. Only by investing in, uplifting, and co-designing with these educators can societies ensure that the technological revolution in education results not in dehumanization, but in the profound reaffirmation of our shared humanity.

Chapter 15

Community Integration and Parent Collaboration in an AI-Enhanced Education System

In an educational era defined by intelligent machines, data-driven personalization, and digital acceleration, the role of community and parental collaboration emerges not as a supplement but as a structural necessity. As artificial intelligence reconfigures the modes, timelines, and boundaries of schooling, families and communities must be actively integrated into the educational ecosystem—not only as stakeholders, but as co-educators and agents of influence. This chapter explores the evolving nature of family-school-community partnerships in the age of AI, articulates the implications for educational equity and inclusion, and offers a comprehensive framework for collaboration that supports human-centered, technologically-augmented learning environments.

The traditional boundaries that once separated the school from the home, or the classroom from the community, are being fundamentally redefined. Learning no longer occurs solely within fixed physical spaces, prescribed curricula, or time-bound school calendars. Rather, it increasingly unfolds across networks of people, platforms, and intelligent agents that operate in real time and across multiple domains. In such a context, educational continuity and student success depend on the seamless coordination of support systems that include parents, caregivers, civic leaders, religious institutions, libraries, nonprofits, and technology providers. These actors form a distributed ecosystem of learning that both complements and extends formal schooling.

Artificial intelligence further intensifies the need for collaborative infrastructure. Intelligent tutoring systems, predictive learning algorithms, and adaptive assessments rely heavily on student data—much of which may originate or be affected by out-of-school contexts. Understanding how a child learns cannot be divorced from understanding the social, emotional, and familial conditions in which that learning takes place. The home environment increasingly becomes a key site for technology-mediated learning, requiring parents to engage not only as caretakers, but as facilitators, supervisors, and sometimes interpreters of AI-driven educational experiences.

Simultaneously, AI introduces new risks and asymmetries. Parents and communities that lack access to digital tools, robust connectivity, or technological fluency may find themselves excluded from meaningful participation in their children's learning journeys. Furthermore, opaque algorithms, commercial platforms, and proprietary software may obscure or limit parental understanding of how educational decisions are made—undermining both trust and accountability. These developments compel education systems to reimagine community engagement not as a one-way flow of information, but as a participatory and ethical partnership that foregrounds transparency, equity, and shared responsibility.

To meet these challenges, a new paradigm of parent-community collaboration is required—one that positions families and local actors as integral to educational design, implementation, and evaluation in AI-enriched contexts. This paradigm must be built on mutual trust, reciprocal knowledge-sharing, and the recognition that the cultural, emotional, and ethical foundations of learning are co-constructed by schools and the societies they serve.

The chapter that follows examines this paradigm in depth. It begins by deconstructing the shifting nature of the parent-school relationship in a digital learning environment. It then analyzes how community institutions can serve as anchors for distributed, place-based AI learning. The chapter outlines inclusive strategies for bridging digital literacy gaps among parents and caregivers, and offers a framework for transparent communication about algorithmic tools. It concludes with policy and practice recommendations for embedding parent and community voice into the design and governance of AI-powered education systems.

By examining the intersection of artificial intelligence, community collaboration, and parental involvement, this chapter affirms a fundamental truth: while machines may personalize content or automate tasks, they cannot replace the human relationships, contextual wisdom, and cultural grounding that families and communities bring to education. In this emerging era, the village is not obsolete—it is essential.

Redefining the Parent-School Relationship in a Digitally Mediated Learning Environment

The infusion of artificial intelligence into education compels a critical reconfiguration of the traditional parent-school relationship. Historically, parental involvement in education was primarily facilitated through scheduled parent-teacher conferences, volunteer opportunities, report card reviews, and periodic communication via newsletters or phone calls. These modes, while valuable, were largely reactive and episodic, reflecting the temporal rhythm and spatial containment of brick-and-mortar schooling. In contrast, AI-enhanced education introduces a paradigm of continuous, data-driven, and remote learning that requires an evolved model of parental engagement—one that is dynamic, digitally fluent, and co-productive in nature.

The digitally mediated learning environment repositions the parent not merely as a supporter of school-based instruction but as an active participant in a co-regulated learning process. AI tools that provide real-time feedback on student progress, generate predictive performance reports, or personalize learning paths invite parents into an ongoing dialogue with both the learner and the instructional system. In this configuration, parental engagement must be proactive, sustained, and informed by a foundational understanding of how intelligent systems function within the educational context.

One of the most notable shifts is the **temporal expansion of parental engagement**. AI-enabled dashboards and communication platforms allow for constant monitoring of student activity, creating opportunities for parents to intervene, guide, or support learning on a daily basis. While this can increase responsiveness and accountability, it also introduces the potential for **hyper-surveillance**, stress, and micromanagement. Education systems must therefore provide clear guidance on the **purpose, boundaries, and best practices** for parental use of AI tools, ensuring that involvement is constructive rather than invasive.

Simultaneously, the **spatial transformation of learning**—with instruction and assessment increasingly occurring at home or through hybrid models—places new demands on families to establish learning-conducive environments, supervise digital engagement, and manage student motivation. These responsibilities are particularly burdensome for parents with limited digital literacy, inflexible work schedules, or inadequate access to devices and connectivity. Thus, the digitalization of education must be accompanied by targeted efforts to **support and empower parents**, especially those in under-resourced communities.

Another core dimension of this transformation involves the **interpretation of algorithmic outputs**. Many AI-powered platforms generate data-rich profiles of student behavior, engagement, and achievement. However, without appropriate scaffolding, these data visualizations may be unintelligible or misinterpreted by parents. Schools must therefore develop **digital literacy programs for caregivers**, equipping them with the skills to accurately understand, contextualize, and act upon algorithmic insights. This includes clarifying the limitations of predictive analytics, addressing concerns around data privacy, and offering human mediation in cases of ambiguity or concern.

Furthermore, the parent-school relationship must now account for the **ethical oversight of AI in learning**. Parents are legitimate stakeholders in discussions about algorithmic bias, platform selection, data governance, and student autonomy. Mechanisms for parental input—such as digital councils, feedback forums, and participatory design committees—must be institutionalized to ensure that family values and cultural considerations are reflected in the deployment of educational technologies. The erosion of transparency in algorithmic decision-making processes poses a significant threat to trust; parental inclusion is essential to restoring and maintaining that trust.

Educational institutions must also address the **emotional and psychological implications** of AI-mediated learning for families. Real-time performance monitoring and comparative analytics can generate anxiety, guilt, or pressure among parents, especially when discrepancies arise between a child's performance and algorithmic benchmarks. School counselors, family engagement officers, and educators must provide socio-emotional guidance that helps parents navigate these technologies with resilience and perspective, avoiding deterministic interpretations of data that reduce learners to quantifiable outputs.

Importantly, the redefinition of the parent-school relationship in the AI era must move beyond compliance and involvement toward **shared agency and co-design**. Parents should not be treated merely as end-users of technology or passive recipients of updates. Rather, they must be engaged as **co-creators of learning environments**, curriculum enhancements, and digital safety protocols. Such collaboration demands a rebalancing of institutional hierarchies and a genuine commitment to distributed leadership.

In conclusion, the evolution of the parent-school relationship in a digitally mediated learning environment necessitates a new relational contract—one built on shared understanding, mutual respect, transparent communication, and ethical collaboration. Artificial intelligence, while often abstract and technical in nature, intersects deeply with the social fabric of family life. By equipping, supporting, and empowering parents to engage meaningfully in this new terrain, education systems can create learning ecosystems that are not only more personalized and efficient but also more humane, inclusive, and democratically governed.

Empowering Families Through Digital Literacy and AI Awareness Programs

The successful integration of artificial intelligence in education hinges not only on the technological capacity of institutions but on the digital readiness of families. As intelligent learning platforms extend into homes and require active parental involvement, the absence of digital literacy becomes a critical barrier to equity, agency, and inclusion. Empowering parents and caregivers with the knowledge and skills to understand, navigate, and engage with AI-powered tools is essential for building a resilient educational ecosystem in which families act not as passive observers but as informed and active collaborators.

Digital literacy, in this context, must be defined broadly. It includes not only the ability to operate hardware or access the internet, but also the cognitive, ethical, and interpretive competencies required to engage with dynamic, AI-enhanced educational platforms. This includes reading and understanding algorithmic outputs, interpreting dashboards, responding to performance alerts, protecting privacy, and supporting responsible technology use by children. Without these competencies, families are at risk of misinterpreting AI-generated insights, misusing educational tools, or becoming disengaged from their children's learning altogether.

Educational institutions must therefore establish **comprehensive digital literacy and AI awareness programs** tailored specifically for families. These programs should be localized, culturally responsive, and structured around the principle of inclusive access. Delivery modes may include in-person workshops at schools or community centers, mobile-friendly digital modules, multilingual video tutorials, and live webinars led by educators or trusted community leaders. To reduce stigma or discomfort, such programs should be framed not as remedial interventions but as community empowerment initiatives, rooted in mutual learning and dialogue.

At the core of these programs should be a clear explanation of **how artificial intelligence functions in educational settings**. This includes introducing key concepts such as machine learning, data analytics, personalization algorithms, and adaptive assessments—explained in plain, accessible language. Parents must understand that AI does not make deterministic conclusions but generates probabilistic inferences based on data patterns. By demystifying AI, institutions can reduce fear and skepticism while promoting informed engagement.

A second focus area must be **data privacy and algorithmic transparency**. Parents need to know what types of data are collected about their children, how that data is processed, who has access to it, and how long it is retained. Literacy programs must therefore include guidance on reviewing privacy policies, configuring user permissions, and recognizing data-sharing risks. Additionally, schools must implement open-data protocols and develop **consent frameworks** that are not merely formalities but are accompanied by explanatory materials that help parents make informed decisions.

The third domain involves **critical data interpretation**. Parents often receive performance alerts, predictive risk assessments, or behavioral trend reports from AI-powered platforms. If left uninterpreted or misunderstood, these can lead to undue stress, inaccurate conclusions, or misguided interventions. Digital literacy programs should train parents to approach data with **contextual reasoning**: understanding that low engagement in a given week may be due to illness, family dynamics, or technical issues—not necessarily a deficit in ability or effort. Such training promotes a holistic, compassionate, and non-algorithmic lens on student development.

Moreover, institutions must recognize the **heterogeneity of digital access and literacy** within communities. Families vary widely in their exposure to digital tools, linguistic fluency, and availability of time or devices. As such, digital literacy initiatives must be **multi-tiered and differentiated**, offering basic introductory sessions for first-time users, intermediate support for confident users, and advanced engagement opportunities—such as participatory tech design workshops—for digitally fluent parents. Public-private partnerships may also be leveraged to distribute devices, expand broadband access, and reduce technological costs for underserved families.

A fourth priority area involves **supporting intergenerational learning dynamics**. In many households, children may exhibit higher levels of digital fluency than their parents. This reversal of the traditional authority dynamic can create tensions or disengagement. Literacy programs must offer strategies for **co-learning** and **shared digital exploration**, reinforcing the value of collaborative inquiry and mutual support. Such approaches foster relational trust and position the home as a site of collective empowerment rather than technological intimidation.

Finally, schools must integrate **feedback mechanisms** into all digital literacy and AI awareness efforts. Parents must have channels for asking questions, voicing concerns, and suggesting improvements. These mechanisms not only build trust but also ensure that programs remain relevant, responsive, and community-informed. Periodic assessments, listening circles, and digital helpdesks can institutionalize feedback as a core feature of parental empowerment.

In conclusion, empowering families through digital literacy and AI awareness is not an ancillary objective but a strategic imperative in the construction of equitable, inclusive, and effective AI-enhanced education systems. Parents and caregivers must be equipped not only to navigate digital platforms but to understand the socio-technical systems that shape their children's learning experiences. By investing in parent-centered literacy infrastructure, education systems affirm the foundational role that families play in the moral, cognitive, and technological development of future generations.

The Role of Community Institutions in Distributed Learning Networks

The integration of artificial intelligence into education necessitates a radical reimagining of where, how, and by whom learning occurs. As AI-enabled platforms dissolve the boundaries of the traditional classroom, learning becomes increasingly distributed—occurring across time, space, and institutional domains. In this evolving architecture, community institutions emerge as essential nodes in a decentralized educational ecosystem. Libraries, museums, cultural centers, religious organizations, social service agencies, and local businesses are no longer peripheral to the learning process; they become dynamic collaborators in delivering, contextualizing, and enhancing AI-supported education.

These institutions offer unique value propositions that formal school systems, constrained by curricular mandates and structural inertia, may struggle to provide. They offer **place-based learning**, **cultural grounding**, **intergenerational mentorship**, and **real-world application**—critical complements to algorithmically personalized, screen-based education. In doing so, they extend the capacity of schools to meet the diverse, situated, and developmental needs of learners in ways that artificial systems alone cannot fulfill.

Public libraries are among the most critical actors in this expanded landscape. As hubs of **knowledge access**, **digital literacy**, and **community engagement**, libraries are well-positioned to serve as inclusive AI learning centers. They offer free internet, device access, informational resources, and trained staff capable of assisting families in navigating digital platforms. In many communities, particularly those with limited school resources, libraries function as **equity engines**, reducing technological disparities and supporting academic continuity.

Museums and cultural institutions play a different but equally vital role. These spaces offer **embodied learning experiences**, **historical context**, and **multimodal engagement** that counterbalance the abstract nature of AI-driven instruction. By collaborating with schools, they can create **AI-enhanced exhibits**, **interactive simulations**, and **project-based programs** that link curricular content to cultural heritage and scientific inquiry. These initiatives ground students 'algorithmic learning in **aesthetic, ethical, and communal frameworks**, which are essential for holistic development.

Faith-based organizations and religious institutions contribute to educational equity through **moral formation**, **community trust**, and **out-of-school time programming**. Their deep integration within local neighborhoods enables them to identify learners at risk, provide safe learning spaces, and mobilize volunteers for tutoring or mentoring. In contexts where AI systems may amplify social or cultural dissonance, these institutions offer a stabilizing influence rooted in shared values and communal responsibility.

Local nonprofits and social service agencies offer crucial infrastructure for addressing the **non-academic barriers to learning**—such as food insecurity, housing instability, mental health needs, or exposure to trauma. AI systems, while capable of predicting academic disengagement, cannot remedy the structural causes of underperformance. These organizations, through case management, wraparound services, and family advocacy, provide the contextual support necessary for AI-powered interventions to be effective.

Businesses, particularly those in the technology and innovation sectors, play an increasingly prominent role as both **content collaborators** and **skill-building partners**. Through apprenticeships, hackathons, coding camps, and AI literacy programs, they help bridge the gap between formal education and workforce readiness. When structured ethically and equitably, these partnerships expose students to real-world applications of AI and prepare them for the evolving demands of the digital economy.

To fully leverage the potential of community institutions, schools and policymakers must **intentionally integrate these actors into educational planning and delivery**. This requires shifting from a siloed, school-centric model to a **network-based model** in which learning pathways are co-designed, resources are shared, and data systems are interoperable—while preserving student privacy and institutional autonomy.

One approach involves the development of **Local Education Ecosystem Hubs (LEEHs)**—geographically bounded collaboratives that align schools, community organizations, and civic stakeholders around shared educational goals. These hubs can coordinate AI-driven diagnostics with human-led interventions, ensuring that learners are not only identified through data but supported through collective action. Digital credentialing systems can further enable community institutions to confer micro-credentials or badges, validating learning that occurs outside the classroom and enabling students to build portable, AI-recognized learning portfolios.

Interoperability must be matched by **governance structures that ensure equity and accountability**. Community partners should be engaged through formal Memoranda of Understanding (MOUs) that delineate roles, responsibilities, data protocols, and shared outcomes. Advisory councils composed of educators, parents, students, and community representatives can oversee implementation, mediate conflicts, and guide continuous improvement. Such structures foster trust and transparency while institutionalizing collaboration.

Equally important is **capacity-building** within community institutions themselves. Many lack the technological infrastructure or trained personnel to meaningfully engage with AI tools. Investment in professional development, technology upgrades, and participatory design workshops is essential to ensure that community actors are not reduced to secondary implementers of school priorities but are empowered as full partners in the co-construction of educational futures.

In conclusion, the role of community institutions in AI-enhanced learning must be redefined not as ancillary but as structural. These organizations possess the cultural capital, contextual expertise, and relational networks necessary to humanize AI-driven education and extend its reach across domains of knowledge, identity, and opportunity. As distributed learning becomes the norm, the school must be understood not as a building but as a **node in a living, learning community network**. Only through deep and sustained collaboration with community institutions can education fulfill its mandate in the age of artificial intelligence: to nurture not only intelligent minds but flourishing communities.

Building Trust, Transparency, and Consent in Data-Driven Parent Engagement

The exponential increase in data collection, analysis, and application within artificial intelligence-powered education environments necessitates a reexamination of the trust framework between families and institutions. As schools implement intelligent systems that monitor student progress, personalize instruction, and automate feedback loops, families must be assured that these processes are transparent, ethical, and rooted in a culture of informed consent. Without these assurances, data-driven parent engagement risks devolving into surveillance, manipulation, or exclusion—undermining the very partnerships essential to successful AI integration.

At the foundation of trust lies **transparency**. Parents must be clearly informed about what data is being collected about their children, for what purposes, by whom, and under what legal and institutional conditions. This includes both direct data inputs—such as attendance, grades, engagement metrics—and indirect behavioral or biometric data, including eye tracking, emotional analytics, or keystroke patterns. Data transparency must also extend to the algorithms themselves: their functions, decision-making processes, and the nature of their training data. Institutions should provide **algorithmic disclosure statements** that explain in accessible language how each system operates, what it predicts or influences, and what limitations or biases may exist.

Transparency must be accompanied by **consent frameworks** that go beyond performative checkbox agreements. Informed consent requires that parents understand the implications of data use, are given meaningful choices, and can withdraw participation without academic penalty. Schools must design consent processes that are **context-sensitive, linguistically appropriate, and inclusive of families with varying levels of literacy or digital familiarity**. Consent should be revisited periodically, particularly when systems are updated or new data types are introduced. Moreover, institutions must distinguish between essential data collection required for educational operations and optional data practices associated with third-party platforms or pilot programs.

The issue of **third-party data access** presents one of the most significant challenges to building trust. Many AI tools used in schools are developed and maintained by private vendors who may collect, store, or analyze student data for purposes not directly related to education. Parents must be notified of these relationships and provided with explicit documentation outlining how vendors comply with data protection laws such as the Family Educational Rights and Privacy Act (FERPA) or the Children's Online Privacy Protection Act (COPPA). Where applicable, schools should seek **data use agreements**that restrict commercial exploitation, mandate data minimization, and ensure the right to data deletion.

Establishing trust also involves building **institutional mechanisms for oversight and accountability**. Schools should establish **data ethics committees** that include parent representatives, educators, administrators, and legal advisors. These committees should have authority to review data policies, evaluate risks, and recommend modifications. In addition, education systems must implement **incident reporting protocols** and **redress mechanisms** in the event of data breaches, algorithmic errors, or unintended consequences. The existence of these structures signals to parents that their concerns are taken seriously and that the institution is committed to responsible innovation.

Beyond procedural mechanisms, trust is cultivated through **relational transparency**. Schools must invest in continuous, two-way communication with families about the role of AI in their children's education. This includes town hall meetings, webinars, newsletters, and one-on-one conferences focused specifically on digital systems and data use. Educational leaders must engage not as gatekeepers of technology but as translators, advocates, and facilitators of community understanding. Teachers, too, should be equipped to discuss AI-related tools with parents confidently and accurately, creating opportunities for shared decision-making.

Special attention must be given to communities that have experienced historical marginalization or institutional mistrust. For these families, engagement must begin with **cultural humility**, **historical acknowledgement**, and **demonstrated accountability**. Data collection practices must avoid deficit-based assumptions or racial profiling, and systems must be audited for potential algorithmic bias. Trust-building in these contexts may require partnerships with community-based organizations or faith leaders who can serve as mediators and cultural bridges.

It is also essential to foster **student involvement** in data transparency processes. Older students should be educated about their digital footprints, rights to data access, and the ways in which their learning is shaped by AI systems. By including students in these conversations, schools reinforce a culture of shared responsibility and prepare young people to become informed digital citizens. Parental engagement in data-driven education should be viewed as a **triadic relationship**-between family, school, and student, with shared agency and mutual respect.

In conclusion, trust, transparency, and consent are not ancillary considerations in AI-enhanced education—they are structural pillars that uphold the legitimacy, effectiveness, and ethical sustainability of data-driven engagement. Parents must be treated as rightful co-governors of educational data practices, not as passive observers of algorithmic systems. Through robust transparency protocols, inclusive consent frameworks, relational engagement, and institutional accountability, education systems can create a foundation of trust upon which transformative, equitable, and human-centered AI-powered learning can be built.

Designing Shared Governance Models for Parent-Community Input

The integration of artificial intelligence into the educational system represents a paradigmatic shift in both instructional design and institutional governance. As AI tools influence not only learning pathways but also disciplinary decisions, placement evaluations, and predictive analytics, the ethical stewardship of these technologies requires participatory oversight. In such a context, **shared governance models** that include structured, meaningful, and continuous parent-community input become essential—not merely as a matter of democratic principle but as a pragmatic necessity to ensure equity, accountability, and social legitimacy.

Traditional models of school governance—school boards, parent-teacher associations, or school improvement councils—have typically operated within the boundaries of conventional pedagogical practices. While these bodies offer critical forums for dialogue, they are frequently limited by informational asymmetries, tokenistic involvement, or lack of decision-making authority. In an AI-enhanced environment, these limitations are magnified: the complexity of algorithmic systems, the opacity of proprietary platforms, and the pace of technological change demand new models of **deliberative, transparent, and informed participation**.

A shared governance model begins with **recognition of parents and community members as co-stakeholders** in educational technology decision-making. Their lived experiences, cultural knowledge, and contextual insight are invaluable for shaping how AI tools are selected, implemented, and evaluated. Governance structures must therefore be re-engineered to include **formalized representation**, **clear jurisdictional authority**, and **capacity-building support** for participants.

One effective approach involves the establishment of **AI Education Oversight Committees (AIEOCs)** at the school, district, or state level. These bodies would include a balanced composition of educators, administrators, students, technology experts, and parent/community representatives. The committee's responsibilities would encompass reviewing AI tool adoption proposals, assessing alignment with pedagogical goals and ethical standards, monitoring performance data, and advising on the procurement of third-party platforms. Critically, these committees should possess **consultative authority** in policy development and **veto power** over tools that fail to meet established criteria for fairness, transparency, or pedagogical value.

To ensure that all participants can engage meaningfully, governance models must be undergirded by **equity-focused capacity-building**. Parents and community members may require orientation sessions on AI functionality, data privacy frameworks, and algorithmic bias. This investment is not remedial but empowering; it affirms that civic oversight of education must be democratized and technically fluent. Institutions should provide stipends, translation services, childcare support, and flexible scheduling to ensure broad and sustained participation from diverse constituencies.

In addition to formal governance bodies, schools should establish **continuous feedback loops** with parents through digital and analog mechanisms. These may include AI transparency dashboards with comment functionality, mobile apps for real-time feedback, structured focus groups, and rotating town halls. Feedback must not only be collected but also acted upon, with transparent documentation of how community input has shaped implementation decisions or system modifications. This fosters institutional accountability and reassures families that their voices influence outcomes.

Another important dimension of shared governance is **participatory technology design**. Rather than adopting pre-packaged AI systems, schools can engage parents and community members in co-design processes—identifying user needs, contributing to feature development, and stress-testing tools in real-world environments. This approach, drawn from the field of human-centered design, increases adoption rates, reduces misalignment, and mitigates risk. Community-led design labs, hosted in libraries or community centers, can serve as hubs for this participatory innovation.

Legal and policy frameworks must evolve to support shared governance. State education codes and district policies should mandate the inclusion of community stakeholders in AI oversight structures and define their roles with clarity. Compliance audits, equity impact assessments, and public reporting requirements should be institutionalized to ensure transparency and deter performative engagement. Policy scaffolding must also protect against conflicts of interest, particularly when technology vendors seek to influence governance processes or outcomes.

Moreover, shared governance must be informed by an ethics of **intergenerational accountability**. AI systems introduced today will shape the educational experiences of future cohorts. Governance bodies must be forward-looking, anticipating unintended consequences, technological dependencies, or cultural shifts. Including youth voices—particularly from historically marginalized communities—enhances both the ethical rigor and temporal relevance of oversight processes.

Importantly, shared governance must be understood not as a static structure but as a **relational process** that evolves with community dynamics, technological innovation, and institutional growth. It requires continual reflection, renewal, and responsiveness. Schools must be willing to decentralize authority, redistribute expertise, and challenge hierarchical assumptions that have historically marginalized non-institutional actors in education.

In conclusion, shared governance models for AI-enhanced education must be built on the principles of representation, transparency, accountability, and co-agency. Parents and communities are not passive recipients of technological change; they are essential co-creators of equitable and humane learning ecosystems. By institutionalizing participatory structures, investing in capacity-building, and embedding ethical foresight into decision-making, education systems can ensure that artificial intelligence serves not as a force of disempowerment but as a catalyst for democratic renewal and community transformation.

Conclusion – Toward a Holistic Family-Centered Model of AI-Era Education

The emergence of artificial intelligence as a pervasive force in education has prompted an urgent reevaluation of the social contract between schools, families, and communities. As learning increasingly migrates into hybrid environments, mediated by algorithms and fueled by data, the educational experience can no longer be confined to the walls of the classroom or the responsibilities of certified educators. Instead, it becomes a multi-nodal, participatory process in which families and communities act as co-educators, ethical stewards, and critical stakeholders. The future of education in the age of artificial intelligence must therefore be **family-centered**, **community-embedded**, and **co-governed**.

The preceding sections of this chapter have articulated a comprehensive framework for building this model—beginning with foundational trust, extending through digital literacy, and culminating in participatory governance. This framework does not position artificial intelligence as a replacement for human agency but as a catalyst for deepened collaboration and relational accountability. In such a model, families are not merely subjects of data; they are interpreters of meaning, advocates for equity, and contributors to innovation.

To realize this model, education systems must first redefine the architecture of engagement. Engagement must become continuous rather than episodic, dialogic rather than directive, and inclusive rather than selective. Digital platforms must be designed not only for efficiency but for ethical communication—providing insight into how decisions are made, how interventions are triggered, and how progress is interpreted. AI should illuminate rather than obscure; it should empower rather than prescribe.

Second, the holistic model necessitates a **cultural shift** in how schools view parental roles. Parents are not barriers to innovation, nor are they simply enforcers of homework compliance. They are dynamic agents of learning whose insights, values, and experiences must inform educational technology design and pedagogical strategy. Particularly in communities facing historical disinvestment, restoring the legitimacy of parent voices is a moral imperative that cannot be addressed through token involvement alone.

Third, schools must cultivate a **networked governance ecosystem** in which decisions about AI adoption, application, and oversight are shared. The institutionalization of parent-led ethics councils, algorithmic audit boards, and co-design task forces creates structural pathways for agency. These structures must be supported by public policy, financial investment, and legal safeguards to ensure longevity, representativeness, and impact.

Fourth, education systems must invest heavily in **interoperable infrastructures** that link schools, community organizations, and families through real-time data sharing, collaborative intervention models, and resource pooling. AI-enabled systems that detect a learner's cognitive struggle must also be able to trigger support from community mentors or counseling services. Predictive analytics must be humanized through contextual interpretation, ensuring that decisions reflect whole-child considerations rather than algorithmic reductionism.

Fifth, the ethical dimension of family-centered AI integration must be continuously reinforced. Data practices must respect privacy, center consent, and avoid bias. Parents must be equipped to understand how AI systems affect their children's learning trajectories and life chances. Furthermore, children themselves must be socialized into understanding how their data is used and how to exercise digital agency within and beyond school systems.

Finally, the holistic model recognizes that **educational outcomes in an AI-driven society are inseparable from civic outcomes**. Schools are incubators of not only knowledge but also democracy, equity, and social cohesion. A family-centered approach ensures that AI-enhanced education does not become a technocratic system serving economic efficiency alone, but a human-centered institution cultivating critical thinking, cultural identity, and participatory citizenship.

In conclusion, the age of artificial intelligence demands not less engagement from families and communities, but more—more informed, more strategic, and more empowered. A truly transformative

AI-enhanced education system must center the family not at the periphery, but at the core. Only by integrating parents and community members into the very design, implementation, and governance of these systems can society ensure that artificial intelligence advances, rather than undermines, the foundational goals of education: human development, social justice, and collective flourishing.

Chapter 16

Governance, Ethics, and Regulatory Frameworks for AI in PreK–12 Education

The accelerating integration of artificial intelligence into PreK–12 education has introduced profound opportunities for personalized learning, early intervention, and administrative efficiency. However, it has also raised significant ethical dilemmas, legal questions, and governance challenges that demand immediate attention from policymakers, educators, technologists, and civil society. As algorithmic systems gain influence over everything from instructional content to behavioral monitoring, a comprehensive and enforceable governance framework becomes essential—not as a reactionary safeguard, but as a proactive foundation for equitable and sustainable educational transformation.

Artificial intelligence, by its very nature, is not a neutral tool. Its outputs are shaped by the data on which it is trained, the assumptions embedded in its algorithms, and the institutional values of those who design and deploy it. In education, these systems are often deployed without rigorous scrutiny, public input, or transparent standards. This can result in unintended consequences such as bias reinforcement, opaque decision-making, or erosion of human judgment in areas requiring moral discernment. The absence of robust regulatory frameworks enables the proliferation of tools that may exacerbate inequality, commodify student data, or automate disciplinary actions without due process.

The purpose of this chapter is to articulate the core principles, institutional models, and policy instruments necessary to govern artificial intelligence responsibly within PreK–12 education systems. It proposes a multi-layered approach that integrates ethical codes of conduct, data protection standards, algorithmic auditing, public oversight mechanisms, and legislative action. Special attention is given to the roles of school boards, departments of education, educational technology vendors, and global standard-setting bodies in constructing an enforceable and adaptive regulatory environment.

This chapter begins by situating the governance of AI in education within broader historical and legal contexts. It then examines the specific risks posed by AI in PreK–12 settings, such as surveillance creep, consent gaps, discriminatory outcomes, and accountability erosion. The discussion proceeds to outline a regulatory architecture composed of institutional responsibilities, procedural safeguards, and community involvement models. The chapter concludes by proposing an actionable roadmap for national and sub-national policymakers to enact coherent, rights-respecting AI governance in education that safeguards both educational integrity and democratic values.

Historical Precedents and Legal Context of Educational Technology Regulation

The development of governance and legal oversight for educational technologies has historically lagged behind the pace of innovation. Prior to the rise of artificial intelligence, the regulation of educational tools primarily focused on issues such as accessibility, data privacy, equity of access, and curriculum content standards. While foundational, these regulatory frameworks were often reactive and fragmented, shaped more by compliance needs than ethical foresight. The emergence of AI, with its predictive and autonomous capabilities, renders many of these legal precedents inadequate, requiring a reevaluation and expansion of governance principles rooted in human rights, transparency, and systemic accountability.

The earliest legal frameworks applicable to educational technology emerged alongside the digitization of school records and student information systems in the 1970s and 1980s. In the United States, the Family Educational Rights and Privacy Act (FERPA) of 1974 remains a cornerstone regulation. FERPA grants parents the right to access, review, and request the correction of student records while restricting disclosure of personally identifiable information without consent. However, FERPA was enacted in an era when educational data resided in physical files or basic databases—long before the advent of predictive analytics, biometric data collection, or AI-powered behavioral scoring.

Similarly, the Children's Online Privacy Protection Act (COPPA), passed in 1998, aimed to protect the online data of children under the age of thirteen by requiring parental consent for the collection or use of personal information. Yet COPPA was primarily designed for commercial websites, not for intelligent educational platforms embedded within classroom instruction. As a result, these foundational statutes, while still relevant, are increasingly insufficient to regulate the complexities introduced by machine learning algorithms that make probabilistic decisions based on sensitive, longitudinal student data.

Internationally, frameworks such as the General Data Protection Regulation (GDPR) enacted in the European Union offer a more expansive vision of data protection, including provisions on algorithmic transparency, the right to explanation, and automated decision-making safeguards. GDPR-inspired principles are gradually informing educational policy discussions in various jurisdictions. However, these policies are often generalized across sectors, lacking the specificity needed to address the nuanced power dynamics of PreK–12 learning environments—where minors cannot fully consent, where institutional asymmetry is pronounced, and where educational impacts may extend over a lifetime.

Precedents also exist in the regulation of high-stakes educational assessments. Standardized testing regimes, particularly in the late 20th and early 21st centuries, were subject to scrutiny regarding fairness, psychometric validity, and accommodations for students with disabilities. These debates established the principle that educational decision-making tools must meet standards of reliability, transparency, and equity. However, AI systems differ in that they are not static tests but dynamic, self-modifying tools that continuously learn from data inputs. This adaptive nature complicates existing validation methods and raises questions about how to evaluate systems whose behaviors evolve over time.

The legal context has also been shaped by broader civil rights legislation. Anti-discrimination laws such as Title VI of the Civil Rights Act and Section 504 of the Rehabilitation Act prohibit educational practices that have disparate impacts based on race, gender, or disability. In principle, these laws could be applied to challenge AI systems that result in inequitable educational outcomes. However, the legal system has yet to fully adapt these statutes to the algorithmic context, where bias may be statistically distributed rather than explicitly programmed, and where causality may be difficult to trace.

Recent developments suggest a growing recognition of the need for AI-specific regulation in education. For example, state-level legislation in California, Illinois, and New York has introduced provisions related to biometric data collection, facial recognition bans in schools, and parental notification requirements for algorithmic systems. At the federal level, legislative proposals such as the Algorithmic Accountability Act and the SAFE KIDS Act aim to extend consumer protections to children in educational settings, though these remain under debate and lack comprehensive adoption.

Notably, the absence of binding international treaties on AI in education leaves much of the regulatory burden to national and sub-national entities. UNESCO and the OECD have issued non-binding ethical frameworks promoting human-centered AI, but these rely on voluntary adherence and lack enforcement mechanisms. This fragmentation underscores the need for jurisdiction-specific yet globally informed governance models that can adapt to local legal cultures while upholding universal principles.

In conclusion, while historical precedents in educational regulation provide valuable foundations, they are insufficient to govern the complexities of artificial intelligence in PreK–12 education. A new legal architecture is required—one that is anticipatory rather than reactive, participatory rather than technocratic, and ethically grounded rather than narrowly procedural. This architecture must address not only the technical dimensions of AI systems but also their social, developmental, and democratic implications within the unique context of education.

The Risks and Ethical Dilemmas of AI in PreK–12 Contexts

Artificial intelligence, when applied to PreK–12 education, introduces a suite of ethical dilemmas and risks that extend beyond those found in other institutional settings. Children, by nature of their developmental stage, dependency, and legal status, require a higher standard of protection than adults. AI's increasing role in shaping academic pathways, behavioral management, and access to opportunities elevates the stakes of governance to matters of long-term equity, autonomy, and democratic integrity. This section identifies and explores the most pressing risks and ethical concerns inherent to AI deployment in the primary and secondary educational space.

1. Algorithmic Bias and Inequitable Outcomes

One of the most critical ethical concerns involves algorithmic bias and the reproduction of systemic inequalities. AI systems trained on historical educational data—data that may reflect patterns of racial segregation, gender bias, or economic disparity—can reinforce those inequities under the guise of objectivity. For example, predictive analytics designed to identify students "at risk" of underperformance may disproportionately target students from marginalized backgrounds, leading to increased surveillance or preemptive remediation that narrows learning opportunities rather than expanding them. In many cases, these systems operate as "black boxes," with little explanation of how predictions are made or which data points carry the most weight.

The ethical failure lies not only in biased outputs but also in the failure to include affected communities in the design, implementation, or evaluation of such systems. Bias is not merely a technical problem; it is a governance failure—a sign of insufficient accountability, transparency, and participatory ethics.

2. Surveillance, Autonomy, and the Erosion of Privacy

AI-powered surveillance technologies—such as facial recognition cameras, keystroke monitoring software, emotion detection algorithms, and wearable biometric devices—are increasingly being introduced in classrooms under the promise of enhancing safety or improving focus. However, these tools raise profound questions about the right to privacy and the long-term psychological effects of constant monitoring. The normalization of surveillance may lead children to internalize a sense of being perpetually watched, undermining the development of autonomy, creativity, and trust.

Furthermore, many surveillance technologies collect highly sensitive data without adequate informed consent from parents or students. The lack of clear data governance frameworks often results in third-party vendors gaining access to behavioral and biometric data for purposes beyond the educational scope, including potential commercialization. This violates the fundamental ethical principle that students 'data should be used solely to support their well-being and development, not to create profit-driven behavioral profiles.

3. Informed Consent and the Rights of Minors

Another key challenge is the issue of informed consent. While legal guardians may technically consent on behalf of minors, the complexity of AI systems, the opacity of data processing methods, and the lack of meaningful alternatives raise doubts about whether that consent is truly informed or voluntary. In many cases, consent is embedded in click-through agreements that provide little clarity and no genuine choice. Furthermore, children lack the legal standing and cognitive maturity to fully understand the implications of how their data is collected, used, and stored.

The ethical principle of assent—respecting the evolving capacities of the child—should guide practices around data sharing and algorithmic decision-making. Educational institutions must adopt a duty of care that exceeds minimal legal compliance, ensuring that children and their families are active participants in decisions about AI use and data practices.

4. Opacity and Lack of Explainability

Many AI systems deployed in education rely on complex machine learning models that are not easily interpretable, even by their designers. This lack of explainability creates a scenario where important educational decisions—such as course placement, disciplinary referrals, or intervention targeting—may be made based on processes that cannot be understood, challenged, or verified by students, parents, or educators.

This undermines foundational principles of due process and procedural fairness. Ethical governance requires that any decision made by or with the aid of AI be explainable in plain language, subject to appeal, and accompanied by human oversight. The inability to interrogate algorithmic decisions, particularly those with significant consequences, is antithetical to democratic education.

5. Automation of Human Judgment and Deprofessionalization
As AI tools become more capable of assessing student progress, suggesting interventions, or even generating instructional content, there is a growing risk of displacing the professional judgment of educators. While AI can augment instructional decisions, it must not replace the relational, contextual, and ethical deliberations that teachers provide. The overreliance on AI may reduce educators to data managers, strip the profession of its intellectual and emotional labor, and reconfigure teaching as a transactional rather than transformational practice.

Moreover, if AI systems are perceived as more authoritative than teachers—particularly in data-driven institutions—then dissenting pedagogical perspectives may be marginalized. This constitutes an ethical breach, as it diminishes the role of human wisdom, cultural nuance, and critical reflection in shaping educational outcomes.

6. Longitudinal Profiling and Deterministic Labeling
AI systems that generate long-term learner profiles based on early assessments can lock students into self-fulfilling prophecies. When data-driven systems label a student as "low-performing," "disengaged," or "gifted" based on predictive analytics, those labels may follow them across academic transitions, affecting teacher expectations, resource allocation, and self-perception. The ethical danger lies in converting potentialities into fixed identities—a form of data determinism that contradicts the developmental and holistic nature of education.

Longitudinal profiling is particularly dangerous in early childhood education, where formative assessments may become permanent markers in AI models. Such outcomes contradict the core educational principle that children develop unevenly, unpredictably, and in diverse ways.

7. Commercial Exploitation and Data Commodification

Many educational AI systems are developed by private vendors who operate under business models that monetize student data through analytics, advertising, or secondary market sales. The commodification of educational data poses a direct ethical threat to the public nature of education. Schools, which are trusted institutions of democratic learning, risk becoming platforms for corporate surveillance and behavioral influence if governance structures do not enforce clear boundaries between educational goals and commercial interests.

Contracts with edtech vendors must include strict limitations on data usage, clear ownership terms, and robust enforcement mechanisms. Ethical governance requires not only contractual protections but also a broader societal debate about the role of commercial actors in shaping public education systems through data-driven technologies.

8. Accountability Gaps and Jurisdictional Ambiguity

In many cases, the implementation of AI systems in schools occurs without clear lines of responsibility. When a biased outcome emerges from a proprietary algorithm used by a district, who is accountable—the school, the vendor, the state? This jurisdictional ambiguity dilutes responsibility and weakens enforcement. Ethical governance requires a comprehensive chain of accountability, where institutions understand their legal obligations, and families know where to seek redress.

Furthermore, when AI systems operate autonomously, without real-time human oversight, accountability becomes even more elusive. Governance structures must mandate human-in-the-loop designs and ensure that no AI system makes significant educational decisions without a responsible individual who can explain, review, and override those decisions if necessary.

In conclusion, the ethical risks associated with AI in PreK–12 education are not hypothetical; they are emergent and, in many cases, already operational. These risks demand proactive, rights-based governance grounded in child protection, educational equity, and institutional accountability. Without such safeguards, the promise of AI in education may be eclipsed by its potential to entrench inequality, commodify learning, and erode democratic trust in public education systems.

Principles for Ethical Governance of AI in Schools

In response to the escalating ethical dilemmas outlined in the preceding section, a robust framework of governance must be anchored in clear, enforceable, and universally applicable principles. Ethical governance is not merely an abstract ideal; it is an operational necessity that safeguards the integrity of educational institutions, protects the rights of learners, and ensures that technological innovation aligns with the foundational values of democracy, equity, and human dignity. This section articulates the core principles that should guide the design, deployment, and regulation of artificial intelligence systems within PreK–12 education.

1. Human-Centered Design

At the heart of ethical governance lies the principle of human-centered design. All AI systems used in schools must be constructed to serve the developmental, emotional, cognitive, and social needs of students. This requires that systems be tailored to enhance—not replace—human interaction and learning relationships. Technological tools must be designed to support educators, honor the diversity of learners, and uphold pedagogical freedom rather than constrain it through rigid data-driven logic.

Human-centered AI design demands participatory input from educators, students, and families. It requires iterative feedback loops to ensure that the system responds to the lived experiences of its users, not just the computational parameters defined by developers. This principle ensures that technology does not eclipse the core purpose of education: the holistic formation of capable, ethical, and socially engaged individuals.

2. Transparency and Explainability

Transparency is a prerequisite for accountability. All stakeholders—including educators, administrators, students, and parents—must have access to clear, understandable information about how AI systems function, what data they collect, how they make decisions, and how they impact learning. Explainability, a subset of transparency, ensures that decisions made or assisted by AI systems can be interpreted and understood by non-technical users.

Transparent systems foster trust and democratic legitimacy. They allow users to challenge errors, question assumptions, and advocate for redress. Governance mechanisms must mandate that vendors disclose algorithms 'logic, training data characteristics, and performance limitations. In cases where full algorithmic transparency is technically or commercially constrained, oversight boards must be granted the authority to audit and certify systems for educational use.

3. Equity and Non-Discrimination
Ethical governance must ensure that AI systems do not exacerbate existing inequalities or create new forms of exclusion. This requires proactive measures to audit for bias in data collection, model training, and system deployment. Equity must be embedded as a design principle, with deliberate efforts to account for differences in race, socioeconomic status, ability, language, and geographic location.

Governance policies must require disaggregated impact assessments to evaluate how AI affects different student populations. Where disparate impacts are identified, systems must be modified or withdrawn. Equity does not imply uniformity of application; rather, it requires sensitivity to context and the intentional design of differentiated pathways that uphold the principle of fairness.

4. Privacy and Data Sovereignty
Student data must be treated with the highest standard of protection. Privacy is not merely a legal requirement but a moral imperative in environments where minors cannot fully consent and where data misuse may have lifelong consequences. Governance frameworks must ensure that data collection is minimized, purpose-specific, and secured through encryption, access control, and retention limits.

Data sovereignty means that students, parents, and schools must retain control over educational data. Ownership rights should be clearly defined, and data should never be used for commercial profiling, behavioral influence, or cross-sector surveillance without explicit informed consent. Privacy impact assessments must be conducted before the deployment of any AI system, and ongoing audits should monitor for compliance.

5. Accountability and Redress

Every AI system deployed in an educational context must have a clearly identifiable human actor or institution that is accountable for its outcomes. This includes responsibility for errors, bias, harm, or unintended consequences. Governance policies must establish pathways for redress when students are adversely affected by algorithmic decisions. This may include appeals processes, third-party reviews, or ombudsman services.

Vendors must also be held accountable. Contracts must include clauses requiring transparency, data stewardship, and ethical compliance, with penalties for violations. Additionally, oversight bodies must be empowered with investigatory and enforcement authority to hold both public institutions and private companies accountable for their AI deployments.

6. Consent and Participatory Governance

Ethical AI governance must honor the rights of students and families to meaningfully participate in decisions about how technology is used in their schools. Consent must be informed, contextual, and ongoing—not buried in opaque terms of service or assumed through passive enrollment. Schools must create forums where parents, students, and educators can voice concerns, contribute to policy development, and co-design implementation strategies.

Participatory governance may include local ethics councils, parent-teacher technology boards, and student digital rights committees. These bodies must be diverse, empowered, and resourced to influence decisions—not relegated to symbolic roles. Inclusive governance is essential to ensuring that AI in education reflects the values and aspirations of the communities it serves.

7. Sustainability and Interoperability

Governance frameworks must ensure that AI systems are sustainable—technically, financially, and institutionally. Schools should not become dependent on opaque systems from vendors that may go out of business or change business models unpredictably. Ethical procurement practices require open standards, data portability, and long-term support guarantees.

Interoperability is essential for integrating AI systems into existing educational ecosystems without creating silos or redundancy. Governance bodies must establish technical standards that ensure seamless communication between platforms while maintaining data security and educational coherence. Sustainable design also includes environmental considerations, ensuring that AI systems do not contribute disproportionately to carbon emissions or digital waste.

8. Continuous Evaluation and Ethical Foresight

AI governance in education must be treated as an ongoing process rather than a one-time checklist. Continuous evaluation mechanisms are essential to monitor how systems evolve over time, especially in response to new data inputs or software updates. Ethical foresight—the practice of anticipating unintended consequences—must be built into governance protocols.

This includes scenario planning, stakeholder consultations, and ethical impact forecasting. Institutions must adopt a mindset of humility and adaptability, recognizing that no system is infallible and that governance structures must evolve in tandem with technological advancements.

In conclusion, the ethical governance of AI in PreK–12 education must be principled, participatory, and protective. These eight principles—human-centered design, transparency, equity, privacy, accountability, consent, sustainability, and foresight—constitute the moral architecture necessary to ensure that artificial intelligence serves the public good rather than undermines it. They offer a compass for institutions navigating the rapidly changing terrain of AI in education and serve as a foundation upon which regulatory structures can be constructed.

Institutional Models for AI Governance in Education

The implementation of artificial intelligence in PreK–12 education necessitates not only a robust set of ethical principles but also the institutional infrastructure to enact, enforce, and adapt those principles in real-world contexts. Effective governance requires well-defined roles, responsibilities, and accountability structures that extend across multiple layers of the educational ecosystem. This section outlines a spectrum of institutional models that can operationalize ethical governance at local, regional, national, and international levels.

These models must be designed to function both independently and collaboratively to address the multidimensional nature of AI in education.

1. Local School and District-Level Ethics Committees
The most immediate site of AI deployment is the local school or district. These institutions are best positioned to evaluate the day-to-day impacts of technology on students, educators, and families. Establishing AI ethics committees at the local level provides a mechanism for schools to proactively assess the appropriateness of AI tools prior to procurement or implementation. These committees should include educators, administrators, parents, students, and technology experts who can collectively review vendor contracts, conduct risk assessments, and monitor deployment practices.

Such bodies must be granted real authority—not merely advisory capacity—to approve or reject technology based on compliance with ethical standards. Their responsibilities may include approving privacy notices, evaluating algorithmic transparency, and hearing complaints from stakeholders. Localized governance allows ethical concerns to be addressed in context, ensuring that policies are responsive to the unique demographics, pedagogies, and challenges of the community.

2. State or Regional Education Technology Regulatory Agencies
At the state or provincial level, departments of education must expand their oversight capacity to include regulatory offices or technology commissions focused specifically on artificial intelligence. These agencies are responsible for setting baseline compliance standards, accrediting educational AI vendors, and auditing school districts for adherence to data protection and algorithmic accountability rules.

These agencies can also serve as clearinghouses for best practices, providing technical assistance to schools while maintaining central databases of approved technologies. Importantly, state-level bodies can mandate disclosure requirements and enforcement penalties, ensuring a degree of uniformity across districts. By harmonizing oversight while preserving local autonomy, these institutions can reduce regulatory fragmentation and close governance gaps.

3. National Education AI Ethics Councils

National governments must establish centralized education AI ethics councils tasked with policy development, research, and long-term strategic planning. These councils should be composed of interdisciplinary experts, including ethicists, educators, technologists, legal scholars, psychologists, and representatives from marginalized communities. Their role is not to micromanage local education but to define national ethical guidelines, standardize assessment protocols, and ensure that AI in education aligns with constitutional and civil rights frameworks.

Such councils must have a dual mandate: policy advisory and public engagement. They should publish regular reports on the state of AI in schools, evaluate emerging risks, and facilitate public consultations. In times of controversy—such as high-profile incidents of algorithmic harm—they must serve as impartial arbiters capable of conducting independent reviews and issuing policy recommendations.

4. Independent Algorithmic Audit Boards

Given the technical complexity of AI systems, particularly those involving deep learning or opaque models, an independent algorithmic audit board must be created to test and verify the integrity of AI tools used in education. These boards, operating similarly to public utility commissions, should be non-partisan and equipped with forensic data scientists who can evaluate source code, training data, and system outputs for bias, fairness, and accuracy.

Algorithmic audits should be mandatory prior to the deployment of high-impact AI systems, such as those affecting academic placement, disciplinary action, or resource allocation. Vendors must be required to undergo third-party validation and submit to re-audits upon system updates. The existence of such boards reinforces public trust and deters the use of unverified or unsafe technologies in learning environments.

5. Public Procurement and Contract Standardization Bodies

Procurement is a critical governance chokepoint that must be regulated to prevent the adoption of non-compliant or ethically questionable AI systems. National and regional education procurement bodies should create standardized contract language that includes clauses on data ownership, audit rights, student privacy protections, transparency obligations, and algorithmic explainability.

Centralized procurement portals can streamline the vetting process, making it easier for schools to identify AI systems that meet ethical and technical standards. These bodies can also coordinate collective bargaining for licenses, ensuring that public education systems are not exploited by monopolistic or exploitative vendors.

6. Ombudsman Offices and Grievance Mechanisms

To ensure that students, families, and educators have access to redress mechanisms, independent AI ombudsman offices must be established within or adjacent to educational oversight institutions. These offices receive, investigate, and mediate complaints related to AI harms—such as incorrect student classifications, privacy violations, or discriminatory practices.

Ombudsman offices must be empowered to recommend corrective actions, facilitate appeals, and report systemic failures to regulatory bodies. Their existence not only reinforces accountability but also signals a commitment to participatory governance, where individuals affected by AI systems have a voice in correcting injustices.

7. Cross-Sector AI Governance Collaboratives

Given the interdisciplinary nature of AI and its entanglement with other sectors—such as health, law enforcement, and commercial technology—governance structures must extend beyond education alone. Cross-sector collaboratives, convened by ministries or intergovernmental bodies, can help align education-specific AI governance with broader national AI strategies. These collaboratives ensure that policies on data portability, digital identity, and algorithmic ethics remain coherent across domains.

By facilitating dialogue between stakeholders in education, child welfare, digital infrastructure, and human rights, such models foster integrated and anticipatory governance capable of responding to technological convergence.

8. Global Standards Bodies and International Norm-Setting

Education is both a national prerogative and a global public good. As AI systems cross borders, global institutions such as UNESCO, the

OECD, and the United Nations must assume greater responsibility for establishing transnational standards and ethical baselines. Global education AI charters, open-source audit protocols, and model legislation templates can support countries in developing locally appropriate but globally coherent frameworks.

International collaboration also facilitates the monitoring of cross-border data flows, vendor practices, and the use of AI in transnational testing regimes. Multilateral partnerships can enable resource-sharing among countries with different levels of technical capacity, promoting equity in the governance of AI-enhanced education worldwide.

Policy Instruments and Legal Tools for Enforcing AI Ethics in Schools

The enforcement of ethical standards for artificial intelligence in PreK–12 education requires more than voluntary guidelines or aspirational frameworks. It demands a structured arsenal of binding policy instruments and legal tools that hold institutions, vendors, and officials accountable for ethical lapses and systemic failures. These instruments must be both preventive and corrective—capable of guiding implementation while providing recourse when violations occur. This section details the legal and policy mechanisms available to support ethical AI governance within educational contexts, drawing from constitutional principles, international conventions, statutory laws, administrative regulations, and institutional policies.

1. Constitutional Protections and Civil Rights Law

In many jurisdictions, national constitutions enshrine rights that have direct bearing on AI governance in schools. These include the rights to education, privacy, equality, due process, and freedom of expression. Constitutional law serves as the ultimate legal backstop when AI systems violate foundational democratic norms. For example, predictive tools that systematically disadvantage students based on race or disability may be challenged under equal protection clauses. Similarly, AI-driven surveillance programs may face legal scrutiny under constitutional guarantees of privacy or freedom from unreasonable search.

Civil rights laws—such as the Family Educational Rights and Privacy

Act (FERPA) in the United States, the General Data Protection Regulation (GDPR) in the European Union, or national anti-discrimination statutes—provide additional layers of enforceable protection. These laws prohibit discriminatory profiling, mandate consent for data collection, and provide remedies for harms. Schools and vendors alike must comply with these laws or face litigation, fines, or reputational damage.

2. National Data Protection and AI-Specific Laws
Many countries have enacted data protection laws that establish parameters for how student information may be collected, stored, processed, and shared. These laws typically include rights of access, correction, erasure, and portability. In the context of AI, such rights take on heightened importance given the complexity of algorithmic profiling and predictive analytics. Legal frameworks must evolve to clarify how these rights apply to automated systems and what obligations exist for data controllers.

AI-specific legislation—such as the EU Artificial Intelligence Act—further introduces risk-tiered regulations, mandatory disclosures, and bans on certain high-risk applications. When adapted to the educational sector, these laws provide a coherent foundation for banning harmful technologies, regulating opaque algorithms, and certifying ethically aligned tools.

3. Statutory Mandates for Ethical Review and Risk Assessment
Education codes and AI regulatory acts must include statutory requirements for ethical review prior to the adoption of AI systems in schools. These mandates should compel institutions to conduct algorithmic impact assessments, bias audits, and data protection reviews before procurement. Additionally, periodic re-assessments should be mandated to ensure continued compliance, especially after system updates.

Ethical review boards—either internal or external—must be legally empowered to halt, modify, or reject AI deployments based on findings from these assessments. The creation of a statutory mechanism ensures that ethical considerations are not left to the discretion of technology vendors or overwhelmed school administrators.

4. Contract Law and Vendor Accountability

Public procurement contracts are powerful tools for enforcing ethical standards. School districts and ministries of education must include specific contractual clauses that mandate compliance with privacy laws, prohibit unauthorized data sharing, and require algorithmic transparency. Contracts should outline vendor obligations regarding audit access, user training, and responsiveness to complaints.

Failure to meet these terms must carry clear penalties, including financial sanctions, termination of contracts, and exclusion from future bidding. Governments may also create centralized vendor registries that blacklist companies found to have violated student rights or misrepresented system capabilities. Contract law provides the legal infrastructure to regulate private actors whose tools shape public education.

5. Regulatory Standards and Certification Schemes

Administrative agencies must develop technical standards and certification schemes that define acceptable thresholds for fairness, accuracy, privacy, and explainability in AI systems. These standards should be developed through open consultation and updated regularly to reflect technological advances. Certification programs can serve as gatekeepers, ensuring that only validated tools enter the educational marketplace.

Such certifications may be mandatory for high-impact systems—such as those involving student classification, assessment, or intervention. Institutions that deploy uncertified tools should face regulatory sanctions, while students harmed by such deployments must be entitled to compensation or remediation.

6. Legislative Requirements for Student and Parent Rights

Laws must also enshrine the rights of students and families to understand and challenge AI-based decisions. These include rights to:

- Notification: Being informed when AI systems are used in decision-making processes.
- Explanation: Receiving clear, non-technical explanations of how decisions were reached.
- Contestation: Challenging decisions through appeal processes or human review.

- Consent: Opting in or out of certain types of data collection or algorithmic processing.

Statutes that codify these rights make participatory governance enforceable. They shift ethical expectations from policy statements into legally binding entitlements, transforming students and parents from passive subjects into empowered stakeholders.

7. Enforcement Mechanisms and Oversight Authorities
Every legal framework must include clear enforcement provisions. This includes the creation of oversight authorities with investigatory powers, sanctioning authority, and independence from political or commercial influence. These authorities must be able to conduct audits, compel testimony, issue binding rulings, and impose corrective measures.

Educational regulators may be complemented by national data protection authorities, children's rights commissioners, or AI-specific enforcement agencies. Coordination among these bodies ensures comprehensive oversight and minimizes jurisdictional conflicts. Legal redress mechanisms must also be accessible and affordable, particularly for marginalized families.

8. Legislative Sunset Clauses and Technology Moratoria
Given the rapid evolution of AI, legislative mechanisms must include sunset clauses that trigger automatic review or expiration of permissions granted to specific technologies. This prevents outdated systems from remaining indefinitely in use and encourages periodic reassessment of risks and benefits.

In particularly sensitive areas—such as facial recognition, emotion detection, or predictive behavioral scoring—temporary moratoria may be necessary until adequate safeguards are developed. Legislators must retain the capacity to act preemptively when early signs of harm emerge.

In sum, policy instruments and legal tools are indispensable to ethical AI governance in education. Without enforceable rights, regulatory teeth, and institutional capacity, ethical principles remain aspirational. Legal frameworks translate those principles into action, ensuring that artificial intelligence advances not only technologically but also justly within the most formative years of human development.

Case Studies of AI Governance in Global Educational Contexts

To further examine the real-world application of AI governance principles and legal instruments within PreK–12 education, this section presents a series of international case studies. These examples offer insights into how different countries and regions have attempted to navigate the ethical, legal, and institutional complexities associated with AI integration in education. By analyzing successes, shortcomings, and contextual variables, these case studies illustrate the operationalization of governance models across diverse political, cultural, and infrastructural landscapes.

Case Study 1: United Kingdom – Data Ethics and Parental Consent in Predictive Analytics

In the United Kingdom, the integration of predictive analytics into secondary school settings triggered significant public debate in the late 2010s. A prominent case involved the use of a commercial AI tool to identify students at risk of truancy or academic failure based on socioeconomic indicators, behavior records, and attendance patterns. While the system was lauded for reducing dropout rates in pilot regions, it simultaneously raised concerns about algorithmic bias, data privacy, and the erosion of student autonomy.

Parents in multiple school districts challenged the program on grounds that they were not adequately informed of the system's decision-making process or data inputs. This led to investigations by the UK's Information Commissioner's Office (ICO), which concluded that several schools had failed to obtain informed consent and lacked transparency in algorithmic governance.

As a result, the Department for Education issued updated guidance requiring local authorities to conduct Data Protection Impact Assessments (DPIAs) prior to the implementation of predictive technologies. Schools were mandated to disclose algorithmic logic, provide opt-out options for families, and ensure human review of AI-generated interventions. This case illustrates the necessity of combining legal compliance with community trust-building in AI deployment.

Case Study 2: China – Centralized AI Strategy and Surveillance Oversight Gaps

China has emerged as a global leader in AI-driven education, rapidly implementing systems that include facial recognition for attendance, emotion analysis during classes, and AI-generated student performance reports. These technologies are deployed in a top-down fashion as part of the national "Smart Education" strategy, which emphasizes standardization, data centralization, and teacher productivity.

While efficiency gains have been reported, such as improved attendance tracking and streamlined test preparation, critics have highlighted the lack of ethical oversight and civil rights protections. Concerns regarding constant surveillance, emotional manipulation, and data security have been raised by international observers, particularly in schools serving young children.

Despite the rapid scale of deployment, China lacks an independent regulatory agency with the authority to oversee ethical breaches in school-based AI. Civil society participation is minimal, and parents often have no legal recourse to contest system decisions. This case demonstrates the risks of implementing AI without procedural safeguards or participatory governance, even in high-capacity administrative environments.

Case Study 3: United States – Decentralized Governance and Regulatory Patchwork

In the United States, the governance of AI in education is characterized by decentralization. While federal laws such as FERPA and the Children's Online Privacy Protection Act (COPPA) provide baseline protections, enforcement is largely left to individual states and school districts. This fragmented approach has led to inconsistent oversight and a proliferation of unregulated technologies.

In 2021, an investigation by a civil liberties watchdog revealed that several districts were using AI surveillance software to monitor student emails and search histories without adequate oversight or transparency. These tools flagged mental health risks and potential threats, but also mistakenly labeled students for disciplinary action based on benign content. The affected families lacked clear mechanisms for appeals or data correction.

In response, states such as California and New York introduced legislation mandating algorithmic transparency and parental notification. However, the absence of a federal framework limits enforcement and contributes to unequal protections across jurisdictions. The U.S. case illustrates the tension between local autonomy and national standards, highlighting the need for federal coordination in ethical AI governance.

Case Study 4: Finland – Participatory Design and Ethical Foresight

Finland represents a model of ethical and participatory AI implementation in education. Rooted in a national commitment to transparency and social welfare, Finnish schools have embraced AI tools—such as personalized tutoring platforms and adaptive learning systems—through a structured process of public consultation and teacher training.

The Ministry of Education collaborated with universities, parents ' associations, and student unions to create an AI ethics charter specific to education. This charter mandates human oversight of AI decisions, transparent algorithm design, and equitable access across regions. Furthermore, Finland requires independent audits of educational technology providers and prohibits the use of AI for student discipline or behavioral scoring.

An ethical foresight framework guides the introduction of new tools, with pilot testing, feedback loops, and impact assessments embedded into every deployment phase. Finland's example demonstrates the feasibility of harmonizing innovation with rights-based governance in a democratic context.

Case Study 5: Kenya – Equity Challenges and International Vendor Influence

Kenya has made significant strides in digitizing education, including partnerships with global AI vendors offering classroom analytics, digital textbooks, and remote testing platforms. However, the influx of proprietary technologies has raised questions about data sovereignty, vendor accountability, and equitable access.

In rural regions, where internet connectivity is limited and electricity is unstable, AI-enabled platforms have underperformed or remained unused. Meanwhile, wealthier urban schools benefit from data-rich systems that reinforce digital divides. Local advocacy groups have called for legislation requiring open-source standards, language inclusivity, and participatory procurement processes.

In 2022, Kenya's Ministry of ICT and Innovation began drafting a national AI policy framework that includes education-specific provisions. The draft includes clauses on student data ownership, localization of content, and capacity-building for educators. Kenya's case highlights both the promise and the pitfalls of rapid technological adoption in the absence of local regulatory infrastructure.

Case Study 6: Brazil – Litigation and Algorithmic Accountability

In Brazil, the deployment of an AI-based academic tracking system led to legal challenges from parents and educational advocacy organizations. The system used behavioral and performance data to assign students to different instructional tracks. However, several students reported that they were misclassified, denied access to advanced classes, and subjected to automated disciplinary actions.

Civil society groups filed lawsuits alleging that the algorithm discriminated against students from certain ethnic and socioeconomic backgrounds. The courts ruled in favor of the plaintiffs, ordering the system's suspension and requiring a full audit of its design and deployment practices.

Following this ruling, Brazil's National Council of Education issued interim regulations requiring AI systems to undergo prior ethical evaluation, consent-based data collection, and periodic third-party audits. The case underscores the role of judicial mechanisms in correcting governance failures and reinforcing institutional accountability.

Synthesis of Case Studies

These international case studies reveal critical patterns in AI governance across diverse educational systems:

- **Transparency is a universal challenge** across jurisdictions, regardless of governance structure or technological capacity.

- **Parental involvement and student rights** remain underdeveloped in most implementations, even where laws exist.
- **Ethical foresight and participatory design** strongly correlate with responsible deployment and public trust.
- **Vendor influence** can skew priorities toward commercial rather than pedagogical objectives, particularly in resource-constrained settings.
- **Litigation and civil society advocacy** play essential roles in holding institutions accountable when other mechanisms fail.

The lessons drawn from these cases are invaluable for shaping future governance strategies. They illustrate not only what is possible, but what is necessary to ensure that AI in PreK–12 education serves public interest rather than private gain.

Roadmap for Future AI Governance in Education

As artificial intelligence becomes increasingly embedded in the fabric of PreK–12 education, it is imperative to chart a forward-looking roadmap that aligns innovation with equity, ethics, and democratic accountability. This roadmap must not only address current gaps in policy and infrastructure but also anticipate future complexities and opportunities. The trajectory of AI governance in education will shape not only learning environments but also the moral and civic fabric of emerging generations. This final section offers a structured vision for the development of resilient, inclusive, and future-ready governance frameworks.

1. Establishing a Unified Global Framework of Principles

A foundational step in shaping the future of AI governance in education is the development of a globally recognized ethical framework that outlines core values, rights, and obligations. This framework should be developed through multilateral collaboration, involving international agencies such as UNESCO, the OECD, and UNICEF, as well as civil society organizations, education ministries, teacher unions, and student associations.

The framework must include universally agreed-upon principles such as:

- Respect for student dignity and agency

- Commitment to non-discrimination and inclusivity
- Transparency in algorithmic operations
- Accountability and redress mechanisms
- Privacy and data protection by design
- Human oversight in high-stakes decision-making

While allowing for contextual adaptations, this global baseline will serve as a touchstone for national legislation, vendor practices, and institutional policies.

2. Integrating AI Governance into Teacher Preparation and Professional Development

Effective governance cannot rest solely on policymakers and technologists. Educators are on the front lines of implementation and must be equipped to identify, question, and respond to ethical concerns in AI deployment. The future roadmap must include the integration of AI ethics, digital governance, and algorithmic literacy into teacher training curricula.

Professional development programs should include modules on:

- Interpreting algorithmic outputs and decision logs
- Understanding data rights and consent protocols
- Managing AI-assisted assessments and feedback tools
- Identifying bias and inaccuracy in real-time applications
- Engaging students and families in ethical discussions

Incentivizing these trainings through certification, micro-credentials, and salary enhancements can support the widespread adoption of governance-conscious teaching practices.

3. Mandating Algorithmic Impact Assessments (AIAs) for All Educational Technologies

A future-ready governance regime must institutionalize algorithmic impact assessments (AIAs) as a legal and operational prerequisite for all educational AI tools. AIAs function as predictive evaluations of the potential social, pedagogical, and ethical effects of a given system before deployment.

These assessments should include:

- Description of the AI system and its intended purpose
- Inventory of data inputs and processing methods
- Identification of affected student populations
- Risk analysis related to equity, bias, and privacy
- Proposed mitigation strategies and human oversight mechanisms

Mandatory public disclosure of AIAs enhances transparency and allows civil society, parents, and educators to participate in governance before harms occur.

4. Building National AI Education Governance Hubs

Governments should establish specialized governance hubs that consolidate policy development, ethical review, vendor regulation, and stakeholder engagement. These bodies must be empowered with both technical capacity and legal authority, ensuring that they are not merely symbolic but operationally robust.

The hubs should:

- Maintain databases of approved and banned technologies
- Issue certifications and revoke non-compliant tools
- Serve as repositories for ethical complaints and resolutions
- Conduct regular reviews of emerging technologies
- Collaborate with global governance institutions

These national hubs must also be sufficiently independent from political or commercial pressures to uphold the public interest.

5. Requiring Open-Source Transparency for Core Educational Algorithms

To foster trust and enable third-party verification, critical algorithms used in educational decision-making must be made open-source or, at minimum, auditable by independent authorities. Proprietary claims must not override the need for transparency when student welfare is at stake.

Regulatory requirements for transparency should include:

- Public release of core algorithm logic or pseudocode
- Documentation of training data sources and model limitations

- Clear explanations of decision paths for end-users
- Independent repositories for benchmarking and validation

Open-source practices can democratize AI governance and prevent the entrenchment of black-box systems in public education.

6. Embedding Student and Family Rights into AI Governance Charters

Rights-based governance must become a defining feature of the educational AI ecosystem. Future policy instruments must explicitly define and protect the rights of students and families with respect to AI technologies.

These charters should guarantee rights such as:

- Notification of AI system use
- Explanation of algorithmic decisions
- Consent for data processing
- Access to human review or appeals
- Portability and deletion of student data

These rights must be embedded into both law and practice, with penalties for institutions and vendors that fail to comply.

7. Enforcing a Moratorium on High-Risk Applications Until Adequate Safeguards Exist

Certain AI applications—such as biometric surveillance, emotion recognition, and behavioral scoring—present elevated ethical and psychological risks. A proactive roadmap must include legislative moratoria or bans on such tools until scientifically validated safeguards and ethical justifications exist.

During the moratorium period, independent research institutions must be funded to:

- Assess long-term developmental impacts on students
- Investigate risks of psychological manipulation or social sorting
- Explore alternative interventions that preserve human dignity
- Develop child-centered impact measurement frameworks

This approach embodies the principle of precaution, privileging safety over speculative benefit.

8. Creating International Educational Technology Tribunals

To adjudicate cross-border disputes and hold multinational vendors accountable, the global governance roadmap must include the creation of international educational technology tribunals. These bodies can provide a venue for:

- Filing complaints related to transnational AI harms
- Resolving conflicts between national regulatory systems
- Enforcing global ethical standards and audit rulings
- Establishing restitution or remediation mechanisms

These tribunals would act as ethical and legal backstops in an increasingly globalized AI landscape.

9. Institutionalizing Ethical Foresight and Scenario Planning

Given the velocity of technological change, governance systems must not only react to current issues but anticipate future disruptions. Ministries, school boards, and policy think tanks should establish units dedicated to ethical foresight and scenario planning. These units should simulate potential futures in which AI reshapes pedagogy, social relationships, and institutional accountability.

Scenario models should explore:

- The impact of AI tutors on teacher roles
- Future labor market requirements for digitally educated citizens
- Risks of algorithmic segregation or data-driven stratification
- Societal consequences of AI-facilitated educational surveillance

Incorporating foresight into strategic planning transforms governance from reactive to proactive.

10. Embedding Democratic Participation into AI Governance

Perhaps the most critical element in a future-ready roadmap is the democratization of governance itself. Policies must be co-created with educators, parents, students, and civil society organizations, not merely imposed by technocrats or political elites. Mechanisms for democratic input must include:

- Participatory budgeting for educational technologies
- Public hearings and stakeholder consultations
- Student advisory boards at the institutional level
- Crowdsourced ethical review processes
- Digital feedback loops for policy revisions

This participatory approach ensures that governance reflects the lived experiences, concerns, and aspirations of those directly affected by AI.

The roadmap for future AI governance in PreK–12 education is neither linear nor universally prescriptive. It must be adaptable, pluralistic, and deeply rooted in the ethical imperative to protect and empower students during their most formative years. Governance must evolve in tandem with technology, anticipating not only what AI can do, but what it should do. By embedding ethics, transparency, and democratic accountability into the design and deployment of educational AI, societies can ensure that innovation serves humanity—beginning in the classroom and extending to the future of civilization itself.

Chapter 17

AI-Literate Leadership – Training Principals and Superintendents for the Next Era

The rapid evolution of artificial intelligence within the educational landscape has redefined not only the nature of classroom instruction but also the responsibilities of those entrusted with leading educational institutions. As AI technologies become embedded in every facet of schooling—from curriculum personalization and resource allocation to behavior prediction and performance analytics—the roles of principals and superintendents must undergo a profound transformation. These administrators can no longer function solely as instructional leaders and compliance officers; they must emerge as *AI-literate stewards*, equipped to critically evaluate, ethically guide, and strategically implement intelligent systems that affect entire learning communities.

AI-literate leadership does not merely imply familiarity with technological trends. Rather, it demands deep conceptual fluency in algorithmic logic, data governance, ethical risk assessment, and digital equity. It calls for the ability to interrogate vendor claims, shape institutional policies, engage diverse stakeholders, and forecast long-term educational and social implications. The principal or superintendent who lacks this literacy risks becoming a passive consumer of opaque technologies rather than an active guardian of educational integrity, child protection, and democratic accountability.

The urgency of cultivating AI-literate leadership is compounded by several converging dynamics. First, the decentralization of technology procurement allows local leaders significant discretion in selecting and implementing AI tools, often without centralized vetting or oversight. Second, the data-driven pressures of accountability frameworks incentivize the adoption of technologies that promise efficiency and predictive precision, regardless of their ethical or pedagogical soundness. Third, parents, communities, and governing boards increasingly demand transparency and justification for how technology reshapes teaching, learning, and surveillance.

Moreover, many AI systems, once adopted, become deeply entrenched in institutional workflows and cultural routines. These technologies tend to produce path-dependent effects, where initial design decisions reverberate over years through feedback loops, norm shifts, and infrastructure lock-ins. As such, early administrative decisions carry disproportionate weight, influencing whether AI amplifies human potential or entrenches systemic inequity.

The preparation of AI-literate educational leaders must therefore be intentional, rigorous, and anticipatory. It must integrate into leadership licensure programs, principal academies, and superintendent professional development pipelines. The traditional emphasis on instructional leadership, operational management, and community engagement must expand to include digital governance, algorithmic ethics, and strategic foresight.

This chapter aims to provide a comprehensive roadmap for training AI-literate leadership across PreK–12 institutions. It begins by examining the evolving leadership demands created by AI integration. It then outlines the core knowledge domains and competencies necessary for effective AI stewardship. Case examples from both domestic and international contexts illustrate institutional successes and failures in leadership readiness. The chapter concludes with policy recommendations and programmatic models for building leadership pipelines equipped to manage the complexities of the AI-augmented educational era.

The ethical and strategic responsibilities of educational leaders have never been greater. By equipping them with the tools to lead in an AI-driven world, societies can safeguard the integrity of education while harnessing its transformative potential. Educational administrators must not be the last to understand the tools they deploy, nor the first to shield flawed systems from critique. They must instead serve as informed intermediaries—champions of innovation that is principled, inclusive, and guided by the highest ideals of child development and public education.

Leadership Challenges in the AI-Augmented Educational System

The incorporation of artificial intelligence into the PreK–12 ecosystem introduces a new spectrum of leadership challenges for school principals and superintendents. These challenges extend beyond mere technological oversight; they intersect with institutional ethics, educational equity, student privacy, pedagogical philosophy, and long-term policy alignment. To adequately respond, leaders must confront uncertainties and contradictions embedded within AI-enhanced education, navigate competing stakeholder demands, and manage infrastructure that is both technical and cultural in nature.

1. Lack of Foundational Understanding of AI Principles

A primary challenge lies in the lack of foundational understanding of how AI systems operate. Many school leaders, trained in traditional pedagogical models, do not possess sufficient technical fluency to question vendor claims, identify algorithmic limitations, or evaluate the implications of model training data. As a result, these leaders often rely on third-party assurances rather than independent analysis when approving AI adoption.

Without the ability to interpret key features such as machine learning logic, data pipelines, or model drift, leaders may inadvertently introduce systems that marginalize certain student populations or produce opaque, non-auditable outputs. This knowledge gap also compromises their ability to lead informed discussions with staff, parents, and school boards, thereby weakening institutional trust and accountability.

2. Navigating Vendor Pressure and Commercial Interests

Educational institutions, particularly those in underfunded districts, are often targeted by aggressive marketing campaigns from AI vendors offering "solutions" to achievement gaps, behavioral monitoring, and instructional inefficiencies. These vendors frequently frame their products in terms of efficacy metrics, return on investment, or predictive precision—language that appeals to outcome-driven accountability cultures.

Principals and superintendents face the challenge of resisting this pressure without appearing anti-innovation or risk-averse. In many cases, procurement decisions are made without independent ethical review, long-term cost analysis, or input from data governance experts. Furthermore, vendor contracts often contain vague terms regarding data ownership, algorithmic updates, and long-term institutional dependencies, leaving schools vulnerable to future exploitation or technological lock-in.

3. Balancing Innovation with Privacy and Consent Protocols

Another complex leadership challenge is balancing the promise of personalized, data-driven instruction with the imperative to uphold student privacy, autonomy, and informed consent. AI systems often require continuous data collection on student performance, engagement, and behavior, raising questions about consent, surveillance, and digital dignity.

Leaders must weigh the instructional benefits of such systems against their ethical implications. For example, a principal may support the implementation of an AI-based writing feedback tool that captures keystroke data but must simultaneously ensure that students and parents understand what data is collected, how it is stored, and how it will be used. Without a clear framework, school leaders are often left improvising policy, risking non-compliance with national regulations such as FERPA or GDPR and losing community trust.

4. Ensuring Equity in AI Deployment and Access

Artificial intelligence systems can unintentionally exacerbate existing educational inequities if they are not deployed with explicit attention to equity and inclusion. Many AI tools are developed using datasets that do not reflect the cultural, linguistic, or cognitive diversity of student populations. If left unchecked, this leads to bias in outputs and the marginalization of already underserved communities.

Leaders must ensure that AI systems do not reinforce discriminatory tracking, punitive behavior scoring, or biased intervention triggers. However, this requires a level of data literacy and cultural awareness that is not uniformly present in current administrative training. It also demands inclusive stakeholder engagement processes, which may slow down implementation but are essential to responsible leadership.

5. Managing Organizational Culture During AI Transitions

The integration of AI tools into school operations and pedagogy fundamentally alters institutional workflows, teacher autonomy, and student-teacher dynamics. Leaders must manage the cultural disruption that accompanies such technological transitions. Resistance may arise from educators concerned about deskilling, students wary of surveillance, or parents fearful of data misuse.

Change management in this context requires more than communication strategies; it requires empathetic leadership, participatory design processes, and continuous professional support. Principals and superintendents must act as translators—converting abstract technological potentials into clear educational narratives that honor human agency and pedagogical intentionality.

6. Absence of Clear Guidelines and Regulatory Frameworks

In many educational jurisdictions, there is a marked absence of clear policy guidelines, legal frameworks, or ethical charters governing the use of AI in schools. This regulatory vacuum places the burden of governance on local leaders who often lack the institutional backing to make informed, consistent, and lawful decisions.

In such environments, school leaders are forced to interpret vague directives or create ad hoc policies, exposing themselves and their institutions to legal liabilities and reputational risks. The lack of legal infrastructure also complicates issues such as parental appeals, algorithmic audits, and cross-school comparisons, further isolating administrators in their decision-making processes.

7. Limited Time and Capacity for Strategic Foresight

School leaders are often consumed by daily operational demands—disciplinary issues, staffing concerns, emergency protocols, and budget oversight. This limited bandwidth leaves little room for engaging in strategic foresight, ethical deliberation, or scenario planning regarding AI technologies.

As a result, AI-related decisions tend to be reactive rather than proactive, driven by crisis management or top-down directives rather than long-term educational vision. Leaders need protected time and structured support to engage in thoughtful, anticipatory planning that aligns AI implementation with institutional missions and community values.

8. Ethical Isolation in Decision-Making

Principals and superintendents often operate in isolation when it comes to ethical decision-making around AI. Without advisory bodies, external audit partners, or inter-institutional dialogue networks, these leaders may internalize ethical stress or normalize questionable practices. Furthermore, fear of public backlash may discourage open acknowledgment of missteps or failed implementations.

Institutions must build governance ecosystems where leaders can share challenges, consult with peers, and receive confidential ethical guidance. Ethical leadership is strengthened not by unilateral decision-making but by dialogue, reflection, and shared accountability.

The challenges confronting educational leaders in the AI era are multidimensional, spanning the technical, ethical, managerial, and relational domains. These challenges cannot be resolved through intuition or experience alone; they require a new form of leadership—anchored in digital fluency, equity consciousness, strategic foresight, and participatory governance.

The next section will outline the core competencies and domains of knowledge necessary for developing AI-literate leadership in PreK–12 systems.

Core Competencies for AI-Literate Leadership in Education

To effectively lead within AI-augmented educational systems, school principals and superintendents must acquire a defined set of competencies that enable them to navigate the complexities of intelligent technologies while upholding educational integrity, equity, and democratic values. These competencies span technical literacy, ethical reasoning, strategic implementation, stakeholder engagement, and adaptive governance. The cultivation of these capabilities must become an integral component of modern educational leadership development programs.

1. Algorithmic Literacy and Model Interpretation

A fundamental competency for AI-literate leaders is the ability to comprehend the logic, function, and limitations of the algorithms deployed within their institutions. This includes understanding how machine learning models are trained, how they generalize from data, and how they evolve over time through feedback mechanisms.

Leaders must be able to:

- Distinguish between supervised, unsupervised, and reinforcement learning paradigms.
- Interpret the significance of model accuracy, precision, recall, and fairness metrics.
- Identify potential sources of bias in training data and algorithmic outputs.
- Evaluate the explainability and auditability of AI tools used in student assessment, behavior monitoring, or resource allocation.

This foundational understanding enables leaders to critically evaluate AI products, participate meaningfully in procurement decisions, and recognize the implications of algorithmic deployment on school outcomes and culture.

2. Data Governance and Privacy Regulation Expertise

AI systems in education rely on the continuous collection, storage, and analysis of vast quantities of student data. Educational leaders must possess a firm command of data governance principles and relevant privacy regulations to ensure compliance and protect student rights.

Key areas of expertise include:

- Understanding the legal requirements of data protection laws such as FERPA, COPPA, GDPR, and regional equivalents.
- Implementing protocols for data minimization, encryption, retention, and third-party access.
- Developing institutional policies around informed consent,

opt-in/opt-out procedures, and data breach response plans.
- Articulating a data ethics framework that aligns with community values and protects student dignity.

Effective data governance allows leaders to steward AI adoption in a manner that earns community trust and withstands regulatory scrutiny.

3. Ethical Reasoning and Risk Assessment

Ethical literacy is essential for navigating the complex moral terrain of AI-enhanced education. Leaders must be able to recognize ethical dilemmas, articulate normative concerns, and evaluate the consequences of technological decisions.

This competency includes the ability to:

- Assess the potential for bias, harm, or unintended consequences in AI deployment.
- Apply ethical principles such as justice, autonomy, beneficence, and non-maleficence in institutional decision-making.
- Conduct structured ethical impact assessments during technology adoption cycles.
- Facilitate stakeholder dialogues around contentious or uncertain ethical issues.

Such reasoning is not supplementary to leadership but central to sustaining human-centered educational environments in an age of automation.

4. Digital Equity and Inclusion Strategy

AI-literate leaders must be champions of digital equity, ensuring that technology does not exacerbate historical disparities in educational opportunity. Equity literacy in the AI context involves proactive strategies to address systemic biases and ensure all students benefit from innovation.

Core competencies include:

- Conducting equity audits on AI-driven practices and technologies.
- Engaging marginalized communities in technology planning

and evaluation.

- Ensuring linguistic, cultural, and neurodiversity inclusion in system design.
- Advocating for equitable infrastructure, such as broadband access and adaptive interfaces.

By embedding equity into all aspects of AI governance, leaders transform technology from a tool of exclusion to a catalyst for inclusion.

5. Strategic Foresight and Scenario Planning

Anticipating future developments is essential for AI-literate leadership. Leaders must be able to engage in strategic foresight, mapping plausible futures and preparing institutions to adapt responsibly.

This includes:

- Identifying emerging technologies and pedagogical trends.
- Constructing scenario matrices to explore technological, political, and societal developments.
- Developing contingency plans for disruptive shifts, such as major algorithmic failures or legal reforms.
- Aligning long-term institutional missions with technological trajectories.

Strategic foresight enables leaders to guide schools through uncertainty with vision and resilience.

6. Vendor Evaluation and Procurement Oversight

AI procurement is no longer a neutral administrative task; it is a strategic and ethical responsibility. Leaders must possess the tools to evaluate vendor claims, negotiate fair contracts, and demand accountability.

Key procurement competencies include:

- Designing ethical request-for-proposal (RFP) frameworks.
- Requiring vendors to submit algorithmic impact assessments and bias mitigation reports.
- Mandating transparency in pricing, data handling, and performance guarantees.

- Structuring contracts with clauses for audit access, termination conditions, and student data non-commercialization.

A rigorous procurement approach prevents technological dependency and safeguards institutional autonomy.

7. Change Management and Culture Transformation

The successful integration of AI requires deliberate culture change. Leaders must manage this process with empathy, clarity, and inclusivity.

Skills in this domain include:

- Developing and communicating a shared vision for AI-enhanced education.
- Facilitating faculty buy-in through co-design and capacity-building.
- Supporting teachers through professional development and collaborative experimentation.
- Responding to resistance with transparency and iterative feedback loops.

Without intentional culture work, even the most promising AI tools will fail to take root or will generate organizational backlash.

8. Community Engagement and Public Communication

AI-literate leaders must be effective communicators, capable of demystifying complex technologies for non-technical audiences. Community engagement is not merely a compliance task—it is a democratic imperative.

Communication competencies include:

- Explaining the benefits and risks of AI in plain language.
- Hosting public forums, listening sessions, and stakeholder workshops.
- Providing clear documentation about technology usage, data rights, and grievance procedures.
- Responding to public concern with responsiveness and accountability.

Transparent engagement reinforces public trust and supports the legitimacy of leadership decisions.

9. Institutional Ethics Infrastructure Development

AI-literate leaders must help construct organizational structures that institutionalize ethical reflection and governance. This means embedding ethical review processes into the decision-making apparatus of schools and districts.

This competency involves:

- Establishing ethics committees or digital governance boards.
- Integrating ethical checkpoints into procurement and deployment cycles.
- Training internal staff to serve as digital ethics liaisons or ombudspersons.
- Developing codes of conduct specific to algorithmic decision-making.

Such infrastructure enables institutions to move beyond reactive compliance toward proactive ethical stewardship.

The leadership competencies required in the AI era are both expansive and essential. They demand a reimagining of educational leadership as a technologically fluent, ethically grounded, and community-anchored profession. Training programs must evolve accordingly, integrating these competencies into the very core of leadership formation and evaluation.

Models for Training and Certification of AI-Literate School Leaders

The urgent need for AI-literate leadership in education necessitates a fundamental redesign of how principals and superintendents are trained, licensed, and supported throughout their careers. Traditional leadership preparation programs, often rooted in administrative theory and instructional supervision, must expand to address the technical, ethical, and strategic dimensions introduced by intelligent technologies. This section explores existing gaps in leadership development and proposes innovative models to prepare and certify school leaders for governance in AI-integrated learning environments.

1. Redesigning University-Based Leadership Preparation Programs

Most educational leadership programs housed within colleges of education are not currently equipped to produce AI-literate leaders. Their curricula largely focus on instructional theory, legal compliance, budget management, and school improvement planning. To remain relevant and effective, these programs must undergo a comprehensive curricular transformation.

Key changes should include:

- Required coursework on **artificial intelligence fundamentals**, including algorithmic logic, data ethics, and machine learning applications in education.
- Cross-disciplinary collaboration between **colleges of education, computer science departments, and public policy schools** to create integrated leadership pathways.
- Case-based learning modules analyzing real-world AI use cases, implementation pitfalls, and best practices.
- Practicum experiences that place aspiring leaders in **AI-enhanced school settings** where they can shadow implementation processes and engage with ethics committees.

Universities must recognize that producing AI-literate leaders is not optional—it is foundational to their social responsibility in the digital era.

2. Embedding AI Competencies in Leadership Licensure and Certification

State departments of education and credentialing bodies hold significant power in shaping the competencies required for principal and superintendent licensure. These agencies should expand their standards to explicitly incorporate AI governance and digital ethics.

Recommendations include:

- Mandating competency in AI risk assessment, data governance, and algorithmic transparency as part of licensing examinations.

- Including AI literacy indicators in professional growth frameworks used for administrative evaluation.
- Requiring documentation of AI-related professional development for license renewal.
- Creating micro-credentials or stackable certificates in AI and digital leadership that count toward formal credentialing.

Credentialing reforms ensure that AI literacy becomes a norm rather than an elective skill among educational leaders.

3. State-Sponsored Leadership Academies with AI Leadership Tracks

Several states operate public leadership academies that offer intensive training for aspiring and sitting school administrators. These institutions are ideal platforms for embedding specialized AI tracks tailored to public school contexts.

Such tracks should feature:

- **Immersive simulations** where participants lead hypothetical schools through AI adoption scenarios involving equity dilemmas, data breaches, and stakeholder negotiations.
- **Team-based projects** that challenge leaders to design responsible AI implementation plans tied to district priorities.
- **Facilitation by multidisciplinary faculty**, including ethicists, technologists, equity advocates, and veteran school leaders.
- **Networking cohorts** to create ongoing peer support systems around AI issues.

Leadership academies can serve as agile, practice-oriented complements to more theoretical university programs.

4. Partnership Programs with Industry and EdTech Providers

Private sector partnerships, when ethically structured, can enhance leader training by exposing participants to the tools and decision-making frameworks used in the development of educational AI. However, these partnerships must avoid vendor capture and maintain critical independence.

Recommended approaches include:

- **Fellowship programs** where school leaders work alongside ethical product development teams to understand model design and deployment.
- **Case exchange programs**, where industry leaders learn about public education constraints, while administrators gain exposure to innovation processes.
- Collaborative research and **pilot evaluations** that allow for co-designed implementation with transparent auditing mechanisms.
- Clear **firewalls** to prevent undue commercial influence on leadership certification or policy decisions.

Well-governed partnerships can advance mutual understanding between education and technology sectors without compromising public interest.

5. Online and Hybrid AI Leadership Credentialing Programs

Given time and budget constraints faced by many school leaders, accessible online programs are essential for expanding AI literacy. Leading universities and nonprofit organizations should develop asynchronous and hybrid credentialing programs focused on AI in education.

Key features include:

- Modular design allowing for **customizable pacing and depth**, covering topics such as algorithmic ethics, procurement practices, and digital equity.
- **Scenario-based assessments** that test practical application of AI principles.
- Capstone projects where leaders audit their own institutions' technology usage and propose reforms.
- **Accreditation by independent educational leadership bodies**, ensuring rigor and recognition.

Digital credentialing lowers access barriers while promoting scalable professional learning models.

6. District and Regional Leadership Development Pipelines

Individual districts or consortia of districts can develop internal leadership pipelines that prioritize AI fluency. These programs leverage local contexts and allow leaders to apply learning immediately within their institutions.

Effective pipeline components include:

- **Mentorship programs** pairing novice leaders with AI-experienced administrators.
- Internal innovation grants for leaders to **pilot responsible AI initiatives**.
- Professional learning communities focused on emerging technologies and ethical leadership.
- Collaboration with **regional education service agencies** to pool resources for shared training opportunities.

Localized leadership development creates institutional continuity and cultivates district-wide capacity.

7. Role of National Principal and Superintendent Associations

National leadership associations can play a transformative role in shaping the field's response to AI. These organizations should become hubs of AI-related resources, convenings, and standards development.

Strategic initiatives may include:

- Publishing **position papers** and ethical guidelines on AI use in schools.
- Hosting **annual conferences** with dedicated AI leadership tracks.
- Offering **tiered AI literacy assessments** to help members self-evaluate and plan growth.
- Advocating for **federal investment** in AI-specific leadership training infrastructure.

By mobilizing professional networks, associations can normalize and elevate AI literacy across the educational leadership profession.

Equipping school leaders with the skills and mindsets required for AI governance cannot be achieved through isolated workshops or surface-level awareness. It requires a systemic, multilevel transformation of leadership preparation and credentialing ecosystems. By embedding AI competencies into all stages of the leadership pipeline—from university programs and state licensure to professional associations and local pipelines—educational systems can prepare a generation of administrators capable of stewarding technology in ways that honor human dignity, democratic participation, and educational excellence.

Global Case Studies of AI-Literate Educational Leadership in Action

To ground the discussion of AI-literate leadership in real-world contexts, this section presents a series of global case studies where principals and superintendents have demonstrated proactive, ethical, and strategic engagement with artificial intelligence. These cases illuminate both the opportunities and pitfalls of AI integration, offering practical insights for educational leaders navigating similar challenges. The selected examples span multiple continents, school sizes, socioeconomic contexts, and technological maturities, demonstrating the universal relevance of AI governance in education.

1. Finland: Human-Centered AI Deployment in the Espoo Municipal School System

The city of Espoo, Finland, has garnered international recognition for its deliberate and ethically grounded approach to educational technology. In 2023, the Espoo Education Department piloted an AI-driven learning analytics system designed to personalize mathematics instruction across ten primary schools.

Key leadership practices included:

- Establishing a **municipal ethics council** to oversee technology decisions, including parents, educators, researchers, and technologists.
- Requiring **algorithmic transparency reports** from vendors before procurement.
- Conducting **community workshops** to build public understanding and allow for input on system design.

- Training school principals in **data privacy regulations**, AI bias detection, and instructional alignment.

Rather than outsourcing responsibility to external providers, Espoo's leadership took ownership of AI governance, positioning technology as a tool to support human-led pedagogy rather than replace it.

2. United States: Digital Equity and AI Ethics in the Chicago Public Schools

Chicago Public Schools (CPS), one of the largest urban districts in the United States, has emerged as a national model for equity-focused AI leadership. In 2022, CPS implemented an AI-based early warning system to predict high school dropout risk using attendance, academic performance, and behavioral data.

Under the leadership of the district's Chief of Schools, CPS took several proactive steps:

- Collaborated with **local universities** to evaluate the algorithm for racial bias and adjust weighting to reduce false positives among Black and Latino students.
- Created an **Ethical AI Use Task Force** comprising school leaders, students, and civil rights advocates.
- Embedded **digital equity training** into all principal leadership development sessions.
- Published a **public-facing AI policy** outlining rights, appeals processes, and non-retaliation clauses for flagged students.

The case of CPS highlights the role of AI-literate leadership in centering ethics, transparency, and inclusion within data-driven systems.

3. Singapore: AI-Focused Leadership Development Through the NIE and Ministry of Education

Singapore's Ministry of Education, in collaboration with the National Institute of Education (NIE), has integrated AI into its national school leadership training agenda. Recognizing that AI would transform curriculum, assessment, and classroom management, the country invested in building future-ready leadership pipelines.

Program features include:

- A mandatory **AI in Education module** for all aspiring principals, focusing on governance, implementation, and equity implications.
- A **Digital Sandbox Initiative** allowing school leaders to test AI tools in controlled settings before full deployment.
- Ongoing **principal learning journeys** where school leaders visit global innovation hubs to study AI integration firsthand.
- Use of **reflective practice journals** and ethical dilemma simulations as part of certification processes.

Singapore's centralized and anticipatory approach demonstrates how national coordination can prepare leaders at scale for AI disruption.

4. Kenya: Grassroots Leadership in Low-Resource AI Implementation

Despite limited infrastructure, a consortium of public schools in Nairobi County, Kenya, implemented an AI-supported literacy intervention in partnership with a local edtech startup. The system used speech recognition to assess phonemic awareness and provide adaptive reading feedback in both English and Kiswahili.

Key leadership strategies included:

- Mobilizing **community participation** through church groups and parent associations to build local legitimacy.
- Training school leaders not only in technology use, but in **ethical trade-offs** related to data ownership and commercial partnerships.
- Coordinating with the Ministry of ICT to ensure compliance with national **data sovereignty** laws.
- Implementing a **peer mentoring system** where more digitally experienced principals supported others.

This case illustrates that even in low-resource settings, school leaders can assert agency and shape AI adoption to reflect community needs and values.

5. Australia: Principal-Led AI Governance Framework in New South Wales

In New South Wales, a coalition of public high school principals collectively developed an AI governance charter after concerns emerged about predictive grading algorithms influencing teacher autonomy. With support from the state Department of Education, they launched the **AI Leadership Accord**—a voluntary but widely adopted framework.

Elements of the Accord included:

- Commitment to **human-in-the-loop** design in all AI applications affecting students.
- Annual **ethical reviews** of technology tools by a rotating panel of principals.
- A shared **procurement checklist** to evaluate vendor claims and ethical risk.
- Integration of AI ethics into teacher performance evaluations and school improvement plans.

By organizing horizontally across schools, principals created a governance infrastructure that both protected professional integrity and elevated the role of AI-literate leadership.

These global case studies reveal that effective AI leadership does not require uniform tools or identical conditions. What they share is a deep commitment to ethical deliberation, community engagement, and institutional transparency. Principals and superintendents who lead responsibly with AI do so by placing educational values above technological novelty and by embracing their role as both stewards of innovation and guardians of equity.

Recommendations for Policymakers, Training Institutions, and School Boards

The integration of artificial intelligence into educational environments demands a corresponding evolution in how school leadership is prepared, supported, and regulated. The following recommendations target three critical stakeholder groups—policymakers, training institutions, and school boards—each of which has a unique and essential role to play in building a robust ecosystem for AI-literate educational leadership. These recommendations are intended to serve as a roadmap for structural transformation, capacity building, and sustainable governance.

A. Recommendations for Policymakers

1. Establish National Leadership Standards for AI Literacy
Policymakers at the national and state levels should revise principal and superintendent standards to explicitly incorporate AI-related competencies. These standards should include:

- Algorithmic literacy
- Data governance and privacy compliance
- Ethical decision-making frameworks
- Equity-centered technology deployment
- Public accountability mechanisms

Codifying these expectations ensures consistency across leadership pipelines and aligns AI literacy with existing professional requirements.

2. Fund Statewide and Regional AI Leadership Development Programs
Governments should provide dedicated funding for the design and delivery of professional learning programs focused on AI integration in educational leadership. These programs may include:

- AI fellowships for school leaders
- Train-the-trainer models for district capacity building
- Microcredential systems recognized for license renewal
- Online courses offered through public universities

Sustained investment will democratize access to high-quality training and mitigate disparities across regions.

3. Mandate Transparency and Ethical Use Policies for School AI Tools
Legislation should require that any AI system procured for use in schools be accompanied by:

- Algorithmic transparency documentation
- Independent bias audits

- Publicly accessible ethical use policies
- Grievance and redress mechanisms for affected stakeholders

Such mandates safeguard student rights and support leaders in making informed decisions.

4. Create a National Registry of Approved AI Educational Technologies
Establishing a centralized repository of vetted AI tools, complete with ethical evaluations and regulatory compliance documentation, would assist school leaders in procurement. Policymakers should task an independent body with maintaining this registry.

5. Incentivize Cross-Sector Collaborations and Innovation Labs
Government agencies should create innovation grants that encourage collaboration among educational institutions, AI researchers, and technology developers to co-design tools and training tailored to school leadership needs.

B. Recommendations for Training Institutions

1. Revise Curricula in Leadership Preparation Programs
Colleges and universities must embed AI governance into the core curricula of educational leadership programs. Suggested curricular enhancements include:

- Required courses on data ethics, algorithmic bias, and policy analysis
- Case study seminars on AI implementation challenges in schools
- Practicums focused on leading digital transformation initiatives
- Cross-enrollment opportunities with computer science and public policy programs

Institutions must treat AI literacy as fundamental to 21st-century leadership.

2. Establish Research Centers Focused on AI and School Leadership
Universities should host interdisciplinary research centers that study the intersection of AI, education policy, and school administration.

These centers would:

- Generate field-relevant evidence to guide leadership training
- Develop open-access resources for practitioners
- Host symposia and policy roundtables
- Serve as convening bodies for regional and national networks

These centers can accelerate knowledge dissemination and innovation in leadership development.

3. Partner with School Districts for Co-Designed Training Pathways
Training institutions should collaborate directly with school systems to create responsive, context-specific learning experiences. These partnerships can yield:

- Embedded professional development residencies
- Joint credentialing frameworks
- Community-engaged research on AI impacts
- Scalable mentorship models leveraging district expertise

Such partnerships ensure that training remains relevant, practical, and grounded in lived experience.

C. Recommendations for School Boards and District Leaders

1. Adopt Local AI Literacy Standards for School Leaders
School boards should adopt policies that set expectations for AI-related knowledge and behavior among principals and superintendents. These policies can be based on national standards but should be tailored to local priorities.

2. Require AI Governance Training as Part of Onboarding and Evaluation
Districts should incorporate AI ethics, procurement review, and digital equity training into the onboarding process for new administrators. Annual evaluations should include assessment of how AI is being managed, including attention to transparency, inclusiveness, and educational alignment.

3. Establish AI Advisory Committees with Community Representation
School districts should create standing advisory bodies to provide

oversight and community input on AI deployment. These committees may include parents, students, educators, data scientists, ethicists, and civil rights advocates.

4. Allocate Budget for Ethical Audits and Impact Evaluations
District budgets should include line items for third-party evaluations of AI tools. These audits should assess:

- Fairness and bias
- Effectiveness and academic alignment
- Data privacy compliance
- Student and community perception

Ongoing evaluation supports evidence-informed leadership and reduces the risk of harm.

5. Foster a Culture of Professional Learning and Ethical Reflection
District leaders must model a commitment to continuous learning and open dialogue about the implications of AI. Strategies include:

- Hosting ethics workshops for administrators
- Offering stipends for AI professional development
- Encouraging experimentation through innovation zones
- Creating internal reflection spaces such as digital ethics roundtables

Such a culture empowers school leaders to lead with confidence, humility, and moral clarity.

The success of AI-literate leadership cannot rest solely on the shoulders of individual principals and superintendents. It requires coordinated efforts across policy, academia, and governance. These recommendations offer a blueprint for structural transformation, helping institutions move from reactive adaptation to strategic foresight. By operationalizing these proposals, education systems can cultivate a new generation of leaders equipped to navigate the ethical, technical, and democratic challenges of the AI era.

The Future of Educational Leadership in the Age of Artificial Intelligence

The integration of artificial intelligence into the education sector marks one of the most consequential transformations in the history of public schooling. While much of the discourse has centered on the instructional impact of AI—how it changes teaching, personalizes learning, and redefines assessment—an equally urgent transformation is occurring in the realm of educational leadership. Principals and superintendents, long regarded as instructional leaders and organizational stewards, must now emerge as strategic AI-literate administrators capable of navigating unprecedented ethical, technical, and systemic complexity.

The future of educational leadership in the AI era will not be defined by passive adaptation, but by principled agency. Leaders who succeed will be those who understand that technology is not neutral. They will recognize that algorithmic tools encode values, amplify existing inequities if left unchecked, and have the potential to either enhance or undermine democratic education. As such, the modern school leader must be both a technological interpreter and an ethical safeguard, a data-informed strategist and a human-centered advocate.

The evolution of school leadership in this era entails several paradigm shifts:

1. **From Manager to Futurist**
   The 20th-century principal managed day-to-day operations. The AI-era principal must anticipate long-term consequences of technological systems, guide change with foresight, and prepare institutions for uncertainty.
2. **From Gatekeeper to Facilitator of Innovation**
   Instead of acting as a gatekeeper of top-down mandates, the AI-literate leader fosters a culture of inquiry, experimentation, and responsible innovation, while maintaining rigorous ethical guardrails.
3. **From Compliance Officer to Equity Steward**
   AI systems often exacerbate disparities unless carefully managed. The leader of tomorrow must actively interrogate the equity implications of every technological deployment and champion inclusive design and use.
4. **From Instructional Supervisor to Algorithmic Ethicist**
   While deep instructional knowledge remains essential, school leaders must also possess fluency in how algorithms affect

teaching, evaluation, discipline, and student identity formation.

5. **From Local Administrator to Global Collaborator**
   In a digitally connected world, educational leaders engage in cross-border dialogue, learn from global case studies, and contribute to international conversations on educational technology governance.

This redefinition of leadership roles necessitates corresponding changes in professional preparation, support structures, and institutional expectations. No single workshop, course, or tool can produce the level of fluency, discernment, and vision required. Rather, systems must be redesigned to elevate AI literacy as a core leadership competency—on par with instructional supervision, legal compliance, and fiscal management.

There is also a moral imperative underpinning this transformation. The adoption of AI in education presents unique risks to student agency, privacy, and dignity. School leaders, by virtue of their proximity to implementation, are often the first line of defense against potential harms. Their decisions—on what tools to adopt, how to communicate with stakeholders, how to handle data, and how to ensure accountability—have profound, long-lasting consequences.

Therefore, cultivating AI-literate leadership is not a luxury or an elective; it is a prerequisite for preserving public trust in education. It is a condition for ensuring that innovation does not come at the expense of equity, and that efficiency does not eclipse empathy.

As schools continue to evolve into hybrid environments—part physical, part digital—the role of the school leader must evolve accordingly. The leader who thrives in this era will be the one who holds firm to timeless educational values while embracing new tools with critical discernment and visionary purpose.

Educational institutions, governments, and communities must now act decisively. They must build the infrastructure for leadership development that aligns with the gravity and pace of technological change. They must support those willing to lead with courage, insight, and accountability in the age of artificial intelligence.

The future of educational leadership has arrived. The question is not whether schools will be led in an AI-rich context, but whether those leading them will be ready. The responsibility is collective. The time is now.

Chapter 18

AI in the Guidance Office – Redefining Counseling and Career Readiness

The traditional school guidance office, once characterized by paper transcripts, college brochures, and annual face-to-face counseling sessions, is undergoing a radical transformation. As artificial intelligence permeates every sector of society, its integration into school counseling and career readiness functions is redefining the scope, structure, and purpose of student support services. In this emerging paradigm, AI-powered platforms assist with academic planning, emotional monitoring, behavioral forecasting, college matching, skills profiling, and even personalized pathway predictions. These systems offer both unprecedented opportunities for student empowerment and sobering risks of datafication, bias amplification, and depersonalized care.

This transformation demands a reconceptualization of the school counselor's role. No longer can guidance be confined to reactive intervention or logistical advisement. The 21st-century counselor must be equipped to interpret algorithmic outputs, critically evaluate AI-powered recommendations, and uphold ethical safeguards within digital infrastructures. Counselors are increasingly tasked with mediating between machine-generated insights and human values, often in contexts where predictive analytics intersect with the most personal dimensions of student identity—such as future aspirations, socio-emotional development, and mental health.

The expansion of AI into the guidance office also reshapes the very definition of "career readiness." In a labor market increasingly driven by automation, platform economies, and skills obsolescence, students must prepare not only for specific jobs but for lifelong learning, adaptability, and hybrid career paths. AI systems that map individual aptitudes to labor market trends can be powerful tools—but only if counselors possess the knowledge and discretion to use them in ways that support equity and agency, rather than reinforcing socioeconomic stratification.

At the policy level, the infusion of AI into student services introduces complex questions about data consent, long-term profiling, surveillance, and the appropriate balance between personalization and standardization. Counseling technologies often ingest sensitive data from multiple domains—academic records, attendance logs, disciplinary histories, online behavior, and social-emotional surveys—aggregating a multidimensional portrait of the student. Without clear protocols and oversight, these systems risk violating student rights, institutionalizing bias, and commodifying personal trajectories for third-party interests.

This chapter seeks to critically examine the integration of AI into school counseling and career readiness systems. It explores the evolving functions of the guidance office in the age of AI, evaluates the types of technologies being deployed, analyzes the benefits and limitations of predictive systems, and identifies the competencies necessary for counselors to act as ethical stewards of student futures. Drawing on international examples, current research, and best practices, it outlines policy frameworks and implementation strategies that can ensure AI enhances—rather than erodes—the human dimensions of student support.

The task before educational institutions is not merely to automate advising functions, but to reimagine them. The future of school counseling must be proactive, data-informed, and deeply human. To achieve this, guidance professionals must be prepared, supported, and ethically anchored in a technological landscape that is both rapidly advancing and morally complex.

The Expanding Role of AI in School Counseling and Student Support Services

Artificial intelligence is reshaping the scope and function of school counseling by expanding both the capacity and complexity of student support services. Whereas traditional counseling roles focused primarily on academic advising, postsecondary guidance, and crisis intervention, AI systems now augment these responsibilities through continuous, data-driven analysis. This transformation is not merely technological—it is conceptual, redefining what it means to provide meaningful, equitable, and anticipatory student support in a rapidly evolving educational landscape.

1. Predictive Analytics and Early Warning Systems

One of the most widely adopted applications of AI in school counseling is the deployment of predictive analytics platforms that identify students at risk of academic failure, chronic absenteeism, or social-emotional disengagement. These systems analyze multivariate data sets—including grades, test scores, attendance patterns, behavioral incidents, and course selections—to produce risk scores or flag early intervention needs. Counselors are notified when a student's indicators cross a threshold, prompting targeted outreach.

While such systems increase efficiency and enable proactive intervention, they also introduce significant ethical and practical concerns. The accuracy of predictions is contingent upon data quality and algorithmic transparency, and false positives or negatives can have profound consequences for student identity and opportunity. Additionally, there is a risk of pathologizing students through algorithmic labeling, particularly if counselors lack the training to contextualize outputs within the broader socio-cultural realities of students 'lives.

2. AI-Powered Academic Planning and Course Advising

AI platforms increasingly support counselors in academic planning by automating the analysis of graduation requirements, credit accumulation, and course prerequisites. Some tools also integrate college entrance criteria, aligning course selections with institutional expectations. Advanced systems incorporate adaptive scheduling, allowing students to simulate different academic pathways and receive real-time feedback on eligibility for specific careers or postsecondary programs.

This capacity enhances personalization, but it also shifts the counselor's role from manual recordkeeping to strategic oversight. Counselors must now guide students through digitally generated pathways while preserving the flexibility to accommodate interests, identities, and non-linear trajectories. In this context, human interpretation and relational expertise become even more critical, as students may interpret AI recommendations as deterministic rather than suggestive.

3. Career Pathway Recommendation Engines

AI-based career guidance tools assess student interests, strengths, personality traits, and performance data to recommend potential career paths. These systems often integrate real-time labor market data, projecting growth sectors, salary expectations, required credentials, and employability skills. Advanced models utilize psychometric analysis, natural language processing, and cognitive profiling to build nuanced student profiles.

Although these platforms promise efficiency and relevance, they carry the risk of reinforcing socioeconomic and racial stratification if the underlying data reflect historical biases. For instance, algorithmic models trained on current workforce data may channel students from marginalized backgrounds into lower-wage careers while steering others toward more lucrative paths. Counselors must, therefore, act as critical mediators—challenging the assumptions embedded in algorithms and ensuring that student aspirations remain the driving force.

4. Social-Emotional Monitoring and AI-Driven Wellness Tools

A new generation of AI tools aims to monitor and support student mental health by analyzing emotional cues from written assignments, chat logs, wearable devices, and online behavior. These systems flag signs of anxiety, depression, or trauma and suggest interventions or referrals. Some platforms even offer chatbot counseling, providing 24/7 emotional support based on trained therapeutic scripts.

The potential benefits of these tools—especially in under-resourced schools—are significant. However, the implications for privacy, consent, and student autonomy are equally profound. Without robust safeguards, emotional data can be misinterpreted or exploited, particularly when shared with third parties. Moreover, automated responses may depersonalize critical moments of distress, undermining the trust that defines effective counseling relationships.

5. College Admissions Matching and Portfolio Optimization

AI is also transforming the college admissions process by assisting students in identifying institutions that align with their academic profiles, financial circumstances, geographic preferences, and career goals. Some platforms use AI to optimize student applications by suggesting essay revisions, highlighting achievements, and identifying scholarship opportunities.

Counselors leveraging these tools must ensure that the process does not become transactional. College matching must remain grounded in the holistic development of the student, emphasizing fit and purpose over prestige or probability. Additionally, the use of generative AI in application materials raises important ethical considerations regarding authorship, authenticity, and admissions equity.

6. Real-Time Student Dashboards and Longitudinal Portfolios

Many districts now deploy comprehensive AI-enhanced dashboards that consolidate student data into dynamic visualizations. These platforms enable counselors to monitor academic progress, intervention history, social-emotional metrics, extracurricular involvement, and more—all in one interface. Some systems include predictive overlays and suggest next steps for counselors.

While such tools provide a comprehensive view of student development, they also raise questions about surveillance, data permanence, and institutional bias. Counselors must be vigilant in ensuring that dashboards do not reduce students to data points, but rather support holistic, human-centered advisement.

The expanding role of AI in school counseling is both a technological frontier and a philosophical crossroads. Artificial intelligence has the potential to enhance personalization, improve equity, and increase access to timely support. Yet without careful stewardship, it also risks commodifying student data, narrowing opportunity structures, and undermining the relational core of educational guidance.

The counselor of the AI era must evolve into a data-savvy, ethically grounded, and critically engaged professional who understands both the capabilities and limitations of technology. As AI systems continue to shape the form and function of student support services, the preservation of human dignity, contextual nuance, and developmental integrity must remain at the center of every decision.

Personalization Versus Standardization – Ethical Tensions in AI-Guided Counseling

Artificial intelligence has introduced a powerful paradox into the field of school counseling: while its promise lies in unprecedented personalization, its architecture is inherently based on patterns, clustering, and probabilistic generalization. This tension between individualized support and systemic categorization raises fundamental ethical questions for school counselors tasked with guiding students through some of the most consequential decisions of their lives. The challenge is to ensure that personalization does not become prediction, and that standardization does not override the uniqueness of each student's story.

1. The Algorithmic Nature of "Personalization"

Many AI-based systems claim to personalize recommendations by analyzing student data and producing individualized insights. In practice, these systems typically rely on clustering algorithms, regression models, or decision trees that group students based on common features—grades, attendance, test scores, socioeconomic indicators, behavioral patterns, and so forth. Personalization, in this context, is not a bespoke process but a function of matching a student to a statistical category.

While this method may improve efficiency and offer useful guidance, it poses significant limitations. It risks misclassifying students whose trajectories deviate from dominant trends, failing to account for outliers or unique aspirations. Furthermore, such systems often lack the qualitative insight that counselors gain from lived interaction—such as family context, unquantifiable interests, resilience in adversity, or evolving passions.

Counselors must remain vigilant in interpreting AI-generated outputs not as definitive guidance, but as tools to inform deeper dialogue. Overreliance on algorithmic personalization without human oversight can lead to deterministic counseling that reinforces existing inequities.

2. The Standardization of College and Career Readiness Metrics

AI systems often embed standardized definitions of success, mapping students to college or career pathways based on predefined indicators. These indicators may include academic rigor, test scores, aptitude assessments, or labor market forecasts. While such metrics provide structure, they also carry implicit assumptions about what constitutes a "viable" future.

For example, a student who excels in creative arts may be discouraged from pursuing a non-STEM field if the system privileges high-paying technical careers. Similarly, students from lower-income backgrounds may be funneled toward vocational pathways due to systemic biases in the underlying data, regardless of their academic potential or personal ambitions.

This standardization can constrain opportunity rather than expand it. Counselors must recognize that success is not universally defined and that AI-generated pathways must be mediated through a culturally responsive and student-centered lens.

3. Ethical Implications of Predictive Profiling

Predictive analytics play an increasingly central role in AI-guided counseling. These systems forecast likelihoods—of graduation, college completion, career success, behavioral incidents, and more. While such tools can be instrumental in early intervention, they also introduce serious ethical dilemmas.

Predictions can become self-fulfilling. When students internalize algorithmic assessments of their potential, it may influence their motivation, self-perception, and risk tolerance. A student labeled as "unlikely to succeed in college" may forgo higher education not because of ability, but because of perceived inevitability.

Moreover, predictive systems may reflect historical inequities. If a model is trained on biased datasets—where students of color, students with disabilities, or low-income students have faced systemic barriers—those same patterns may be replicated and institutionalized in future recommendations.

Counselors must approach predictive tools with caution, treating them as diagnostic instruments rather than judgments of worth.

Transparent communication with students about how data is used, what predictions mean, and how to challenge or contextualize them is essential to preserving student agency.

4. Data Ownership, Consent, and Student Autonomy

The personalization promised by AI is fueled by the collection and processing of vast amounts of student data. This includes academic records, behavioral logs, biometric data, and digital activity patterns. The ethical use of this data requires clear consent mechanisms, transparent ownership policies, and rigorous data protection standards.

Yet, in many school systems, students and families are not adequately informed about what data is collected, how it is used, or who has access. Consent is often embedded in lengthy enrollment forms or hidden within software agreements that are not easily understood by students or parents.

True personalization must be grounded in informed consent and respect for autonomy. Counselors should advocate for transparent data governance and ensure that students retain the right to access, challenge, and request deletion of their data where appropriate.

5. Equity and the Digital Divide

The promise of AI to personalize guidance assumes equal access to the digital tools that enable such services. In practice, disparities in technology infrastructure, internet connectivity, device availability, and digital literacy often mean that some students benefit more from AI-enhanced counseling than others.

Students in under-resourced schools may encounter outdated platforms, limited AI integration, or insufficient training for counselors. Others may face language barriers, cultural mismatches, or skepticism toward data collection rooted in historical mistrust.

Personalization that is only available to privileged groups becomes a mechanism for deepening inequality. Counselors must advocate for equitable access to AI resources and ensure that personalization does not become a luxury good.

6. Preserving the Human Dimension of Guidance

Perhaps the greatest ethical tension in AI-guided counseling lies in the balance between technological efficiency and human connection. Personalized algorithms may offer accurate suggestions, but they cannot replicate empathy, trust, or the nuanced understanding that defines effective counseling.

There is a risk that overreliance on AI may deskill counselors, reduce face-to-face engagement, or diminish the relational depth of student support. Institutions must recognize that AI is a tool, not a substitute. The counselor-student relationship remains central to meaningful development, even in the most technologically advanced environments.

Educational systems should design AI integration in ways that augment human interaction, not replace it. Tools should serve as supports for deeper conversations—not as replacements for them.

The ethical tensions between personalization and standardization in AI-guided counseling reflect broader societal questions about justice, autonomy, and the role of technology in shaping human development. While artificial intelligence can dramatically enhance the reach and responsiveness of student support services, it must be employed with humility, scrutiny, and a commitment to equity.

Counselors stand at the intersection of machine logic and human complexity. Their role in interpreting, contextualizing, and mediating AI outputs is critical to ensuring that technology serves, rather than subverts, the holistic mission of education. As AI continues to evolve, so too must the ethical frameworks, professional practices, and institutional safeguards that govern its use in the guidance office.

New Competencies for AI-Aware Counselors – Training and Credentialing Pathways

As artificial intelligence becomes increasingly embedded in the practices of school counseling, the role of the guidance professional must evolve beyond traditional competencies. The counselor of the AI era is not only an academic advisor and emotional support resource but also a data interpreter, ethical mediator, and technology integrator. This redefinition of responsibilities necessitates a corresponding shift in professional training, certification, and ongoing development.

1. Understanding Algorithmic Foundations and Limitations

A core competency for modern counselors must include a foundational understanding of how AI systems function. This includes knowledge of:

- Data types used in AI models
- The basic principles of machine learning and natural language processing
- The meaning and limitations of predictive analytics
- How clustering and classification algorithms make decisions

Although counselors need not become computer scientists, they must acquire a working literacy in AI in order to critically engage with the tools they are expected to use. This allows them to detect when an algorithm might be misapplied, misinterpreted, or in conflict with ethical norms.

This foundational knowledge should be introduced in graduate programs and reinforced through continuing education modules tailored to the educational context.

2. Data Literacy and Visualization

Counselors must become proficient in reading, interpreting, and communicating data visualizations that are now embedded within student dashboards, risk-monitoring tools, and pathway planning platforms. Key competencies include:

- Identifying meaningful trends and anomalies in longitudinal student data
- Understanding how metrics are calculated and what they represent
- Communicating data insights clearly to students, families, and faculty
- Recognizing potential biases or distortions in the data or interface

Without these skills, counselors may defer to automated summaries, losing the ability to challenge problematic interpretations or provide nuanced, context-specific guidance.

3. Ethical and Legal Knowledge in Data Use

AI systems in counseling often process sensitive data, raising significant legal and ethical concerns. Counselors must be thoroughly trained in:

- FERPA (Family Educational Rights and Privacy Act) and applicable state laws
- Data consent and opt-out frameworks for students and parents
- Ethical guidelines for technology use in education
- Managing third-party vendor relationships and data-sharing protocols

Additionally, counselors must develop the capacity to identify when an AI system may produce discriminatory outcomes or disproportionately impact vulnerable populations. Ethical literacy must become a dynamic part of the counseling skillset, not an optional add-on.

4. Cultural Competence and Bias Interrogation

AI systems often reflect the cultural assumptions and historical inequities embedded in their training data. As such, counselors must be trained to interrogate:

- How student identity categories are encoded in AI tools
- The impact of socioeconomic, racial, gender, and linguistic bias in algorithmic recommendations
- The potential for technological tools to marginalize students based on non-normative behaviors or goals

Cultural competence must evolve to include a digital dimension—one that ensures technology serves all students equitably, regardless of background.

5. Counseling in Hybrid Human-AI Systems

In the AI era, counseling is increasingly mediated through hybrid systems that combine human judgment and machine outputs. Counselors must learn how to:

- Integrate AI recommendations with professional intuition and interpersonal insight

- Discuss AI-generated suggestions with students without deferring to them as absolute
- Co-construct plans with students that honor both data and personal values
- Advocate for modifications to systems that do not align with ethical or pedagogical principles

This competency transforms the counselor into a hybrid interpreter—one who can navigate both the human and algorithmic aspects of decision-making without compromising dignity or personalization.

6. Communication with Stakeholders in the AI Ecosystem

Counselors must also become fluent communicators with multiple stakeholders involved in the AI implementation process, including:

- Students and parents
- Teachers and administrators
- IT and data teams
- Policy makers and software vendors

This requires technical fluency, ethical clarity, and advocacy skills. Counselors must be able to ask hard questions, raise concerns, and articulate student-centered values in multidisciplinary conversations.

7. Professional Credentialing and Micro-Certifications

Given the pace of technological change, traditional credentialing systems may be too slow to equip counselors with relevant AI competencies. An emerging solution is the use of micro-certifications or stackable credentials in:

- AI literacy for educators
- Data ethics in schools
- Predictive analytics interpretation
- Technology equity and access

These certifications can be delivered through partnerships between universities, school districts, and educational technology providers. They should be updated frequently and aligned with professional development standards recognized by national counseling organizations.

8. Institutional Support and Continuous Learning

Professional development cannot occur in a vacuum. Institutions must provide:

- Protected time for counselor training and interdisciplinary learning
- Access to updated research, case studies, and best practices
- Peer learning networks and mentorship structures
- Incentives for AI-related skill acquisition, including promotion pathways

Counselors must be supported not only in acquiring knowledge, but in integrating it into practice in meaningful and sustainable ways.

The infusion of artificial intelligence into school counseling demands a new professional identity—one that merges deep relational expertise with technological fluency, ethical discernment, and cultural responsiveness. Developing this identity requires systemic reimagining of training pathways, credentialing standards, and institutional priorities.

The counselor of tomorrow must not only respond to student needs but anticipate them through informed interpretation of data, critical engagement with AI tools, and a steadfast commitment to justice. With appropriate preparation and support, counselors can become the ethical backbone of AI integration in education—ensuring that technology serves human flourishing rather than undermining it.

Case Studies in AI-Integrated Counseling – Global Models and Lessons Learned

To understand how artificial intelligence can be meaningfully and responsibly integrated into student counseling systems, it is instructive to examine real-world applications across diverse educational systems. These case studies provide valuable insights into implementation strategies, policy alignment, training approaches, and systemic challenges. They also illustrate the cultural and contextual variability that must be considered when designing AI-powered guidance models.

1. Singapore: National-Level Integration with MySkillsFuture

Singapore's Ministry of Education has implemented *MySkillsFuture*, a national AI-driven career guidance platform that supports lifelong learning and skills development. Beginning in secondary school, students engage with the system through personalized learning journeys, career interest assessments, digital portfolios, and AI-powered job-matching algorithms.

Key features include:

- A centralized government data infrastructure that tracks skills development and labor market demand.
- AI career matching based on psychometric profiling and real-time job market data.
- Integration with national upskilling initiatives, allowing students to see how educational paths align with long-term employment trends.

Lessons learned:

- Government ownership and alignment with national employment goals can accelerate adoption.
- Equity concerns must be addressed to ensure low-income or marginalized groups are not filtered into narrow career tracks.
- Counselor training is critical to ensure they are not displaced by the platform but positioned as interpreters and mentors.

2. Estonia: Digital Citizenship and AI-Ready School Infrastructure

Estonia, known for its advanced e-government systems, has built a robust digital ecosystem that supports AI integration in education. In counseling, Estonia's schools utilize *eKool* (eSchool), a centralized data platform that integrates academic records, behavioral data, and student preferences to support guidance professionals.

AI is used to:

- Predict student disengagement through behavioral analytics.
- Suggest individualized academic pathways based on national testing and interest inventories.
- Facilitate early intervention for at-risk students, flagged

through data dashboards.

Lessons learned:

- Seamless digital infrastructure enables interoperability across educational tools.
- Ethical data governance frameworks, including student data ownership rights, are essential for maintaining public trust.
- Systems must be localized and adaptable, rather than standardized across all schools.

3. United States: Localized Innovation in AI College Counseling Tools

In the United States, AI-powered guidance tools are typically developed and deployed by private vendors, leading to varied adoption and implementation. One notable example is *Naviance*, a platform used in thousands of U.S. schools that combines career interest inventories, college application tracking, and AI-driven recommendations.

Some schools complement Naviance with platforms like *YouScience* (aptitude-based career matching) and *ScholarPath*(real-time scholarship and vocational opportunity tracking). However, decentralized decision-making leads to disparities in access, implementation fidelity, and training.

Lessons learned:

- Without national standards, implementation quality depends heavily on district resources.
- Privately developed tools must be evaluated rigorously for bias, accuracy, and data ethics.
- Counselors must be central to the evaluation and deployment process to ensure the tools are student-centric.

4. China: Surveillance-Driven AI in Education Guidance

China's educational AI platforms often emphasize behavioral monitoring and predictive analytics. Some school systems use facial recognition and AI-powered video analysis to monitor student engagement, fatigue, and even emotional state in classrooms. These insights are reportedly integrated into student profiles used for academic counseling.

Applications include:

- AI-predicted student trajectories based on biometric and performance data.
- Early identification of "underperforming" students for remedial intervention.
- Social credit-style assessments integrated with educational planning.

Lessons learned:

- High surveillance approaches raise significant concerns about autonomy, consent, and psychological safety.
- Technological capacity does not equate to ethical maturity; strong regulatory frameworks are essential.
- The model illustrates the danger of using AI to normalize hyper-standardization and reduce students to behavioral metrics.

5. Finland: Human-Centered Digital Ecosystems for Counseling

Finland has embraced a balanced approach to AI in education that emphasizes student agency and teacher autonomy. The *KouluAI* initiative focuses on using AI to support—not replace—human educators and counselors. AI systems provide predictive insights, but final decisions remain with educators.

Key attributes:

- Transparent AI design, including explainable algorithms and open-source tools.
- Co-design of platforms with counselors, educators, and students.
- Ethical AI curriculum incorporated into teacher and counselor training.

Lessons learned:

- Participatory design enhances trust and adoption.
- Explainability and transparency mitigate risks of overreliance on AI.
- AI systems should be seen as co-pilots, not autopilots.

6. United Kingdom: Targeted Pilot Programs and Ethical Oversight

The UK has experimented with AI-based early warning systems and university readiness tools in select pilot programs. In the *FutureReady* initiative, students receive personalized dashboards showing skill gaps, suggested courses, and employer connections based on AI analysis.

These tools are typically:

- Integrated with regional job boards and apprenticeship systems.
- Overseen by local authorities to align with community development goals.
- Evaluated against ethical frameworks set by bodies such as the UK's Centre for Data Ethics and Innovation (CDEI).

Lessons learned:

- AI integration benefits from alignment with local labor and education strategies.
- Ongoing evaluation by independent ethical boards supports responsible deployment.
- Without equitable digital access, such innovations may reinforce educational stratification.

Case studies across global contexts demonstrate that AI integration into school counseling is not a uniform process, but a complex negotiation of culture, infrastructure, values, and governance. While some systems prioritize national strategy and efficiency, others emphasize human-centered design and ethical safeguards. Still others reveal the dangers of unchecked surveillance and algorithmic overreach.

The most promising models share common characteristics: transparency in algorithmic function, meaningful counselor involvement, clear ethical oversight, and adaptability to local contexts. These principles provide a foundation for future models that uphold the dignity, diversity, and potential of every student.

Policy Recommendations for Ethical and Effective AI Integration in School Counseling

The implementation of artificial intelligence within school counseling must be guided not only by technical innovation, but by deliberate and ethically grounded policy frameworks. Without structured oversight, AI systems risk becoming opaque, inequitable, or misaligned with the core values of education. The following policy recommendations provide a blueprint for districts, governments, and educational institutions seeking to responsibly and effectively integrate AI into the counseling function.

1. Establish National and Local AI Ethics Guidelines for School Counseling

Governments and school systems must adopt comprehensive AI ethics frameworks tailored to educational counseling. These guidelines should include:

- Requirements for algorithmic transparency, explainability, and auditability.
- Guidelines for avoiding bias and ensuring fairness in predictive modeling.
- Safeguards against overreliance on AI in high-stakes decisions (e.g., college admissions, disciplinary actions).
- Protocols for student and parent consent, data usage, and data retention.

Such frameworks should be co-developed with counselors, technologists, ethicists, educators, and representatives from affected communities. Periodic review mechanisms must be instituted to adapt to technological change.

2. Mandate Counselor Involvement in AI Design and Implementation

Counselors must be central stakeholders in the selection, development, and deployment of AI tools used in their practice. Policy should require:

- Representation of counselors on procurement committees for AI software.

- Counselor input in the co-design of platforms and dashboards.
- Training for counselors before and after rollout to ensure effective, ethical use.

By embedding human judgment and frontline experience into the technological decision-making process, schools can ensure that AI tools are aligned with real student needs and contextual realities.

3. Require Algorithmic Transparency and Explainability in EdTech Contracts

School districts and ministries of education must insist on contractual language that guarantees algorithmic transparency from vendors. This includes:

- Access to documentation explaining how AI decisions are made.
- Visibility into the datasets used to train algorithms and their limitations.
- The right to audit algorithms for accuracy, fairness, and compliance.

Such provisions empower counselors and administrators to scrutinize the tools they are expected to trust—and to intervene when outcomes raise concerns.

4. Fund Targeted Professional Development and Credentialing Programs

Governments and accrediting bodies must fund large-scale, accessible, and recurring professional development focused on AI literacy for school counselors. Policy recommendations include:

- Mandatory AI ethics and data literacy modules in graduate counseling programs.
- Credentialing incentives for micro-certifications in AI-powered counseling tools.
- Public-private partnerships to provide cost-effective access to training resources.

A skilled workforce is foundational to any AI integration strategy. Without robust training, even the most advanced platforms will fall short.

5. Ensure Equity in AI Access and Usage Across Schools

AI counseling tools must not become a mechanism for widening the gap between resource-rich and underfunded schools. Policy must require:

- Equal access to AI infrastructure, devices, and bandwidth across school districts.
- Subsidized licensing or open-source platforms for low-income institutions.
- Local language and cultural adaptation to reflect student populations.

Policies must ensure that no student is denied access to personalized support due to geography, socioeconomic status, or demographic factors.

6. Establish Independent Oversight Bodies for Continuous Evaluation

To ensure accountability, independent AI oversight boards should be established at national or state levels. These boards should be tasked with:

- Monitoring the impact of AI systems on student outcomes and well-being.
- Reviewing cases of AI-related harm or ethical violations.
- Recommending modifications, suspensions, or discontinuation of problematic tools.

Oversight should be transparent, public-facing, and include representation from diverse stakeholder groups, including students and families.

7. Create Feedback Loops and Student Advocacy Mechanisms

Policy should mandate that every AI tool used in counseling be accompanied by clear feedback mechanisms, allowing students and counselors to:

- Flag inaccurate, discriminatory, or confusing outputs.
- Request explanations or review of algorithmic decisions.

- Challenge or override AI-generated pathways based on qualitative factors.

In addition, student rights to data access, correction, and deletion must be clearly articulated and enforced through digital rights legislation.

8. Align AI Counseling Tools with Labor Market and Civic Goals

Counseling platforms should be designed not only to optimize individual outcomes but to support broader civic, economic, and democratic goals. Policy should incentivize:

- Integration with national workforce development strategies.
- Exposure to civic engagement, entrepreneurship, and public service pathways.
- Inclusion of non-linear, creative, and emergent career options in AI models.

Such alignment ensures that AI systems serve the full range of societal needs—not just those that are easily quantifiable or profitable.

Policy plays a decisive role in shaping whether artificial intelligence in school counseling becomes a liberating force or a mechanism of control. The integration of AI must not be left to chance or convenience. Instead, it requires a coordinated architecture of ethical principles, legal safeguards, training infrastructures, and democratic oversight.

Educational policy makers must rise to the challenge of ensuring that AI tools amplify the human-centered mission of school counseling. With deliberate design, transparent implementation, and continuous improvement, artificial intelligence can enhance the effectiveness, inclusivity, and ethical grounding of guidance systems. Without such foresight, it risks becoming an invisible gatekeeper—one that reinforces exclusion under the guise of personalization.

Preserving Human Dignity in an AI-Augmented Guidance System

As artificial intelligence continues to reshape the landscape of school counseling, educational institutions face a pivotal decision. They can either relegate human agency to the margins, entrusting critical student decisions to predictive models and opaque algorithms, or they can harness AI in service of a more responsive, equitable, and humane vision of student guidance. This chapter has demonstrated that the future of the guidance office hinges not on the sophistication of the technology alone, but on the moral and strategic frameworks that govern its use.

The transformative potential of AI in student support is unmistakable. It can detect risks early, surface unseen talents, match students to opportunities with unprecedented precision, and alleviate administrative burdens from overstretched counselors. It can provide continuity in fragmented systems, expand access to information, and democratize career exploration through data-driven personalization. When implemented ethically and strategically, AI can be a powerful ally in ensuring that no student is left unseen or unsupported.

However, the promise of AI must not obscure its dangers. Predictive systems are only as reliable as the data they ingest and the assumptions they encode. Without vigilant oversight, these tools may replicate systemic biases, narrow student options, and reduce rich human potential to algorithmic probabilities. A guidance office mediated by AI must never lose sight of the student's right to agency, privacy, and personhood. In educational counseling—where trust, empathy, and human understanding are paramount—the erosion of these values would constitute a grave failure.

The role of the counselor, therefore, becomes even more vital in the AI era. Rather than being displaced by machines, counselors must evolve into interpreters of data, defenders of equity, and navigators of complexity. They must embody the bridge between algorithmic insight and human context, advocating for students in systems that may not always recognize nuance or injustice. With proper training, support, and ethical grounding, counselors can lead the integration of AI in a direction that enhances—not diminishes—the core mission of education.

Equally important is the role of policy makers, educators, technologists, and families in shaping this future. A shared commitment to transparency, inclusivity, and dignity must underpin every deployment of AI in the guidance ecosystem. This includes investing in infrastructure, establishing robust ethical guidelines, and centering student voice in both design and oversight. The transition must be deliberate, participatory, and anchored in the belief that every student deserves more than a datapoint—they deserve a future built on care, understanding, and possibility.

Ultimately, the question is not whether AI will enter the guidance office—it already has. The question is what kind of guidance system society wishes to build. Will it be one of efficiency at the cost of humanity, or one where machines augment the wisdom and compassion of trained professionals? The answer lies in the choices made today by those entrusted with shaping educational futures.

The AI-augmented guidance office must not become a place where students are sorted, surveilled, or steered without voice. It must become a sanctuary of clarity, empowerment, and hope—a place where data illuminates possibilities, but dignity directs decisions. In this vision, AI does not replace the counselor; it reinforces the counselor's power to see, to listen, and to guide.

This is the charge for the future: to build counseling systems where intelligence—human and artificial alike—serves the sacred task of helping every student find not only a career, but a calling.

Building the Future Through the Child

The twenty-first century is no longer on the horizon—it is fully underway. The rapid acceleration of artificial intelligence, machine learning, and automation is not a prediction but an existential reality, with education standing as both the proving ground and the battleground for society's collective response. This book has traced the seismic implications of this transformation across every developmental stage, from infancy to graduation, across every dimension of learning, leadership, infrastructure, and family life.

The traditional educational blueprint—anchored in standardized testing, one-size-fits-all instruction, and industrial-age job preparation—is now fundamentally obsolete. In its place, a new architecture must emerge: one that leverages intelligent technologies without surrendering the human soul of learning. A structure in which AI supports the cognitive, emotional, and creative development of every learner—while counselors, teachers, parents, and leaders remain ethically grounded guides in a world of data-driven complexity.

Each chapter of this work has served as both a lens and a blueprint: from Head Start to high school, from curriculum design to AI-literate leadership, from equity in digital access to new forms of guidance and career readiness. The path forward is clear—education must be radically reimagined as a lifelong, personalized, interdisciplinary, and technologically symbiotic experience. The school must no longer be a building of knowledge storage but a living system of human growth, powered by AI but led by human values.

This moment demands more than awareness—it demands agency. Policymakers must act not as bureaucrats but as visionaries. Teachers must be trained not merely in pedagogy but in computational literacy and emotional intelligence. Parents must be empowered not just to supervise homework, but to co-shape their child's AI-augmented journey. Counselors must not simply advise, but ethically navigate the algorithmic scaffolding of student life. And students themselves must be taught not only how to adapt to technology, but how to shape it.

Education has always been the most powerful societal lever. In the age of artificial intelligence, it is now the defining test of collective wisdom, foresight, and courage. The institutions that fail to adapt will fracture. But those that rise—those that prepare their children for a world of hybrid cognition, lifelong reskilling, and ethical uncertainty—will create not just stronger economies, but more just, more informed, and more resilient democracies.

Appendix A

Glossary of Terms

This glossary provides definitions of key terms used throughout *The AI-Educated Child* to ensure clarity, consistency, and a shared understanding among educators, policymakers, parents, and stakeholders engaging with AI-driven education reform.

Artificial Intelligence (AI)
A field of computer science focused on creating machines capable of performing tasks that typically require human intelligence, such as decision-making, problem-solving, pattern recognition, and language understanding.

Algorithm
A set of instructions or rules programmed into software to solve a specific problem or perform a task, especially in AI applications like adaptive learning platforms and predictive analytics.

Adaptive Learning
An educational technology approach that uses AI to personalize learning content, pace, and assessments based on an individual student's needs and performance in real time.

AI Literacy
The ability to understand, evaluate, and responsibly interact with AI systems, including foundational knowledge of how algorithms function, their capabilities, limitations, and ethical implications.

Career Readiness
A student's preparedness to enter the workforce with the necessary technical, cognitive, and soft skills, now increasingly linked to navigating AI-influenced labor markets.

Data Sovereignty
The principle that individuals should control their personal data, particularly important in education as student information is collected and processed by AI systems.

Digital Equity
Fair access to technology, internet, devices, and digital literacy education, essential to ensure all students benefit from AI-powered educational advancements.

EdTech
Short for educational technology, this refers to digital tools and platforms that support teaching and learning, increasingly including AI-driven applications.

Explainable AI (XAI)
A subset of AI focused on making algorithmic decisions understandable to human users, particularly important in educational settings to maintain transparency and trust.

Ethical AI
The design and use of AI systems that align with moral principles such as fairness, accountability, privacy, and inclusivity.

Hybrid Learning
An instructional model combining in-person teaching with online or AI-enhanced digital learning experiences.

Machine Learning (ML)
A branch of AI where systems learn and improve from data without being explicitly programmed, forming the basis of many predictive and adaptive educational tools.

Micro-Credentials
Digital certifications earned for completing focused learning experiences, often aligned with specific workforce competencies or AI-related skills.

Predictive Analytics
AI-driven analysis that forecasts student outcomes (such as dropouts or performance levels) based on historical and real-time data.

Personalized Learning
Educational approaches that tailor instruction, content, and pacing to the individual learner's strengths, needs, and interests, often supported by AI tools.

SEL (Social-Emotional Learning)
The process through which individuals develop emotional intelligence, interpersonal skills, and ethical decision-making—a critical complement to AI-based academic tools.

Smart Infrastructure
Digitally integrated physical environments (classrooms, devices, platforms) that support AI-enhanced learning and administrative operations.

Stakeholder-Centric Design
An approach to educational reform and technology development that actively involves teachers, students, parents, and administrators in decision-making processes.

Student Data Privacy
The protection and ethical management of personal information collected from students through educational technologies.

Talent Pathways
Structured academic and career routes that align student learning experiences with emerging opportunities in the labor market, often identified via AI tools.

Appendix B

Frameworks for AI-Educated Reform Implementation

This section provides strategic implementation frameworks designed to guide policymakers, administrators, and school systems through the transition to AI-integrated educational environments. Each framework aligns with a core reform domain addressed in *The AI-Educated Child.*

1. AI Curriculum Integration Framework (K–12)

Phase	Description	Key Actions
Audit & Assess	Evaluate existing curriculum for AI-relevant gaps and opportunities	Conduct curriculum audit; identify STEM, ethics, and data literacy gaps
Design & Align	Develop cross-disciplinary modules to embed AI concepts	Align AI topics with math, science, civics, and humanities learning goals
Pilot & Iterate	Test AI modules in selected schools with teacher feedback loops	Launch pilot programs, gather feedback, adjust design
Scale & Sustain	Roll out refined curriculum nationally with continuous support	Offer PD to educators, update learning materials annually

2. Ethical AI Deployment in Student Services Framework

Pillar	Objective	Sample Policies
Transparency	Ensure students, parents, and staff understand AI decisions	Require explainable AI documentation in all vendor contracts
Consent	Establish informed consent protocols for student data use	Use opt-in policies and granular data sharing preferences
Oversight	Monitor systems for fairness and safety	Form independent review boards and regular audits
Intervention	Allow human override of harmful or flawed algorithmic outcomes	Implement "override rights" for school counselors

3. AI Teacher & Counselor Readiness Framework

Tier	Description	Implementation Actions
Foundational	Build baseline digital and AI literacy	Embed AI modules in pre-service training
Applied	Support use of AI tools in the classroom	Offer in-service PD on AI tools, analytics, adaptive platforms
Reflective	Foster ethical, student-centered use	Conduct case study discussions and ethics workshops
Leadership	Equip educators to shape school AI policy	Certify educators as "AI

		Ambassadors" or innovation fellows

4. AI-Literate School Leadership Framework

Area	Responsibility	Strategic Practices
Vision & Policy	Define AI learning priorities	Draft AI charter, align with national goals
Resource Management	Allocate funding and infrastructure for AI	Budget for devices, internet access, data protection
Stakeholder Engagement	Communicate transparently with staff, families, and communities	Host public forums, create AI-readiness task forces
Impact Measurement	Evaluate AI's educational and equity outcomes	Use both quantitative dashboards and qualitative student feedback

5. AI + Equity Assurance Framework

Equity Focus	**Action Area**	**Tools or Practices**
Access Equity	Devices, internet, and tools	1:1 laptop programs, subsidized broadband
Cultural Equity	Representation in datasets	Audit AI datasets, adjust for linguistic or cultural relevance
Learning Equity	Personalized vs.	Adaptive interventions with educator override

	standardized support	
Opportunity Equity	College and career matching systems	Inclusive AI career pathways with cross-sector employer input

Appendix C

Agreements and Ethics Declarations for School AI Use

This section provides model agreements and ethical declarations for schools, districts, and vendors to adopt when implementing AI technologies in K–12 education. These documents are intended to safeguard student rights, ensure responsible data use, and promote shared accountability.

1. Student Data Privacy and Consent Agreement (Model Template)

Purpose: To ensure students and their guardians understand how AI technologies collect, use, and manage data in the school environment.

Agreement Terms:

- **Scope of Data**: The AI tools in use may collect academic records, behavioral analytics, attendance, device activity, and learning patterns.
- **Consent**: Explicit opt-in consent is required from guardians before any AI platform is activated for a student. A guardian may revoke this consent at any time.
- **Use of Data**: Data will only be used to support personalized learning, intervention planning, and programmatic evaluation. It shall not be sold or shared with third parties unrelated to the educational service.
- **Right to Review**: Guardians and students may request access to all data collected, including algorithmic output and interpretability documentation.
- **Data Retention**: Personal data will be retained only for the duration of the student's enrollment and will be deleted within 180 days of exit unless legally mandated otherwise.

Signed by: Parent/Guardian | Student (14+) | District Representative

2. Vendor Ethics Declaration for Educational AI Systems

Purpose: To establish a standard of responsibility, transparency, and alignment with educational goals for any vendor supplying AI systems to schools.

Key Declarations:

- The vendor affirms that all algorithms used in the system are explainable, auditable, and free from discriminatory bias to the best extent technologically possible.
- The vendor provides full transparency into the origin and structure of training data.
- The vendor shall not use student data for commercial purposes beyond contract delivery.
- The vendor shall cooperate with periodic third-party audits for fairness, data security, and efficacy.
- The vendor affirms compliance with COPPA, FERPA, GDPR (where applicable), and all district-specific data governance laws.

Signed by: Vendor CEO/Principal Officer | District Technology Officer

3. School AI Implementation Ethics Charter

Purpose: A foundational document to guide the values and boundaries of AI usage within a school or district.

Principles:

- **Human Oversight**: All AI decisions will remain subject to human review and educator override.
- **Fairness**: Schools will not use AI systems that disproportionately disadvantage any student group based on race, gender, ability, or socioeconomic status.
- **Transparency**: Students and families will receive plain-language summaries of how AI tools work and how they affect educational outcomes.
- **Informed Use**: All staff using AI systems must receive annual training in ethical AI practices and be certified prior to use.

- **Student Voice**: Students will have opportunities to give feedback on AI tools used in their educational experience.

Ratified by: Superintendent | Board of Education | Parent Advisory Council

Appendix D

AI Prompts for Educators and Counselors

This appendix provides actionable prompt templates designed for use with AI tools such as large language models (LLMs), adaptive learning systems, and predictive dashboards. These prompts are intended to enhance instruction, support student development, and guide personalized learning without diminishing educator judgment or ethical standards.

1. Instructional Support Prompts for Teachers

Goal: Automate lesson planning, differentiate instruction, and identify learning gaps.

- *Prompt for Lesson Planning*:
  "Generate a 45-minute interdisciplinary lesson on the causes of climate change suitable for 8th-grade students, aligned to NGSS and Common Core standards, including one interactive activity and assessment questions."
- *Prompt for Differentiation*:
  "Rewrite this reading passage at three different Lexile levels: 600L, 900L, and 1200L. Maintain scientific accuracy and key vocabulary."
- *Prompt for Misconception Diagnosis*:
  "Analyze this set of student quiz answers and identify the top three common conceptual errors with suggested reteaching strategies."

2. Prompts for School Counselors

Goal: Guide student pathway analysis, social-emotional trends, and intervention planning.

- *Prompt for Career Mapping*:
  "Match this student's interests (technology, music, problem-

solving) and GPA (3.2) to five emerging AI-era careers, with related college majors and required skills."

- *Prompt for Emotional Monitoring*:
  "Summarize patterns in student behavioral data over the last 60 days and flag any anomalies that may indicate social-emotional distress or disengagement."
- *Prompt for Intervention Strategy*:
  "Design a multi-tiered support intervention plan for a 10th-grade student showing chronic absenteeism, based on MTSS and trauma-informed care principles."

3. Prompts for School Leaders and Policy Makers

Goal: Aid strategic planning, equity audits, and future-readiness benchmarking.

- *Prompt for Equity Audit*:
  "Provide a report comparing AI learning tool usage rates across schools by socioeconomic status and identify disparities in access or outcomes."
- *Prompt for Infrastructure Planning*:
  "Design a phased, budget-conscious implementation roadmap to equip 50 schools with AI-supported learning platforms over 3 years."
- *Prompt for Innovation Benchmarking*:
  "List the top five AI-related educational practices adopted by leading international school systems and their measured impact."

4. Prompts for Family Engagement & Learning at Home

Goal: Support at-home enrichment and understanding of AI in education.

- *Prompt for Home Activities*:
  "Suggest five fun, age-appropriate, screen-light activities to teach an 8-year-old the basics of how AI works."
- *Prompt for Parent Education*:
  "Summarize in plain English what adaptive learning means, how it is used in schools, and how families can support it at home."

Appendix E

Templates for AI-Era Education Planning

This appendix includes ready-to-use templates to assist educators, administrators, and policy teams in planning, monitoring, and implementing AI-integrated educational strategies. These templates are designed to be flexible, fillable, and adaptable to school-specific needs.

1. AI Integration Planning Template (School-Level)

School Name: ________________________________
District: ________________________________
Date: ________________________________

Strategic Focus	Current Status	Proposed Action(s)	Responsible Lead	Timeline
Curriculum AI Literacy				
AI Teacher Training				
Data Privacy Compliance				
Infrastructure Needs				
Parent Communication				

2. AI-Enhanced Student Profile Template

Student Name: ___________________________
Grade Level: _________
Profile Created By: _____________________

Category	Description or Data
Academic Strengths	
Social-Emotional Skills	
Career Interests	
AI Tool Usage & Feedback	
At-Risk Flags (if any)	
Recommended Interventions	

3. Family AI Literacy Engagement Tracker

Family Name	Attended AI Workshop	Completed Online Course	Tech Support Requested	Follow-Up Needed

Use this to identify and support households that may need additional education or assistance in navigating AI in their child's schooling.

4. Educator AI Readiness Self-Assessment Checklist

Skill/Knowledge Area	Rating (1–5)	Comments/Needs
Understanding AI's Role in Education		
Using Adaptive Learning Platforms		
Interpreting Predictive Data Reports		
Managing Student Data Ethically		
Teaching AI Literacy in the Classroom		
Communicating AI Concepts to Families		

Instructions: Educators should complete this form each semester to assess growth and identify training needs.

5. AI Tool Vetting and Procurement Form (For Administrators)

Tool Name: ____________________________
Vendor: ____________________________

Evaluation Criteria	Met (Y/N)	Notes
FERPA/COPPA Compliance		
Explainability of AI Decisions		
Customization for Diverse Learners		
Data Security Certifications		

Cost and Licensing Terms		
Ongoing Support and Updates		
Educator Training Provided		

Acknowledgments

This work was born from urgency but sustained by vision. At a moment when the very foundations of education face reinvention, this book represents more than a scholarly roadmap—it is a call to action. Such a work does not emerge from a single voice but from a chorus of thinkers, educators, and advocates who believe deeply in the transformative power of learning, even when the rules of the game are changing.

Gratitude is first extended to the educators—teachers, counselors, curriculum designers, and school leaders—who daily navigate the tension between tradition and transformation. Their courage to adapt, experiment, and reimagine education in the age of artificial intelligence forms the living proof that reform is not only possible but already underway.

Acknowledgment is also owed to the students and families whose lived experiences, often underrepresented in policy debates, have shaped the call for equity, access, and ethical use of technology. Their stories are not footnotes to innovation—they are its moral compass.

This work also reflects the contributions of researchers and policy architects working at the intersection of education, ethics, and AI. Their white papers, field studies, and pilot programs have laid the groundwork for a responsible framework to guide the future of learning.

Special thanks are extended to the builders—technologists, developers, and edtech visionaries—who are writing the code of the classroom of tomorrow. May their work continue to honor not only the intelligence of machines but the dignity of the human learner.

Lastly, this book is dedicated to the policymakers and educational leaders who will read these pages not as critique but as a blueprint. May the courage to act follow the clarity to see.

About the Author

The author of *The AI-Educated Child* is a visionary strategist, technologist, and education reform advocate committed to shaping a future in which every child is equipped to thrive in the age of artificial intelligence. With a professional background spanning business development, automation, and equity-driven innovation, the author brings a uniquely interdisciplinary lens to the challenge of redesigning education for the 21st century and beyond.

Throughout a career grounded in entrepreneurial rigor and real-world problem-solving, the author has launched platforms that merge AI with real estate, digital infrastructure, and economic empowerment—demonstrating an unwavering belief in practical transformation over theoretical discourse. This ethos is reflected in every chapter of this book: actionable, implementable, and written not merely for academic discussion but for institutional deployment.

Motivated by both personal legacy and collective responsibility, the author believes deeply in a future where no learner is left behind by the digital revolution. Through this work, the author challenges policymakers, educators, and communities to rise to the occasion—not to adapt incrementally, but to reimagine fundamentally.

This is not a detached observer of change but an architect of it. A builder of systems. A challenger of convention. A parent. A strategist. A voice from the frontier.

www.ingramcontent.com/pod-product-compliance
Lightning Source LLC
LaVergne TN
LVHW050928210926
848482LV00013B/565
* 9 7 9 8 9 9 9 7 2 8 0 1 2 *